Praise for *The One Who Loves You*

"Luders-Manuel navigates her mixed-race upbringing with courage and grace, and she shares her stories generously. *The One Who Loves You* is **an inspiring must-read for anyone who has ever questioned where they fit in.**"

—**Nabil Ayers**, author of *My Life in the Sunshine*

"With *The One Who Loves You*, Shannon Luders-Manuel establishes herself as a literary luminary. . . . It's a gripping, immensely genuine, and heartfelt story of a daughter and father who love each other, rising above any failings, frailties, and flaws. **Luders-Manuel is a gifted writer with the most genuine heart I've felt beating on the page.**"

—**Lauren DePino**, *New York Times* essayist

"*The One Who Loves You* is **the brave and heartbreaking journey of a tender soul finding her way through faith, identity, and belonging**, without much direction from the ones *she* loves. Luders-Manuel skillfully unearths the nuances of generational trauma held within the confines of race, religion, gender, sexuality, and social class in the Western United States during the turn of the twenty-first century."

—**Maya Washington**, author of *Through the Banks of the Red Cedar: My Father and the Team That Changed the Game*

The One Who Loves You

a memoir of growing up biracial
in a black and white world

Shannon Luders-Manuel

Lawrence Hill Books
Chicago

This memoir is drawn from my memories, letters, conversations with friends and family, and details from the thirty-odd journals I kept between 1988 and 2003. I understand that despite the truth as I know it to be, memory can be subjective and is therefore imperfect. All names but my own and my parents' have been changed to protect the privacy of those mentioned.

Copyright © 2025 by Shannon Luders-Manuel
All rights reserved
Published by Lawrence Hill Books
An imprint of Chicago Review Press Incorporated
814 North Franklin Street
Chicago, Illinois 60610
ISBN 978-1-64160-983-8

Library of Congress Control Number: 2024948105

All images are from the author's collection

Typesetting: Nord Compo

Printed in the United States of America
5 4 3 2 1

For Bobby

"I can say anything, but the things I want to say are trapped in that wide open space so I don't say anything at all."

—Jennifer Lauck, *Blackbird: A Childhood Lost and Found*

Prologue

A WRINKLE IN TIME

Dad was dying. I had seen him only once in the past four years, when my white fiancé had asked for his blessing. Now, ready to say goodbye for the last time, I called him from my cubicle to finalize the details of my flight. After all, I knew he could have changed his mind about my visit, or even about his death itself.

When Dad picked up, all I heard was silence on the other end of the line.

"Hello?" I asked. I heard breathing, so faint I wasn't sure if it was just my imagination. Then I made out mumbles, but I couldn't piece any words together. My heartbeat was suddenly clear in my chest and I felt sweat break out on my forehead.

"Dad?" My question was louder than I intended, mixed with a tone of desperation I didn't know I had on reserve for my father. Was I too late? I checked myself, aware of the heavy silence of accounts payable and the small partitions that separated me from the rest of my coworkers.

"Hi," Dad said, not his characteristically firm *Hello*. "I'll see you soon."

I could tell those words took more energy than I had ever needed to expend for anything, even uphill sprints in cross-country in the hot California air.

My dad was a shape-shifter. A Cheshire cat. Sometimes he was invisible while standing before me, and sometimes his presence beat down on me from miles away. He was a chronic bender of the truth, a fighter with demons of his own creation, a father who wanted to show his love for me but didn't know how.

I had been preparing for this phone call my entire life. Now that it was here, I wanted to run—I just wasn't sure in which direction.

1

OF MICE AND MEN
1981

WHEN I WAS FIVE, my dad moved two towns away, to a house between a gun shop and a pet store. The house looked like a small box planted in the middle of a large square of brown grass. On one of my weekend visits, Mom and I pulled up to find Dad on the roof shooting at birds with his BB gun while my favorite neighborhood fixture, Henry the Goose, waddled by. I didn't like him hurting birds. After all, Henry was a bird and he didn't shoot him. Henry seemed to me just like an old man pacing back and forth in front of his house, making sure everything was OK. He quacked like he was telling you all the neighborhood gossip.

The "gun shop house" was in a flood zone next to the San Lorenzo River, which drained into the Pacific Ocean a couple miles away. Dad said he stepped off his porch one day into the river that had spread to his front step. He and his neighbors were rescued by a local volunteer team and placed on a gym floor with individual cots, just like the ones in a makeshift war hospital. When I heard the news, I wondered what happened to Henry. I imagined him swimming along unfazed, with his head bobbing up and down in the water as he grasped for objects just out of reach.

Dad ambled down from the roof to greet Mom and me. "I got a mattress for Shannon," he said. He put away his BB gun and led us into the house, sparsely furnished with mismatched oak furniture. When I was a baby and my parents were still together, I had slept in a walk-in closet between the bathroom and the bedroom he shared with Mom. Every night Dad snuck past me to take a bath, and every night, I jumped up and said, "Daddy!" I didn't tell Dad this at the gun shop house, but I didn't like sleeping alone in the open living room. I felt closets were the perfect size for hopes and good dreams.

Dad opened the front closet to get the bed, a mattress with a folding steel frame, and he let out a high-pitched shriek. There, sitting on top of it, was a mouse, just like the ones that help Cinderella. I took my hand and reached it high, letting it rest on the small of Dad's back.

"It's OK, Daddy," I said.

He straightened and opened the door again. He looked back at Mom and then back at the mouse. He marched into the closet, and the mouse ran under the mattress. Dad got down on all fours and peeked around the different corners. He put his hand out and touched random objects, and every time he heard a squeak, he jumped out of his skin. All of a sudden, Dad shot his arm forward, stood up straight, and ran out the front door with the mouse hanging by its tail between two fingers of Dad's big hand. I heard the garbage can open and slam shut, and Dad marched back into the house, with his swagger more noticeable than usual. He stood in front of us, put his hands on his hips, and said, "Well, then."

"Well, then," Mom echoed.

Despite almost a full foot difference in height, Mom and Dad stood facing one another, as if squaring off in a silent battle, with an army of memories lined up before them. Mom broke the trance first. She shrugged her shoulders and then shook her arms, like a cat does after being sprayed with the insult of water. She reached over to give me a big hug, said she'd see me tomorrow, and walked out the door.

Like usual, Dad looked at me like I was a toy he wasn't sure how to play with. The TV was on, and I sat in front of it on the carpet. Dad sat on the sagging couch and leaned forward with his hands in his lap. The black-and-white image on the screen was fuzzy but I made out *The Jeffersons*. Sometimes I wished I had a mom like Louise. She was loud and opinionated, and she looked like someone to snuggle up to. But I liked Dad better than George Jefferson. My dad was tall and smart, and when he wanted a woman to do something, all he had to do was look at her and talk softly, and she'd do anything he asked. It didn't work on Mom anymore, because she knew she was Brer Rabbit from the folktale, and he was Brer Fox, who made the Tar Baby to lure Brer Rabbit in. If she got mesmerized by that baby made of tar, put her fingers in that sticky flesh, she'd never get herself loose again, and Dad would have her trapped for good. But the tar in the story was really lemon and sugar, so I figured Dad couldn't be that bad.

After the show, Dad and I did push-ups before I changed out of my Superman shirt and my red shorts with the white stripes at the bottom. I knew girls weren't supposed to wear Superman clothes, but they weren't supposed to have Afros either. The ones I knew had hair they could brush in front of the mirror and watch it get smoother before their very eyes. But I had tough hair you couldn't mess with, and so did my dad.

I counted to twenty as my dad did push-ups, but he was still going, his arms bone and muscle, nothing more. I did five and the pain felt so good that I wanted to keep going forever. It felt better than ballet class where I was supposed to do pirouettes and lift my arms delicately above my head. My tutu was my armor, but I didn't want strangers to ooh and ahh. I wanted them to part before me on the sidewalk in deep respect.

Dad said dumpsters were America's untapped resource, and I figured it must be true. That morning he had pulled out a barbell for him and a dumbbell for me, right from his very own parking lot. We raised our arms high above our heads and pushed the air out through our mouths. I looked at my arm and it too was bone and muscle. Mostly bone.

"These streets are scary, Little Bit," he said as he lowered the barbell to the floor. "You've gotta stay strong or people will take advantage of you. I had a knife pulled on me almost every day in prison, but I knew how to take care of myself."

I nodded, but no one pulled knives on the playground, they just kicked and threw sand as I ran away.

Dad liked to talk about what landed him in prison as if it were a camp story told by flashlight. His eyes lit up as he discussed being the mastermind and the getaway driver for an attempted bank robbery.

Somehow it didn't occur to either of us that a mastermind who gets caught isn't much of a mastermind. It wasn't until Dad had been gone for over ten years that I began to question this story and discovered his crime was stealing TVs off the back of a truck with a bad bunch of twentysomethings. Dad didn't like mediocrity. If he was going to have a prison stint follow him for the rest of his life, he was going to make the most of it by crafting a tale that made him the bold and mysterious hero for his daughter.

"If anyone ever tries to hurt you," he said, "you just tell the Black Prince and I'll take care of them." I didn't know where he got his nickname at the time, but I later learned it came from Jimmie Walker's 1975 comedy album *Dyn-o-mite*, in which he hollers, "The black prince has arrived!" It suited my dad.

I looked at Dad with his cotton ribbed undershirt and his missing front tooth centering a wide smile, his well-worn hands and scruffy, short goatee. As I picked up my dumbbell and reached my hand to the ceiling, I pictured the kids who teased me. Only this time I wasn't running away.

My mom has always stressed that I was born in a period of love. As bits of their history unfolded in my teens and twenties, I understood why she felt the need to protect my origin story. My parents met in "flower power" San Francisco, when my dad, originally from St. Louis, hired my mom to work on a grant proposal for a new Head Start location—a nonprofit for low-income families with children five and under. My dad was forty-four and newly divorced for the third time. He had six children with four women in various states. My mom was twenty-six and had just resigned from a job as a civilian secretary for the coast guard, doubting her secretarial competence but pulled to make a difference. My parents fell in love amid the backdrop of Haight-Ashbury. They weren't into free love; they didn't do drugs. But my dad admired Mom's past activism: marching in protests against the Vietnam War; going door-to-door against the Prop 14 repeal of the Fair Housing Act; and volunteering in support of the Delano Grape Strike.

When my parents met in 1974, my mom was in flux. Her dad had died from a brain tumor two years before, and her mom had just sold the family home outside San Francisco and moved two hours south to Santa Cruz. Then Mom's roommate left to join the navy. Dad was an anchor in unsteady waters, and an exciting one at that. He had read law books in prison in the 1960s and was the first formerly incarcerated person to be hired as an interviewer for Kansas State Employment Services. My parents inspired each other, and when my dad asked my mom to move into his Haight Street apartment, she said yes. Living with my dad was her new political statement. Not against her mother, who had wanted their San Anselmo neighborhood to become more diverse, but against the women who had said "We don't think people should be mixed up like that" when Mom fought against Prop 14 and against all those who decried miscegenation, even though the Supreme Court had declared anti-miscegenation laws unconstitutional in 1967.

But their love story didn't last. While they were together, my father often disappeared overnight. I was born in 1976, three years into their relationship, on United Nations Day. A year later, my dad started another Head Start program but ran out of money, and they lost the apartment. Grandma moved us from the colorful microcosm of Haight-Ashbury to downtown Santa Cruz—equally hippie but strikingly white—just ten minutes from her own house. Dad's drinking, always a problem, intensified. He would be irritable during the week while working as a paralegal trainee for the NAACP until he could binge again on the weekend and pass out.

When I was three, Dad accused Mom of sleeping with the mailman and threw her across the room. Accusing her of infidelity was a frequent tactic he used to deflect attention from his own cheating. Over the years, Mom felt leaving would mean she believed the stereotype about abusive Black male partners, and she understood the difficulties he had faced growing up: his father leaving when he was eight, and his mother going on welfare to support her eight children, of which my dad was almost the youngest; his mother telling him, when as a child he complained about getting beaten up, "You get out there and fight, or I'll give you a worse beating than they ever would." Dad had hit my mom before, but that day, something snapped. She stood shaking in the doorway, with me on her hip, then turned on her heel and never went back.

———————

My earliest memory is of sitting in front of the wall heater with my Pluto the dog puzzle when I was about two years old—when we were still a family unit in our Santa Cruz apartment. One of the pieces was Pluto's big, white bone, and I loved it so much that I wanted to share it with Grandma, my mom's mom, who lived about ten minutes away. The wall heater had horizontal slots, and I pictured strangers slipping letters through them just like they did at the post office. I slipped the bone through one of the slots and glanced out the window at the bright blue sky. I knew it would shoot down into the large opening that must be at the bottom and somehow make it to my grandma's hands. I giggled at how clever she'd think I was. It's fitting that my first memory is of my grandmother, who became more of a mother than my mother was.

Grandma lived in an L-shaped, ranch-style house on a corner lot in an almost all-white neighborhood. Her living room was the size of Mom and Dad's whole apartment. When Mom and I left the apartment, Grandma moved the washer and dryer to the garage and gave me the laundry room. The hot and cold knobs were still on the wall, right above my bed. I deliciously pictured turning them and watching water gush down onto my tile floor before it would seep down the two shallow steps beyond my door.

At night the cat slept under my particleboard bed that sat on top of two end tables. She nestled in the hollow opening that she thought was made just for her. Grandma had the front bedroom, Mom's was the middle, and my mom's younger brother, Adam, who was nine years older than me, had the primary bedroom at the end with his own bathroom. In the dining room between us rested massive chests with intricate detailing from our ancestors in Germany; old dolls propped up inside glass cabinets; and cut-glass dishes, most of which we never used. Right on the other side of my sliding door was the dishwasher that Grandma ran while I slept. It sounded like thousands of people cheering, and they cheered me to sleep on my empty side of the house.

Mom faced a new beginning at the age of thirty. Dad and Grandma both suggested a degree in social work, so Mom enrolled at Cabrillo College, the local community college, with plans to one day transfer to San Jose State. While she was in class, I went to the college's preschool—one of the best in the area—jumping the waiting list through affirmative action initiatives. Amber, a mixed-race girl, was my best friend at preschool, though her race was probably lost on me: she looked white, with tan skin, bright blue eyes, and ringleted, dirty-blond curls. My preschool mates and I picked apples at the local orchard and put them in canvas bags we'd colored with crayons. Sometimes we sang songs inside the teepee on the edge of the school. The grounds were our wonderland.

Mom did work-study hours at United Cerebral Palsy, and I sometimes joined her. She felt at home in communities of those who didn't look or act like everyone else—those whom most others looked down on. She was born with a cleft lip and palate and had ten surgeries before, at the age of seventeen, she said "no more." She didn't stand out much by the time I came around. Her lips were a little uneven, bigger than usual on one side and smaller than usual on the other. Each year on her birthday, she couldn't blow out the candles on her cake—the air coming tepidly out of one side of her mouth, no matter how hard she tried. She'd been teased in school, and even teachers thought she was dumb because of her appearance. Her dad had wondered aloud what sin he had committed to make her come out that way. At United Cerebral Palsy, Mom felt like she was among friends, so I did too, coloring with participants in the activity room and gifting each other our drawings, all of us eager to please.

When Dad picked me up from preschool for overnights, he sometimes came early. "I can't live without you for another minute," he'd say. He and Mom saw a mediator through the court for visitation rights, though I'm sure I didn't know. Dad was for after-school pickups and weekends, when it suited them both. And he had a rule to follow: he couldn't drink when he saw me.

One afternoon Dad and I sat together in the kitchen on his vinyl chairs with brown paisley print. Dad ran Vaseline through his hair with his fingers, and he stopped to take a puff of his pipe before tackling all the tangles with the wide-toothed comb.

"Do Hambone, Daddy," I said.

Dad rolled his eyes but there was a smile on his face. He sat himself tall on the chair, and all of a sudden his hand slapped his chest and his leg, back and forth, back and forth, so fast that it was all a blur before my eyes.

"Hambone, Hambone, where's your wife, in the kitchen, cookin' rice, Hambone."

I didn't know who Hambone was, but when my dad sang about him, his face lit up, so I knew he must be special. I thought he must be skinny because he was called Bone, and he must be funny because he was called a ham.

Dad stopped rhyming and ran his hand through his newly shined Afro.

I dragged over a kitchen chair and sat beside him. The metal legs screeched on the floor, and I was lucky enough to grab the chair without the tear in the seat. I plopped down, hunched over, and slapped my chest and my leg, but I couldn't do the magic. There was no rhythm, and when I opened my mouth to rhyme, I couldn't slap my body at all.

Dad laughed and scooped me up a corn bread patty from the pan. "Don't worry, Little Bit," he said, setting down the plate. "You're a Hambone girl underneath it all."

I looked at Dad's dark-brown hands and then my own mocha ones, and I wondered.

When I was six, Dad moved from the gun shop house to a cabin on a winding street with no sidewalks and tons of trees in between scattered houses. It was like a secret hideaway, and I had my own room with a big window overlooking a forested hill. When I put my bag down and walked around, I saw two deer munching in the backyard. I imagined myself as Flower in *Bambi*—a black-and-white creature surrounded by animals who roam through grassy hillsides and speak to each other in soft tones.

I heard a knock at the door, and opened it to find Naomi, Dad's new girlfriend. Naomi had the same pale skin as Mom. But in my mind, Mom was a girl, and Naomi was a woman. Instead of overalls and a yellow sweatshirt, Naomi wore tight black jeans, leg warmers, and a black leather jacket. Her hair was blond or really gray—I can't remember which—and it was cut short like the twins in *The Parent Trap*. Her voice was gravelly like the women in Mom's Al-Anon group—women, I thought later, who had replaced bad men with bad coffee and cigarettes.

Naomi never cried. Her voice was loud like Dad's, and if he yelled, she yelled back. Sometimes Dad laughed when she yelled. Other times he didn't like it, and in those moments I wanted her to be quiet like Mom taught me through example.

Naomi's strong voice boomed through the front room and into my bedroom. Soon after, her body followed, and she picked me up and hugged me close as if she had come just to see me.

"Hi, Shanna Banana," she said.

"Hi," I said into her shoulder.

Naomi put me back down and I noticed that she held something in her hand. She took her arm from behind her back and presented me with a magic wand. It had a star on top that caught the light, different-colored ribbons that cascaded down, and little bells that tinkled when she shook it.

"Who do you think this could be for?" Naomi asked with a smile. "I'm passing this on to you, because it has magical powers. I put the wand in front of me and closed my eyes, and I wished for a car in gold light. And what do you know? I got a gold car."

I extended my arm out and took the wand, mesmerized that someone else understood the magic in things as much as I did.

"Thank you," I said, as I ran my fingers through the ribbon.

When night came, I awoke with a pain in my side that came with every breath. Precordial catch syndrome, I later learned. A benign condition. I called for Dad but he didn't come. Naomi came instead.

"My blood and my germs are fighting," I told her as she snuggled up beside me—something I interpreted from Mom after she explained why my knee hurt after a scrape. Naomi told me to lie on my other side and the pain would get lost and disappear as it made its way through my body. After a few breaths, I inhaled all the way, just like magic, just like the magic wand. When I woke up the next morning, she was gone. I sat up and looked out the window to find the deer grazing once again.

———————

I saw my younger cousins on my mom's side at least every month—both Joseph and Charlie and their parents, and Adria and Elsie and theirs. Mom and I stayed at their houses for a month when I was six, while Grandma and Uncle Adam took the Greyhound across the country to Disney World. Not that Mom and I hadn't ever had our own vacation. When I was three, Mom and I took the Greyhound bus from California to New Mexico to see her uncle and cousins, then up to Wichita, Kansas, to see my dad's dad and stepmom and aunts and uncles and cousins, then back to New Mexico, then back home to California. We would do the trip again when I was eight.

This summer, my mom told me that staying over with family was our own vacation, but my ears were attuned when the grown-ups thought I wasn't paying attention: Mom didn't want us to be home alone because she was afraid Dad would come and cause trouble like he had before. Not too long before we left Grandma's, Dad had held his BB gun to Naomi's head and threatened to shoot during one of my visits. Naomi told Mom and said she should get full custody. I knew there had been a sense of danger when Mom and I lived with Dad, and I knew from Mom's and her siblings' words that "full custody" meant Dad couldn't take me away. Mom spent our vacation at their kitchen tables, making a plan.

I'll never know if I saw Dad put the gun to Naomi's head or not. My mind had started blocking things long before that happened. It needed a certain reality: Trustworthy male figures. Bambi in the woods. A magic wand that cast the world in a golden light. Chasing actual memories is like running in circles, forever inching toward the target but failing to make contact. As an adult, I once googled 1980s BB guns and felt instantly dizzy at the images before me, as if faced with a bully I had forgotten existed, its form now jumping off the screen. However I learned of Dad's threat from that summer, I carried it with me. In the end, Dad never followed through with setting up the custody hearing, so Mom got it by default.

It wasn't possible to run in circles inside Grandma's house. Instead, Adria and Elsie and I had to run from Uncle Adam's room to mine, turning around, and then turning back around like we couldn't make up our minds. But at their house, we ran round and round in a circle like we were going somewhere. First the kitchen, then the hall, then the living room, then the dining room—then we did it all over again.

One day during our visit, Adria chased me with a balloon. She was almost as old as me but smaller, even though I was the smallest in my class. She had long, straight, sleek hair like a horse's tail, braided down the middle of her back. She ran a bit like Henry the Goose because she was born with one leg shorter than the other. Her feet went *ker-thunk*, *ker-thunk* as they hit the floor.

"The balloon won't pop," she said.

I didn't believe her and I kept running. Faster and faster to get away from the pop that would happen in just a matter of time. I knew the only time a balloon didn't pop was if no one touched it, and then it slowly shrank until it was just like a big raisin full of bad air.

Aunt Deborah called from the kitchen where she was making bread.

"Girls, no running." She talked differently from Mom. More like Grandma or Naomi, who knew they were in charge. Aunt Deborah was Mom's little sister, but Mom asked her for advice about me, and Aunt Deborah never asked Mom for advice about her daughters. During an earlier visit, Adria and I were superheroes while we ran—she Wonder Woman and I Superman. I had run full speed toward the backyard, expecting to jump over the back steps only to ricochet off the sliding glass door I thought was open. The glass door had shattered before me, and Deborah ran over to where I was. Her arms shook as she hugged me to her. Maybe this is why she wanted us to stop today, but I had bounced off that sliding door without a scratch and wriggled out of her arms. I wasn't about to slow down now.

I stopped in my tracks in the living room and pulled Adria into a corner where there was almost no light. The big plant in the crocheted basket that hung from the ceiling loomed toward me with its tentacles outstretched.

"My daddy can shoot your mommy," I said, "so she'll leave us alone."

Adria's eyes got wet and she dropped the balloon.

"Mommy?" Her voice shook. She ran to the kitchen and I dropped myself down on the carpet, my arms and legs all exposed on the floor.

Right when I hit the ground, I felt the balloon squish underneath me. I heard a pop, just like Adria said wouldn't happen. I screamed, covered my ears, and thought, *People never keep their promises.*

2

WHERE THE SIDEWALK ENDS
1984

Sacramento, Calif.

Hello Shannon,

I'm sorry I didn't get to see you. I still don't know what happened with Naomi. I should have made plans to come by way of Greyhound. Whatever clothes you and Dorrie select will be O.K. with me. I've always liked Dorrie's selection of clothing for you. It's just that I wanted to do it together.

I had asked that Naomi leave me in Santa Cruz and I would spend some time with you and Dorrie. Golden West, shopping, and things like that. We need to do things together sometimes. We are apart and yet "fabric reality" is that we are still a "unit." I think I'll have a job as of next week. When that occurs I'll work at it approx. one month & move to Palo Alto which is very close to Santa Cruz. I feel it will be easier to find work there and I'll be able to see you very often, plus send or give you money every week.

Did I say—I love you? ☺ I just did.

Your Father

Robert C.

DAD WAS GONE—REALLY GONE. No more house in Aptos. No more deer or Naomi or BB guns. No more "Daddy can shoot people," because that didn't get you friends. Also no "Daddy was in prison," or "Daddy and Mommy were never married," or "I have five brothers and sisters but I've never met them." I started saying these things only at my appointments with the Black therapist in her office at the circle church.

I walked from my second-grade classroom to the church, which was in the middle of a circle street. The circle street was in the middle of a circle neighborhood, which was called the Circles. Joan sat in a comfy chair and I sat on the couch. She held a clipboard and asked me how school was. I said fine. I thought Mom must have brought me here because there was something wrong with me, but I didn't know what. I didn't know if I had to go back every week because I was answering the questions wrong or right.

I imagine Joan pointed to a dollhouse in the corner. She asked me to play. I noticed her watching me as I picked up a doll and put it back down. Should I play with the Black one or the white one? Her eyes bore into the back of my head as I picked up the Chinese doll. Or maybe she was Japanese. She looked like my cousins, who were a quarter Japanese, and I liked playing with my cousins. So I thought maybe this was a safe choice.

"Interesting," Joan said. "And why did you choose that particular doll?"

"I don't know." Beads of sweat formed on my forehead.

Should I put the doll in the living room or the bedroom? Or maybe the kitchen? Should she be standing up or sitting down? Should I pick up another doll, and if so, which one? Should it go in the same room or in a different one?

Joan scribbled on her clipboard and I froze.

"Keep going," she said with a smile.

At school no one watched you play. The tired grown-ups on yard duty just talked to each other and looked over their shoulder to make sure you hadn't died. No one watched me play at home either, except Uncle Adam. And he didn't watch me like an adult. He didn't look over to make sure I hadn't died. I thought maybe Mom brought me to therapy because I played wrong. But if that were true, who would have seen it?

I picked up a toy truck and rolled it back and forth along the table. I figured nothing could go wrong with a toy truck.

"Do you want to tell me about your daddy?" Joan asked.

"OK."

"Do you know where he is?"

"In Sacramento."

"How do you feel about him moving away?"

I shrugged. "I dunno."

"Do you miss him?"

"I guess so."

"What do you feel when you talk to him?"

How to explain that he was a voice floating into a receiver like God. Someone you think is there but you never see. I couldn't remember what his nose looked like, or if his head really touched the ceiling or if that was my imagination. I thought Mom had found a Black man to pretend to be Daddy and he decided to quit and move away.

In my thirties, Mom told me she walked into the room that day to find me lying on the coffee table in the fetal position. We have no idea why.

"See you next week," Joan said.

Mom got a phone call from Dad right before Thanksgiving. Mom said "uh-huh" and "OK," and then hung up the phone and swore. She sat down beside me at the kitchen table. "Shannon?" Whenever she said my name as a question, I knew she had something important to say—usually something I didn't want to hear. "Your daddy can't make it," she said. "That doesn't mean he doesn't love you."

I figured if Mom had to convince me of Dad's love, maybe he didn't love me after all. Love was a thing that shouldn't need explaining.

When Thanksgiving came around, my house transformed into a fancy affair. The doorbell made its custom ring, "London Bridges," programmed by Uncle Adam, and we opened the door to the Murphys—Aunt Deborah, Uncle Eugene, Adria, and Elsie. Shortly after, my uncle Edward, my aunt Margaret, and my cousins Joseph and Charlie arrived. Both families had a mother, a father, and two kids—two girls for the aunt and two boys for the uncle. Deborah and Eugene had met folk dancing, and Edward and Margaret had met square dancing. Maybe Mom and Dad didn't stay together because they didn't meet dancing, I thought.

The adults sat at the dining room table with its deep-red tablecloth, brought out only for holiday meals. The heavy plates and utensils made their twice-yearly appearance. A silver tray with a handle held apples, grapes, and nuts. My cousins and I sat at the kids' table, with different plates, different utensils, and no tablecloth. But it was just as special. Adria, Elsie, and I wore matching velvet dresses with lace collars that Aunt Deborah had sewn for the occasion, just as she had for Easter, along with matching bonnets. The best part of the meal was always listening to the adults talk about old times. I never remembered much of the stories, but their voices and laughter were enigmatic—and sweet like cotton candy. I tried to hold their words in my consciousness for as long as possible, until they invariably melted away.

Everyone at the kids' table had a dad at the big table but me. Adam was the closest to the role. He was tall enough, though not as tall as my dad. He wasn't the right color, but then neither was my dad. I guessed color got lighter when it went to the kid, not darker. Kind of like how strawberries in a smoothie looked pink instead of red. Uncle Adam made a silly face when I looked over—bared teeth and big eyes, his shaggy hair framing his sixteen-year-old face and falling gently on the collar of his plaid, Western-style shirt. I made a silly face back and sat up a little taller.

My aunts and cousins and other uncles were guests here, but this was my house, my table, my pumpkin pies—everyone came to me. If my family were the circle neighborhood, my house would be the church, in the center, where I saw Joan the therapist. My grandma—slender, seemingly tall, and proper with a playful aura—was the center of the family. Her gray hair was fashioned in a Dorothy Hamill cut that set off her thick, black, square glasses. She wore a blush-colored pussycat bow blouse and slacks for the occasion instead of her usual turtleneck tucked into elastic cotton pants.

Grandma had her own business engraving name tags, buttons, and nameplates, but words themselves were her real passion. She often left the table during dinners to grab off the hall shelf the World Book dictionary, which she had once peddled door-to-door with her sisters. We'd do a deep dive about a word that had come up while we talked: where it came from, how it was used, and how it should be pronounced. Our eyes grew big with wonder whenever we learned something new. Grandma's Boston accent, left over from childhood, made everything sound more important, like a governess instructing a pupil. Once a month, women from Grandma's writing group read pages around the dining room table, their cadences transporting me to adult worlds filled with mysterious emotions and vivid pictures.

My mom had kept a record of my sayings from toddlerhood inside a small World Book notepad, including "In a ponce of days ago" and "Oh, my dearling heart." By age seven, I knew I wanted to be a writer, just like Grandma did. I wrote poems in a little book with strawberries on the cloth cover, hoping to be Shel Silverstein. Sometimes I copied Silverstein's poems into my book and read them to my family, sure they wouldn't be able to tell. As I practiced with my own poetry, I noticed that words of varying syllables made melodies like music. The lines were unsurprisingly banal, but the excitement at creating cadences remained.

After we ate our Thanksgiving meal, the extended family took a walk around the sleepy neighborhood with its wide, empty streets and chirping birds. We cousins stopped for the best fallen leaves we could find, then placed them on the table during our dessert of pumpkin and mincemeat pies. As we dug in, we each shared what made us thankful.

My friend Eric and his sister Karen lived five houses down from Grandma's on the opposite side of the street. They had a mom and a dad and real bedrooms. Sometimes Eric, Karen, and I played on my wooden swing set. We swung Karen high in the air—her blonde hair rising behind her. Eventually she would start to squeal, but she smiled, so we knew not to stop. When she got tired and went home, Eric and I would climb to the fortress at the top of the swing set and disappear under a blanket. Only slivers of light came in through the pink cloth.

Other times I visited Sun, who lived down the street. We watched and rewatched our favorite movie, *Big Bird in China*, and performed tricks with her magic set. But one afternoon when I knocked on Sun's door her mom said she couldn't come play. In fact, she said, Sun could never play again. I saw Sun's face peek out from behind her bedroom curtain. Then it disappeared like a magic trick behind the veil.

"Why can't Sun play anymore?" I asked Mom when I got home.

"Some people just have strange ideas about who can be friends," Mom said with a scowl.

I took to riding my skateboard alone in the parking lot of the Methodist church up the street, or sitting on it as I raced down High Street, flying past the house of another friend as I gently tilted this way and that on the windy sidewalk.

A girl named Sarah lived across the street from Eric and Karen. Her driveway was a half circle with perfectly shaped bushes in the middle. The house reminded me of the Brady Bunch house—all pink with brown and gray bricks mixed in. Her dad drove a blue convertible because he was a doctor, just like Eric and Karen's dad was. Only, their dad looked right at me when I talked to him, and his eyes smiled. Sarah's dad looked up at the sky, straight past me to the bushes, or down at his arms folded in front of his chest as if something really important were hiding between them. Sarah had Eric and Karen over to play inside her pink house. I wanted to enter and turn into a Brady Bunch girl, but I never got past the porch. I heard them watch TV after they rode bikes up and down the street with index cards taped to the spokes to make the sound of a motor. I knocked on the door and Sarah opened it with her straight blonde hair falling to the middle of her back. "Can I play?" I asked. She looked me up and down and said, "No, sorry."

The kids on my street went to an elementary school on the hill, far away from the Circles. Mom said she chose Bay View for its diversity. There were a few brown students like me, but I bragged the most about my classmate Chastity, who had bright pink hair. No one seemed as different as her—in my mind, she was a real live hippie. At lunch on my school playground, I rotated between playing Hot Lava with my friends and swinging on the monkey bars. On the bars, I flew through the air on the dead man's drop and spun around in circles on the low bar. My arms held me just as I held the dumbbell with Dad.

One day, just like most days, I flew this way and that, spinning myself like a top right before it crashes and burns.

"Ew, she's Black." I looked over from upside down and saw a white boy riding by on a bicycle.

That night at dinner, I sat and stared at my plate of spaghetti while Mom, Grandma, and Uncle Adam passed garlic bread and salad.

"What's wrong?" Grandma asked me.

"I wish I was white," I said angrily, surprising even myself with the force of my words.

When I was younger, I had wished Mom were Black, and at the time, I told her so. My desire was likely to assuage the disconnect I felt between me and "normal" parents and children—to exist as a miniature version of a mother, like I saw in those around me. At the time, I didn't see the way my mom's and my mouths pouted the same. The way we both stood awkwardly, hands folded in front of our bodies.

"Too bad," my mom had said back then. "I'm your mother and I'm never giving you up."

Now, in second grade, I determined it was I who was different, not my mother. I was the one who needed to change.

My family sat frozen, their garlic bread and salad tongs held in hands of stone.

Finally, Grandma lifted from the spell of my words. "Most second graders feel unliked," she said. "It's a hard year. One day you will be glad your heritage is just what it is."

But what good is a heritage if it marks you, I thought. Like the *Sesame Street* song, "One of these things is not like the others / One of these things just doesn't belong." Even PBS knew that some differences were just too great.

————————

Mom and I walked to the First Congregational Church up High Street, where I had built-in friends. The church stood tall like the bow of a ship, two stories at the front and one story at the back as it followed the hillside. Light streamed in through the chapel's many windows, and the ceiling was so high that if I made copies of my dad and stacked them on each other's shoulders, I would have to make more copies than I could count on one hand. Mr. Brown wore a black robe with a sash of different colors. The kids came to the front and sat on the carpet near the pulpit when Mr. Brown started his sermon. He told us that Jesus was an important man who, through his own life and his teachings, showed us how to be compassionate and kind. Then Mr. Brown excused us to Sunday school.

The singing was the best part of church. Mom and the other adults turned to different pages in the songbooks that sat in wooden holders attached to the backs of the pews. Mom held the book down low and pointed to the words, her finger moving along with the melody. But one of the songs I knew by heart; it was always the last song before church ended:

Praise God for whom all blessings flow
Praise him all creatures here below
Praise him above ye heavenly hosts
Praise father, son, and holy ghost.

I didn't know what it meant, but I liked that I could always count on it. The adults seemed at peace whenever they sang it, and it marked the end of the sermon and the beginning of cookies and punch.

Before I joined Mom in the big room across the courtyard for mingling, I ran with my white and Samoan friend past the pulpit, behind the stage with the giant cross in the middle, and into the secret back area from where Mr. Brown and the other adults magically appeared during services. We ran down the winding metal staircase into the lower level, with its long hallway and closed offices. Back there, we were in a hidden world privy only to those in the know. The adults at church didn't mind that we roamed in their territory; kids were welcome anywhere. My friend and I giggled in hushed tones as we ran back up again.

Unlike at school, at church we were all connected by a shared belief, a shared God, and a shared feeling of unity. And here we were connected to a Father who was always there, in the chapel, even though we couldn't see him. He was in the soft light filtering through the windows, he reverberated off the walls when we sang. He was in our hearts, filling us up with happiness. His spirit serenaded Mom and me as the wind gently moved through the trees on our walk home.

———————

That summer, the extended family spent a weekend at Joseph and Charlie's grandparents' lake house. All us cousins played Frogger in a room just for games, which I liked better than swimming in the lake with the frogs themselves. The lake was too cold, too green, and seemed to go on forever. Joseph and Charlie showed us the basement. It was nicer than the room on the third floor filled from top to bottom with glass-eyed dolls. And right away, I knew what was supposed to happen in this basement. If the game room was for playing, and the doll room was for avoiding, the basement was for Underground Railroad. I seated my cousins in a line on the floor, each sitting cross-legged, and all facing me, the conductor of the train. Their straight hair of varying hues framed their pale faces, and their attentive gazes waited for my cue as the oldest—and therefore they believed the wisest—cousin. We pumped our arms and said "*choo choo*" at my command. "I don't like it down here," Adria said, as she looked from wall to wall at the long guns in glass cases. They were a collection of another kind: Civil War guns from the Union side. I didn't know the name of the war, but I knew it was my job to tell them about the Underground Railroad. I was the one with the right skin.

Slavery was all I knew about Blackness. That, Mom's Michael Jackson *Thriller* record, and my dad's existence, which was fading. Unbeknownst to me, Mom told Dad of my increasing sadness about him being 150 miles away. While Dad's ex-wives had kept their children away because of his drinking, Mom forever transformed my life by putting her foot down in this critical moment. Dad needed to be there. It was his job as a father, and I hadn't seen him in almost a full school year.

Through reading my dad's letters to my mom in my forties, his abandonment expanded from my personal life story to his own socioeconomic one. Dad missed Sacramento, with its vast Black enclaves, its more affordable rent, and the smattering of other family members who, like him, had migrated from the Midwest.

It just didn't have his daughter.

Sacramento, Calif.

Hello Shannon,
It was great seeing you and we will do it again soon.
I saw you as you were skipping down the street with Dorrie, going to the car.

I thought, "There goes my baby girl and I'm going to miss her Berry, Berry much."

Tell Funshine Bear hello for me and tell him to eat all his meals. I will call you sometime. I love you.

Your Daddy,

Robert C.

3

A CHILD'S CHRISTMAS IN WALES
1985

East Palo Alto, Calif.

Hello Daughter,

Thanks for the beautiful Easter card. I like the message in it.

    I'm getting settled but don't have a house as yet.

    I've started working, and it will take a paycheck for me to do that, so it will be a few weeks.

    Just as quickly as I get a place I'll have you up for as long as possible.

    I'm not having a good time because I miss seeing you. Southern Pacific commute trains run thru here and we can ride it sometime. The main thing is I'm much closer to you now. I will NEVER be separated from you! I love you.

    Your father,

    Robert C.

DAD MOVED FROM SACRAMENTO to a house in East Palo Alto, an hour from Santa Cruz, on a street that followed the light-rail. I didn't know at the time, but he worked so hard to move closer to me that he spent a few nights at Hospitality House, a San Francisco shelter. In my thirties I pulled his letters out of a manila envelope and googled each return address to see where they had originated. I even enlisted my mom to drive with me to a few locations. But this was my journey, not hers, and I chastised myself when the trip gave her a panic attack. She spoke ill of my father so infrequently that I had minimized the extent of her trauma.

One Saturday back in 1985, Mom dropped me off at Dad's new house for an overnight visit. Dad drove his ex-girlfriend Naomi and me to the large city park with Duante, a cousin on his side of the family who was eight like me.

I hung from the jungle gym rings just like I did at school, but this time I wasn't alone. Duante swung beside me, in swim shorts and no shirt, looping his legs over the top of the bars. Duante was a mini version of Dad, with long longs and a chest that rippled even though it was mostly flat. But he was also a version of me. The few other people that I knew in Dad's family were old, but Duante and I stood at the same height, his darker body a mirror of mine. He was an automatic friend.

In preschool, Mom had kept my hair in an Afro. Now it came to the middle of my back like a poofy triangle, and Mom kept it in two big braids, except for the two puff balls at the top that Grandma made with scissors. Dad took out the braids and the puff balls and brushed out my hair into its triangle with the Afro top. He didn't like it when my hair wasn't free.

Naomi flashed pictures of Duante and me as Dad stood by with a suave smile. Though she wasn't Dad's girlfriend anymore, they still cared about each other.

When Duante and I were done with the bars, we headed over to a blue wagon with red wheels set up on blocks. We climbed to the top, and Duante steered the invisible horse while I pumped my fists for being the best horse rider. With him, I didn't need to play Underground Railroad. Being a horse rider was so much better. We got to feel the sun on our bodies, the wind whistling through the oak trees. And we got to be on top of the world, not underneath it. It was my first experience with Black joy, simple happiness with another Black person in a nation that tried to keep us down. That day, instead of a white boy saying "Ew" as he rode by me on a bicycle, I had a Black boy beside me, validating my existence.

As Naomi took more pictures, I imagined them making their way to Dad's wall so he wouldn't think to move away again. I glanced over at him every once in a while to make sure he hadn't evaporated like trick liquid on hot asphalt when you get too close to it on the road. Before we headed to the swimming pool, we had a picnic of fried chicken, watermelon, oyster crackers, and punch. Dad lit a cigarette and took a puff as he crossed one leg over the other and leaned forward to rest his elbow on his knee. He handed Naomi a cigarette, and she held it carefully between her fingers. My dad often shifted between loquacity and silence, and today was a silent day. There were no stories about his exploits. Instead, he was regal, even in his thrift store ensemble of wide-leg jeans, a button-up tan shirt, and a brown faux-leather peacoat. His eyes on me made me feel alive, like Pinocchio turning into a real boy or the Velveteen Rabbit becoming a real bunny.

Duante threw oyster crackers up in the air and tried to catch them in his mouth. Sometimes he won, but most times he didn't. I scarfed down more watermelon. The juice ran down my chin a little, and I wiped it away with the front of Naomi's blue shirt, which I put on over my rainbow bathing suit. The juice broke the heat and filled my stomach with air conditioner goodness. I watched the sun above us as it waved through the leaves. It teased me with its penchant for disappearing so slowly that darkness would eventually come without warning.

After we ate, Duante and I took turns running up the steps of the slide and tumbling into the pool. Normally I didn't like the icy coldness of pools or the feeling of my bare skin on plastic slides that forced me to crash at the bottom. But the slide was small and my dad was tall as he watched from his chair near the pool. Naomi jumped in and splashed Duante and me with water. She lifted me onto the concrete by the side of the pool and told me to jump on her shoulders. She paraded me this way and that as Duante made circles around us. When she put me back down, I dog-paddled to the other side of the pool, then put my head underwater and swam back like a frog. I couldn't hear anything except the water as it rushed past my ears. My arms reached out in front of me in a quick motion and then pushed to the sides as they moved me forward. On land, I got nowhere fast. My shoes hit concrete with uncertainty as I followed someone who told me where to go. But underwater, my body floated with just the power of my arms and legs as they guided me to my destination.

All of a sudden I felt something move in my stomach. It sloshed just like the pool water, except it was inside me. I grabbed my stomach to bend forward as much as I could. Naomi guided me to the edge of the pool, where I saw Dad crouched down with his hands out to pull me forward. He gripped gently around my arms and led me to the pool's edge. I took a gulp of air and then threw up watermelon juice all over the concrete, mixed with seeds for good measure.

It was the very best day.

———————

After fourth grade, when I was ten, Mom and I moved over the hill to San Jose so she could be closer to San Jose State, where she was getting her master's degree in social work. Now to get to Grandma's we had to drive half an hour over the Santa Cruz Mountains, winding our way to the top and then back down. Our apartment was a little bigger than Grandma's living room. I slept on the top of Adam's old bunk bed, and Mom had the bottom. We were closer to Dad now, just thirty minutes and on the same side of the hill, but I only saw him about once a month.

Our complex was called the Sunnybrook Apartments, but everyone called it the Sunnybrook Zoo. I got used to seeing lights from police cars outside our window. One morning Mom and I walked to the carport to see a perfect little hole in the back window of our tan Toyota Tercel that looked the size of a stray bullet. The glass fell out all the way to fifth grade, leaving a trail behind us.

We had a bottom apartment our first year there. One afternoon a friend from the complex and I went upstairs to bug the high school kid while Mom was at college. The high schooler wasn't home, but his dad had us come in anyway. I don't remember what he said; all I remember was the gun lying boldly on the table. I made an excuse to leave. The gun seemed to follow me down the stairs and into my apartment, burned in my mind. I told Mom about the gun when she got home. A couple days later, she and I heard the dad's girlfriend screaming from upstairs. Mom called the police, and as the screaming continued, we hid out in the manager's apartment and called again. We never saw the girlfriend after that. Mom got me enrolled in an after-school program so I wouldn't walk into apartments when she wasn't home.

By sixth grade, we had moved to a second-floor apartment. We became one of the manager's favorite tenants, which was handy since Mom couldn't always pay rent on time if her stipend was late. We helped the manager, a round woman from Greece, paint apartments when tenants moved out. At the apartment next to ours, it was difficult painting over the places where the boyfriend had punched the wall. I was glad I would no longer hear his screaming that seemed to thunder out from our bathroom mirror—a thin layer between us and destruction.

A few days before Christmas, the extended family gathered at Grandma's house for caroling, run by Aunt Deborah. In Grandma's living room, Aunt Deborah accompanied our singing on the grand piano, taking requests for "O Holy Night," "The Twelve Days of Christmas," and "Joy to the World." Sometimes some of us joined in on instruments: Uncle Eugene, Adria, and me on violin; Elsie on cello; Uncle Adam on French horn; and sometimes Aunt Deborah switching from piano to the accordion. A few years later, Aunt Deborah made carol books with each family member on the cover. Grandma barely had a musical bone in her body, but she liked to watch her progeny play, and she sang along with fervor. The Murphys didn't believe in God, but they belted out religious carols all the same, as a Western historical tradition. Mom believed, and I believed, but inside ourselves. God was something for Sunday morning.

This year, like some others, I also joined the Murphys at the San Jose Dance Theatre's classic *Nutcracker* ballet. My cousins and I wore our velvet dresses with lace collars, white tights, and matte white Mary Jane shoes with an itty-bitty heel. Back home, my *Nutcracker Suite* cassette tape (with Leonard Bernstein and the New York Philharmonic's rendition of *Peter and the Wolf* on the other side) was on its last legs. My ears were in ecstasy as I took in the familiar songs live, and my eyes danced along with the ballerinas onstage. *The Nutcracker* spoke the language of my imagination, with visions of giant rat armies and trees that grew through the ceiling.

At intermission, we gathered in the atrium along with the other guests. Just like when I joined the Murphys for Rodgers and Hammerstein

musicals—*South Pacific, The King and I, The Sound of Music*—I felt out
of place in the large hall filled with mostly white heads, and, at the *Nutcracker*, dressed fancier than most I saw every day, in clothes bought
at stores I never entered. Mine was the sole Afro in the building, as far
as my eye could see. Adria took my hand and squeezed it three times,
which meant that I should squeeze back just as many. It was a game we
often played as we lay in bed when I slept over. One-one. Three-three.
Four-four. Two-two. I forgot my Afro and the color of my hand as I
squeezed back in rhythm.

On the way home, both Adria and Elsie took my hands and laid their
heads on my shoulders. I couldn't fathom why they fought over me, but
they did, insisting I sit between them even when Uncle Eugene wasn't
in the front passenger seat. Adria lifted her head from my shoulder and
patted my Afro. "I love your mop," she said. Elsie popped her head up
and patted it too. "Boing! Boing!" They giggled as they looked at me with
sparkling, reverent eyes. I envied their life, and I had no idea that they
envied mine. I wished for their expensive mummy sleeping bags that kept

them extra warm and made swishing noises when they moved; they envied my pink Strawberry Shortcake one that was more in line with our young ages. I envied the way their parents guided them through schoolwork; they envied my freedom to play.

Even though Mom and I had moved away, we were still first and foremost part of the Santa Cruz foursome, especially at Christmas. With my aunt's family I was a tagalong, but with Grandma and Uncle Adam, I was the child.

Every year, the four of us put on our winter coats and boots and trudged through the tree farm in the Santa Cruz Mountains, our breath pushing out of our mouths like see-through clouds—the only time and place it ever did. When I was ten, my fifth-grade year, each step took us farther into the farm until nothing else existed except us and the silent trees. Out here we breathed deeply, as if inhaling the fir smell would prolong the Christmas season for as long as it stayed in our bones. Every New Year, after we took down the tree, Grandma vacuumed up the fallen fir needles, and the smell emanated from the vacuum cleaner until the next Christmas.

Uncle Adam picked a bigger tree each time we went to the farm, and this time was no different. We chose one with the same fullness on all sides, and a top that would hit the ceiling if it were any taller. Uncle Adam sawed the tree while Grandma held it steady; Mom looked up in wonder at the treetops. Once they got it loose from the trunk, we carried it back to the parking lot like hunters carrying a deer. Some of the sap got on my hands and I tried to wipe it on a dry part of the base. As we reached the clearing, I ran as fast as I could, away from what I knew was coming.

What I deemed the "spider web machine" was deafeningly loud, rude, and insistent. Workers put each tree into the machine, and when it came out the other end, it was covered in a web rope trap that sucked all the breath out of it and pulled all its arms so tight that I was sure it was suffocating. In preschool I hallucinated spiders and webs on more than one occasion, culminating in panic attacks. That day I hid in Grandma's orange Volkswagen camper, in the backseat across from the stove. The heaviness of the tree asserted itself on the roof as we made our way home through the winding roads.

Back home on the front porch, Grandma and Uncle Adam cut the white ropes off the tree while it leaned up against the house. The tree breathed a sigh of relief as Grandma and Adam hauled it inside and placed it in the corner of the living room in front of the big windows, which was now a majestic, harmonious throne thanks to the tree's presence.

On Christmas Eve, Grandma and Adam sat with Mom at the Christmas service at our old church in Santa Cruz. It was the only day of the year they came, and not for the religion. That year, all the other kids and I were children outside Bethlehem in our musical production of *Amahl and the Night Visitors*, about a disabled boy and his mother who take in the three wise men for the night on their way to meet Jesus. On our walk home, we passed the yearly live manger scene outside the Lutheran church. Mary, Joseph, and Baby Jesus stayed immobile inside their straw manger, with twinkling lights illuminating their faces in the crisp night. They had white skin, just like "Amahl" at church, but in my picture book, he was tan like me.

One block farther and we were home. The grown-ups ate cheese fondue while I had my special plate of spinach ravioli. The angel chimes went *ting, ting* as they circled above the candles, their trumpets raised high. After dinner we opened presents before bed while the Mormon Tabernacle Choir serenaded us from the record player. Each year we took turns playing Santa for handing out gifts, usually either Adam or me. The gifts had perfect wrapping paper and labels, which Grandma would neatly fold to avoid making a mess. We all oohed and aahed as each person took a turn being the center of attention while slowly opening their gift with feigned nonchalance. In addition to my other presents, I always unwrapped homemade peanut brittle from my step-grandma in St. Louis, whom I'd met twice.

We didn't exchange many presents, believing more in the magic of the holiday than what we could get from the mall. When I thought we were done for the night, Uncle Adam handed me a simple white envelope.

"Open it," he said with a big grin.

Inside the envelope I found a single white note card that said, Look in the Microwave. My eyebrows furrowed and I looked around the room for an explanation. Uncle Adam, Grandma, and Mom all stared at me with goofy grins. I knew Adam must be up to something. I walked to the kitchen and turned the light on. I opened the microwave and found another note: Look in the Hall Bathroom. My face brightened and I walked with quickened steps to the mirrored room that I usually hated to enter for fear someone would be standing behind me in the glass. LOOK IN THE DISHWASHER. LOOK IN THE COOKIE JAR. LOOK IN YOUR CLOSET. LOOK ON THE HALL CHAIR. I stared in amazement at the chair that held a card I hadn't noticed each time I ran past it. I picked the card up off the delicate seat and read, LOOK ON THE FRONT PORCH. I wondered how many more cards there were and wondered what I'd find at the end. Another book? A stuffed animal? A box of my favorite cereal? As my mind filled with possibilities, I stepped out the front door to find everyone gathered behind Adam's red bicycle. A ribbon was tied to each handlebar, a basket rested in front, and the bicycle shined with reborn newness.

"Is that mine?" I asked. My family's faces stared back at me with an intensity that overwhelmed me. I longed to move toward them but also longed to escape their piercing stares of happiness.

"Yes," Uncle Adam said. "Merry Christmas."

I ran toward him and wrapped my arms around his middle, careful not to disrupt his polo shirt, his perfectly pleated pants, or his softly feathered, light brown hair.

"Tomorrow, I'll teach you to shift gears," he said.

Even though Christmas Eve was always filled with presents, my favorite part of the holiday was Christmas morning. We woke up slowly and sat around the living room in our pajamas with cups of hot chocolate in our hands and the faint smell of embers from the fire the night before. Grandma's voice had a warm morning raspiness, and it was one of the few times of the year that I saw her completely still. She sat in the wicker rocking chair in her fuzzy blue robe, facing Mom and me on the gold, velvety couch. Adam rested his back against the couch from his seat on the floor. We opened our stockings at the same time, but at a slow pace just like with the presents, so we could lift out the first surprise to the last surprise as a group and not as separate, self-centered people.

I knew somewhere in each stocking would be a tangerine, filberts, and my favorite: maple sugar candy. As we dug deeper, we found silly presents that Grandma always seemed to have on hand: Scotch tape, floss, and other household items. When we were through excavating, we placed our empty stockings next to us and stared at our piles with pride. I soaked in this perfect moment for as long as I could, and hoped that the clock would stop ticking and the sun would stop rising. I hoped that we would forever be Grandma, Mom, Uncle Adam, and me, silent in the living room in our pajamas with nothing in between us except air and light and warmth.

Dad didn't seem to fit into this world, and I didn't wish that he did. He was a missing figure, but not from Grandma's living room. I was too young when my parents had split to remember when we had all been together. I wanted Dad to pick me up in his Chrysler and take me on adventures—to the ocean, to the forest, back to the pool. I wanted him to call me every night. I wanted him to make me corn bread patties and let out my hair. I wanted to know whether his absence was due to forces he couldn't control or whether, most times, he just couldn't make the effort. The less I saw of him, the less I knew who he was.

———————

In fifth grade, I got a chance to learn an instrument in my school's music program. My arm was too short for my first choice, the flute, so I chose the violin, which Adria and Elsie had been playing since they were little. And since they were in a gifted program at their school, I knew I should be in one too. I took the test one afternoon after school in an empty classroom. Mom sat with me as the teacher moved from page to page. Each question left me more confused than the last. I didn't understand why, at a public school, I was supposed to know the name of the pope, or what the seven sacraments were. She flipped to a new page and asked me what was wrong with the black-and-white nature drawing. "The shadow is going the wrong way," I said. I was confident about that answer, but then there were more questions about God and Jesus and church. Mom and I went to our new Congregational church every Sunday, and Adria and Elsie didn't go to church at all. I thought they must be brilliant to know all this stuff about God without even believing in anything.

A few days later, Mom picked me up from school and handed me a homemade book tied with a small piece of twine. Mom had written the title in her neat handwriting: "I Like Shannon, I Love Shannon." I flipped through all the ways Mom loved me. One page read:

*She can make up lots of different kinds of games, and stories,
and poems.*

    *She likes white people, and Black people, and Vietnamese peo-
ple, and Greek people, and Mexican people, and Spanish people,
and Japanese people, and disabled people. She likes all different
kinds of people.*

The book was bittersweet, an obvious clue that I didn't get into the
program. I thought maybe the teacher got short with me when I asked
a question in class because I was the only Black girl in the room. Adria
and Elsie were part Japanese, like their dad. That must have been the
difference between us.

Mom was mad about the test, but she didn't tell me at the time. She
wonders if the public school gave me a religious test just to fail me. Just
to make sure a Black girl didn't make it into the program. Whatever the
reason, the test seemed proof that I had misjudged myself, that I was
not, in fact, smart.

Grandma saw a difference between me and my cousins too. One day
she and Uncle Adam proudly gave the cousins personalized name badges
they created on their engraving machine. Adria's said something akin to
Violin Virtuoso Adria. Elsie's probably said she was a 4-H Master.
Mine said, Thank You Girl Shannon. My ears burned when I read what
had been etched in plastic, atop an engraved heart with heart-shaped
vines on either side. I said thank you. That's the best that could be said
of me. That was what Grandma thought when she looked at me: I had
an appropriate reaction—not even an action.

True, I didn't get straight As. I didn't like 4-H, and I dropped Girl
Scouts after a week, when my wraparound skirt fell down in the parking
lot during tag before the meeting started. I had just started playing violin,
while Adria and Elsie had been playing for years. Grandma probably never
realized the weight of those four words. But that name badge would be
reinforced for the rest of my life as I learned that people wanted, above all
else, for me to smile, for me to reflect back their generous and accepting
nature. My wide smile expressed an innocent docility. I was trained not
to demand, nor ask for, anything. So began a lifelong lesson in a Black
woman's place, even with people who don't mean to put her there.

San Jose, Calif.

Hello Daughter,

How are you doing in school and at home? Are you going to be in any plays or such this month? When you're going to be involved in any activity be sure to let me know in time so I can make it.

I'm still getting the brakes fixed and when that's done I'm coming to see you, probably in a couple of weeks.

As I keep fixing this and that the car will finally become reliable from bumper to bumper and I can visit any time and often.

I'll call before I come down and, remember I'm Robert Conrad "Martin Luther King" Manuel. The one who loves you . . .

Your Father,
Robert C.

4

THE BLUEST EYE
1986

"I'M NOT GOING TO BE AROUND MUCH LONGER," my dad said when I was ten. At the time, I believed him. Doctors had cut him open like a frog in science class to remove stomach cancer. He said they almost lost him on the operating table. At ten I thought "lost" meant he wandered down the halls with his IV bag in hand. I could just picture how the wheels of the metal rod squeaked as they ran against the tile floor, with the nurses and doctors unaware which way he had turned as he looked back at the empty hallway with a devilish grin. Only later would he tell me that he looked down on himself from a corner of the room as they shocked his body back to life. He chose to stay, he said, because he knew he was destined for greatness.

Dad had an apartment in a small, blue triplex on a long, straight road in San Jose, with precisely planted trees between the sidewalk and the curb. Like always, my dad lived in the Black part of town, while I lived in the white part. His house had two picture windows, one on each side of the front door, and roses that attempted to reach the windowsills. Inside, we watched *Wheel of Fortune* and then played on our own official game board before bed. I saw him a little more often now that we lived in the same town, and he even bought us a parakeet to complement the one I had at home.

"Dad, I have an idea for a game," I told him one afternoon at the Rose Bush House. "It's for playing double Dutch alone. Two robots are at either end and make the ropes go."

"That's a wonderful idea," Dad said with a smile, not indicating that he was just playing along. He took out his typewriter and set it on the kitchen table, then found a piece of paper from a drawer in the living room. Together, we typed up a letter from me to Mattel. Below, Dad had me draw the contraption, complete with an on-off switch and speed control. At the bottom I typed, "Will I get paid? It's OK if I don't." Dad made a copy of the letter and promised to mail it. Later I would understand how silly my idea was, but I never forgot how seriously Dad took me. He feigned belief so I would believe in myself.

The next morning, as Dad and I stepped out of the house, a Black neighbor and her daughter were standing in the shared driveway. The girl was a foot taller than me, older, and with a tight Afro. She was wearing faded black jeans and a tucked-in tank top, and she stood with a swagger just like Dad's, slightly leaning to one side. It was a Black swagger, I knew. My Cabbage Patch Kid rested on my hip, and the neighbor girl looked from me to the blue-eyed, blonde-haired doll, Amy, with a confusion. (My other Cabbage Patch Kids were at home: brown-skinned Karina and white-skinned baby Mercy.) I said hi sheepishly, aware of my doll's complexion for maybe the first time. The neighbor girl said hi back, and then silence. Dad and the woman talked closely, their bodies inches apart. Dad told the girl and me to stand in front of the house for a picture. We stood awkwardly by the rosebushes while Dad snapped his Polaroid with an approving smile. As he immortalized me in his Black world, I wondered if he hoped some of my whiteness would wash off me by my proximity to the neighbor girl.

Dad had a new part-time job with the NAACP, where he worked as a representative in the Social/Economic Research and Development office. I didn't know what that meant, but I was proud he was helping people. The office was in a two-story building on the corner of a quiet, neighborhood street. Dad and I walked into the front hallway that opened out into a big room for meetings with a couple small rooms and a staircase off of it. When we first stepped inside the building, I blinked to adjust my eyes to the lesser light and held my stuffed beagle Dominic under my arm. The ceiling lights were dim against the heavy walls and wood floor. I walked forward and heard the wood creak underneath my feet. Dad ambled up to a man who was busy sweeping as he whistled to himself.

"Hi, George," Dad said.

George's face lit up and he held the broom still. "Hey there, man!" They shook hands, and Dad stepped slightly backward to put his hand behind me and gently guided me forward.

"This is my daughter, Shannon. Shannon Dorrie." Dad liked to include my middle name, which is Mom's nickname, short for Dorothy. Mom told me once that it was Dad who named me.

"Hi," I said with a little wave.

"Shannon here plays the violin, can you believe that? My little musician." Dad seemed to grow even taller than his six-foot self. My violin was a loan from Aunt Deborah, who also paid for the Suzuki lessons I took with my cousins. At our recitals, my poofy hair and stiff uniform, which seemed like it could stand upright from its cheaper fabric than that of my cousins', felt out of place next to the silky black hair and equally silky uniforms of the mostly Asian ensemble. But that was the fabric Mom could afford.

"Your daddy here talks about you all the time," George said. "I'm honored to finally meet the famous Shannon Dorrie."

I smiled, surprised that this man knew who I was. Dad took me farther into the big room, where grown-ups lingered and talked with each other over potato chips and diet soda. "Shannon Dorrie" came out of Dad's mouth again, along with all the proper introductions. The grown-ups grew silent and turned their gaze in our direction. Their eyes twinkled as they took me in, competing for Shannon Dorrie handshakes and even a chance to hug me as if I were a long-lost daughter. They knew my age, my grade, and that I lived in town with my mom. I didn't tell them that Dad talked about me but not much to me, that he only asked if I worked hard in school before starting to list all the good he did in the community, like writing to his congressmen and helping neighbors cut through red tape to find services. I didn't tell them that I never knew if he was really going to see me when he said he was, and that I could count the number of visits we'd had that year on one hand. That he called me a violin virtuoso but never came to a recital. Instead I smiled and said, "Thank you."

Dad had his own desk in one of the small rooms on the first floor, with a window overlooking the street. Now that I'd made my rounds with his friends, he sat in his tall chair and made phone calls to important people and said important things. His voice was like honey that trickled sweetly but powerfully into the telephone. He was a taller and skinnier version of the images I saw in my book on Martin Luther King, whom Dad admired more than anyone. His having worked for the NAACP would impress me for decades—a gold standard in the fight for Black equality.

My stuffed dog Dominic and I played War on the floor. Dominic and my Cabbage Patch Kids made excellent companions. I shuffled the cards and then dealt half for him and half for me. I flipped over our top cards to see whose was highest. When it was his, he got both cards, and when it was mine, I did. We played and played as the sun sank lower in the sky, with the light slowly leaving Dad's window.

Pictures of me at different ages dotted the bulletin board above Dad's desk—a baby picture, and a few school photos, the most recent with my Afro style. Now instead of hair that reached the middle of my back, it was short all over, thanks to a lice outbreak in third grade. At first I had grieved my full tresses as Mom snipped closer and closer to my scalp. But now I had hair like Dad's again—something that bonded us even while we were apart.

Hair bonded Mom and me too, especially when I was little. She'd comb it out every morning while I watched *Sesame Street* on the living room floor. At first it hurt, but I soon developed the thick scalp she promised would develop. She always cut my hair herself, some times better than others, and always in an Afro, because that's what she knew how to do. She apologized for her limitations when she looked back on my hair-care journey, but she was more hands-on than many white mothers of mixed-race daughters in the 1980s and '90s, long before YouTube tutorials and best-selling hair-care guides.

Next to the photos of me on Dad's office wall was a newspaper clipping titled PAINTINGS OF BLACKS REMOVED: NAACP INVESTIGATES CHARGES, with Dad's name in one of the paragraphs, listed as "an official at the San Jose office." After Dominic the dog and I finished war, I asked Dad for a piece of paper and a pencil. I took them back to the floor and,

with my rudimentary skills, drew Dad the paralegal as he sat at his desk and made important phone calls like the president.

For my birthday month in October, Dad took me to Golden West for a giant birthday pancake, a tradition of the past couple years. This year, his friend Cheryl from work came with us. Cheryl was white like mom, and younger, with perfectly feathered, long brown hair. Once she came with Dad and me to the Rose Garden. Today we sat in a brown uphol-stered booth by the door, and the pancake came, delivered on a sheet, with SHANNON spelled out in the whipped butter, just like always. Only this year, they didn't measure right, and the last *n* trailed under the *o*.

After the waiter and waitress sang "Happy Birthday," Cheryl excused herself to the bathroom.

Dad turned to me when she rounded the corner. "Cheryl is going to move in, and we might even get married."

"OK," I said. No one I knew was married except my two sets of aunts and uncles. I didn't know why he'd want to get married, but she seemed like the type of woman men marry. She dressed right and spoke right and smiled right. And I could tell she genuinely liked me. If they did marry, she wouldn't take Dad away. Maybe I'd even see him more, just like when he was with Naomi. A few months ago, Dad had asked me what I thought of him getting back together with Mom. Mom and Dad together felt like pairing up random strangers off the street. I couldn't remember us ever being a family. And I knew Mom well enough to know she'd say no.

When Cheryl came back to the booth, I sliced into my birthday pancake and put a decadent forkful in my mouth. As I began to chew, I noticed a strange sensation and looked down at my baking sheet. Some of the tinfoil had come off with the pancake.

"Is it OK to eat tinfoil?" I asked with my mouth full.

Dad said "No," louder than he seemed to intend. I shot up and walked to the bathroom, opened the empty stall, and deposited the chewed food into the toilet. As I flushed, I was sure Dad had just saved me from death. I could picture the siren getting louder as the ambulance reached Golden West, and the paramedics lifting me onto the gurney. "I'm so sorry," the waiter would say, with a tear in his eye. "I shouldn't have put the pancake on tinfoil." "You almost killed my daughter," my dad would respond with quiet rage. Who knows what danger would have befallen me if he hadn't been there to save me, I thought.

It would be the last time I saw him in such a heroic light.

Things weren't all bad at the Sunnybrook Zoo. After our first year there, Mom and I moved from our downstairs apartment to one upstairs, with a steady wash of light streaming in from the windows. In fifth grade I'd had to go straight from school to an after-school program because Mom had late classes. But after I brought home a bad final report card, she decided to take a lighter class load for my sixth-grade year so she could spend more time looking after me.

We didn't feel like mother and daughter but like two people trying to get by in the world with only each other—and no Grandma to pick up the slack since she now lived almost an hour away. At night we took baths together and drew on each other's backs with special chalk. I made letters on Mom's small, slightly freckled back and made her guess what I wrote, usually "I love you." When I got chicken pox, which Mom had almost died from when she was seven, Mom doted over me with talcum powder baths and dotted calamine lotion on my skin. We had "toothbrushing parties," Mom's clever way of making even routine hygiene seem like special time together.

In our sparse living room, free of even a television just like at Aunt Deborah and Uncle Martin's, we colored together on the floor. Mom always shaded in the outlines perfectly and then filled in the white spaces a degree lighter, with perfect angled strokes. I studied her creations that never veered outside the lines as I tackled my own pages. In winter, we took a spontaneous road trip up Mount Hamilton to play in a bit of snow in an open park. We often wandered by footfall through the hills above our apartment complex and took in the city from the trails of brown grass.

One night as Mom and I drove toward home, we decided to follow searchlights to their destination. We meandered through the neighborhood, with the moon and the streetlights making patterns across the dashboard, until we reached a used car lot where the searchlight shined like a pot of gold at the end of a rainbow.

I spent every Saturday night listening to the weekly countdown on the local pop radio station and meticulously documenting the results in my journal. Some nights I called the female DJ, who graciously asked me questions about my life and seemed interested in my answers. She even returned my letters on station letterhead. One afternoon I got Mom to drive me to the station, an act she said she never would have had the courage to do herself at my age. The DJ wasn't there, but I left the station with a T-shirt and a high from those who had welcomed me warmly.

School was a different story. I took the bus to Edwin Markham Middle School the first year after Latino parents won a fifteen-year battle to prove the district was segregating students with intent. The campus felt enormous as I navigated my way through the halls. The lockers were gone. Too many bomb threats, I heard.

Two eighth-grade Black boys liked to harass me as I passed them in the halls. "Afro!" they shouted. One of the boys was in choir with me, and while he wasn't exactly nice there either, he only got brave with his other friend around. I wondered if they were friends with another boy who, when I passed him in the halls, called out, "You're pretty. Pretty ugly!" I turned away from him and closed my mouth to hide my buckteeth and adjusted my suspenders attached to my black pleated pants.

Before the busing, Markham had been a white school. As "Shannon Manuel," I found myself in a remedial dual-language math class where students spoke both English and Spanish, even though I hadn't been behind in fifth grade. In October, after being out for two weeks with chicken pox and doing my work on my own, the teacher presented me with Student of the Month. When he announced it upon my return, I sat at my desk, dumbfounded. "Go up there, idiot," a student chided. I walked up sheepishly to accept my certificate. Shortly after, Mom talked to the school counselor and had me transferred to a nonremedial class.

It took a while to find a friend at Markham. In fifth grade I had befriended a white girl on the school bus. She teased me, but she was also the only girl who bothered to talk to me. One afternoon she invited me over with another friend, and the two of them wrapped me up in duct tape. When I got home, I told my mom what had happened. Mom pulled out the phone book, walked over to the corded phone, and dialed her number.

"Is your mom there?" she asked. "Well, Shannon has something to tell you and I'm going to be listening when she does. And I'm going to call back to make sure your mom knows what you've been doing."

Mom handed me the receiver, and I took it, my hand shaking. "Hello? I don't like it when you wrap me up in masking tape, and when you make fun of me on the bus. And I don't want you to hit me anymore."

Mom's eyes grew wide at the mention of hitting. She took the receiver back. "Did you hear that?" she asked. "Good."

My sixth-grade year, I made friends with Sandy, a shy white girl I could tell held no ill will toward anyone. She had inconsequential brown hair and scraggly clothing much like mine. We were instant friends, providing a shield for each other against the onslaughts of preteen angst. She was my first real friend since Santa Cruz.

Sandy would never think of hitting, or teasing, or wrapping someone in masking tape. We never hung out outside of school, but she became my best friend. For the yearly talent show, we performed "Anything You Can Do" from *Annie Get Your Gun*. Onstage, I forgot all the hand gestures we'd practiced, and my voice shook, but it didn't matter—we learned at the end of the talent show that the winners were chosen by applause from the audience. As social outcasts we never had a chance. Still, together we had dared to push back against our wallflower status and raise our voices in a crowded room. I even talked to the counselor about the two boys who teased me in the halls, and whatever he said to them worked.

I graduated that year with top honors.

———————————

Every Labor Day and Memorial Day my extended family and I camped at "the Land," a large area of forest in the Santa Cruz Mountains owned by Aunt Deborah and Uncle Eugene's friend. They had all met at an Eastern European folk dancing class at UC Santa Cruz around the time I was born. The friend had taken Deborah and Eugene to his land to practice, and over the years, he came to host two Land Dance weekends a year. About fifty people, mostly families, still come from Silicon Valley to the remote location behind a closed gate. Participants drive down, down, down a dirt road, switching back and forth and back and forth under canopied trees, until you feel like you're headed into the earth itself. At the very bottom is the Land, complete with a giant folk dance deck in a clearing, a little outdoor sink with a counter, and a firepit for meals. Participants sleep in tents wherever they can find a spot off the trails. To use the bathroom, a camper carries a flag down a trail and sits on a log wedged between two trees. After using the roll of toilet paper that sits on the log, we were to cover over the area with a shovel.

The Land was mostly for Eastern European folk dancing, but I didn't notice any difference between my family and the many Jewish ones who took part. We were all one family, and my aunt and uncle seemed to hold a special place in the community as unofficial cofounders. I didn't know how to "dance Black," my hips attached tightly to the rest of my middle. But I knew some of the folk dance numbers by heart, my legs and feet lifting this way and that as we danced in a circle to scratchily recorded songs from long ago and far away, booming through an A/V system, with words I couldn't understand. It wasn't my culture, but the Land was as home to me as the one I lived in. I'd heard the folk tunes and live music since I was a baby, or maybe even in the womb.

That year, after Memorial Day, the Murphys and I went back to the Land in June to celebrate my cousin Adria's birthday, a week or two before the end of the school year. We had the expanse to ourselves. Sandy's birthday was the same day as Adria's (and coincidentally also the same day as Dad's). Sandy's mom and her boyfriend were going out of town to a motorcycle convention, so I asked Sandy if she wanted to tag along to the Land. Adria welcomed Sandy like family. We hiked, lounged on the raft in the pond to catch newts, and roasted marshmallows in the dark around the firepit. On Sunday, after we'd returned to the Murphys', Sandy's parents came to pick her up. They looked us over and then couldn't get her to the car fast enough. At school the next day, Sandy said she couldn't see me anymore. Her mom hadn't known until then that I was Black or that my cousins were part Japanese. I wondered why someone so concerned with who her daughter spent time with left her alone on her birthday for a motorcycle convention.

From that moment, losing Sandy was a first and lasting reminder that friends could be torn from me, even if they didn't want to be. That I was marked with something inferior. In 2015 during a move, Sandy found my birthday card to her, which she had hidden inside her doll all those years ago. She cried when she found the card and then sought me out on Facebook. After thirty years, our friendship was restored. Getting Sandy back was getting back something that had been taken from me—a happy ending to my sad story.

Later that summer, Mom got married. She said she knew Gary was safe because of Mrs. Ford—the elderly Black woman Gary took care of in Dad's old neighborhood. Mom said any white man who sacrificed his time to help an old Black woman must possess a warm heart, unlike the man she had dated right before Gary, who had grabbed my wrist and insisted I say please before he'd let go. Mom quickly let him go, out the front door. But harassment isn't always so obvious; sometimes it sneaks up on you.

Mom had started dating that spring after her Al-Anon sponsor said her sadness was probably loneliness. That didn't make sense to me; Mom was never alone. She had me. And she had Al-Anon, which she still attended religiously, even though she hadn't been with Dad in nine years. After talking with her sponsor, Mom went to events hosted by Parents Without Partners until she and Gary met at a dance. He was a Christian Scientist, a few years older than Mom, and seemed even older, with prematurely gray hair and a face wrinkled from working as a gardener for the city. Gary was the opposite of my dad: where one was witty beyond measure, able to have philosophical conversations with anyone, the other was a stick-in-the-mud who never had much to say. Mom and Gary dated for six months before they got married in Grandma's backyard.

The sky was extra blue that day—as if Jimmy Cliff were telling me to "look straight ahead, there's nothing but blue skies," despite the invisible cloud that hovered over me. Family and friends stood on the lawn and on the patio under the trellis as the wind chimes tinged overhead. Mom and Gary recited their vows to Mr. Brown, our old minister from Santa Cruz. Mom wore a dark blue linen dress with a Peter Pan lace collar and a simple white wreath on her short, permed hair. I stood beside her, proud to be her maid of honor in spite of whom she was marrying. Adria and Elsie were to my left, all of us in prairie dresses and patent leather shoes. Gary's son, Nick, who was a year and a half younger than me, was his best man, no doubt feeling as dubious about the union as I did. After the ceremony, Nick sat on the edge of the lawn and dug up flowering weeds with a scowl. His hair was so blond that it was almost white. His younger cousins were easy to spot in the crowd, with similar near-white halos.

My family locked arms and danced in a circle to a familiar folk dance tune, but I didn't feel like celebrating. Instead, I squeezed past and ambled up to the barbecue and grabbed a hot dog from the food table. I looked up to the blue sky through the trellis and hoped its brilliance wasn't in vain.

The day after the wedding, Mom and I moved from our apartment to Gary's three-bedroom, one-thousand-square-foot home in the suburbs.

The first time I saw Gary's house, it was shrouded in smoke from his bad fireplace. The firemen had just been there, probably after receiving a call from a neighbor. When we stepped inside, the carpet rolled in places on the living room floor, like stuck waves. His old roommate, a middle-aged Mexican man named Hollywood, had poured water on it to clean it. My room was currently being repainted from Hollywood's black to a cheerful white. Gary had offered me the bigger room, but I wanted to be as close to Mom as possible, even if by just two or three steps.

At Gary's, I had a room with a door, but the door shut Mom out. Or shut me away from her. In fact, now she was locked away with two doors between us. If I ever wanted to reach her, I had to get past the sleeping giant first. A giant who spoke in an alternatingly gentle voice—almost babyish—and one that boomed off the thin walls of the small house with no notice, attacking whoever was close by. It was a marked difference from the steadiness of Uncle Adam, the only other male I had lived with past toddlerhood. As an adult, Mom would tell me that Gary often didn't remember his rages. It was as if he entered a different state and then blacked it out when he came to.

"Why do you like Gary even though he yells?" I asked Mom one afternoon in the car, made brave by her inability to look me in the eye.

"Well, the yelling isn't good, but your dad hit me, and that was worse." I wondered why either had to happen. Weren't there men who didn't hit or yell?

Dad called me one day to give some very urgent advice. I took the call on top of the washing machine, with the cord of the telephone gently snuggled in the door jamb. "Your mother will always be your mother, your father will always be your father, but that man will never be your father." Gary didn't feel like my father anyway. But neither did my father. Fathers were supposed to be a steady presence, sitting in an easy chair in the living room, smoking a pipe and watching the news. They were supposed to tell corny jokes and rib their wives just a little bit. They were supposed to grill their daughters about their day, and not just in spurts on the telephone. They were supposed to be a rock that their daughters sometimes resented but also leaned on—someone to hold on to, someone to keep them afloat.

When I was in seventh grade, Dad moved to a duplex in a closer neighborhood, but he felt farther away. He no longer worked for the NAACP. His light brown house sat on a plot of light dead brown grass.

For a Saturday visit, rarer than they had been the year before, Mom dropped me off and then drove around the corner out of sight. I knocked on Dad's door, but no one answered. I turned the knob and stepped inside. The house was silent, with an eeriness like right before an earthquake. The ground didn't start to shake, so I stepped forward through the house. The living room was empty. The kitchen was deserted. Light filtered out of the open bedroom door and into the hall. I followed the light and rounded the corner, and I stepped into whatever was waiting in the shadows. My dad was face down on the bed. His breathing was heavy like sleep, but it was three o'clock in the afternoon. The air smelled pungent, like that of the homeless men with empty bottles who shuffled as they asked for change.

I touched the heel of his shoe.

"Dad?" I whispered.

Dad didn't respond to my touch. I placed my hand on his blue shirt, putting the faintest pressure on the low of his back.

"Dad?"

He was never quiet. He never lay down. He should have been lecturing me, teasing me, sneaking pictures of me picking my nose. We should have been watching *The Jeffersons* or driving to the Rose Garden with Cheryl, who had vanished. I wondered if my dad was dead. But dead people didn't breathe. I wondered if he was in a coma, but people didn't fall into comas on their own bed. Instead—I knew from TV—they're in the hospital, surrounded by friends and family, with someone who loves them holding their hand, urging them to return to the land of the living.

I walked around Dad's bed and stood next to his head. His eyes were open but he didn't see.

"Dad?"

Then I noticed a woman I'd never seen before. She was standing behind the open bedroom door. She wobbled slightly as she took off her black leather coat. Her weave rustled stiffly as she took off her polka-dot shirt. She was trying to unsnap her bra while doing a striptease. She hummed softly, but no one was watching. No one but me.

I thought about the movie *La Bamba*, which Mom and Gary had taken me to see in the theater while they were dating. In the movie, the singer Ritchie Valens's brother always has a bottle in his hand. One night he bangs on his mom's door, begging to see his baby daughter. He screams into the abyss, with eyes on fire. Dad was the opposite of screaming, but I felt in that moment the same way I had watching the brother in the movie, and I didn't know why. I didn't know that when I was a baby, my dad had often disappeared overnight, and sometimes for days. I didn't know he had regularly passed out three or four times a week from drinking.

"Mom?" I said into Dad's phone receiver after darting out of his bedroom with the stripping stranger hiding behind the door. "Can you come get me?"

I waited on the porch until Mom pulled up. Neither Dad nor the stranger came to check on me. When Mom arrived, she walked inside. Dad and the stranger were sitting at the kitchen table—the stranger's shirt opened wide, exposing her bra.

"You shouldn't have done that in front of my daughter," Dad said loudly to the stranger, who stayed silent.

"I'm taking Shannon home now," Mom said, her head reaching up as high as it could from her small frame, as if a marionette had granted her a few more inches.

Somehow she knew not to ask me what happened, and even if she had, I didn't know how to explain what I saw. I sat in the backseat with what my mom would later say was a face closed like a fist. We left my father behind, a man who had lain dormant as he sought to escape a world he told me was beautiful.

5

A TREE GROWS
IN BROOKLYN
1988

IN SEVENTH GRADE, Punky Brewster was my best friend. I knew it was just a TV show, but I also knew it was real—that Punky, a spunky orphan, and the girl who played her, Soleil Moon Frye, were one and the same. Mom bought me Punky's dog, Brandon, from Toys "R" Us. I carefully cut out the two pictures of Punky from the cardboard box he came in and carried them around in my pocket. Over the next few months, the cardboard grew soft, almost cloth-like. Creases formed across Punky's face. She was becoming part of me.

Toward the end of my mile walk home from school, before crossing over to my street, I talked silently to the Punky Tree—a tall oak tree next to the sidewalk that I just knew held Punky magic. Whenever I walked underneath those branches, Punky's spirit emanated from the gently rustling leaves. I had parents, but since my live-in family had changed four times, I felt like she and I spoke the same language. We were both displaced, both believed in goodness, both had to carve our own way. The tree applauded me each day for getting through school, and it reassured me I could get through the next.

At home, my Cabbage Patch Kids were just as real as Punky. They had their own fabric high chairs with rubber handles that attached to the kitchen table. My Cabbage Patch Kids and I talked about everything: I mediated arguments; I taught them reading, writing, and arithmetic with workbooks from the teacher's store; I made sure they got to bed on time. But they couldn't come to school with me. Only Punky could.

Union Middle School was different from Markham, my previous school. Where Markham had felt like chaos, Union felt like order. Kids were white and rich. The school was just over the city line in wealthy Los Gatos. My neighborhood bumped up to the line so closely that Union was the public school for kids on my block. I had no bullies, but I also had no friends. Every afternoon I came home to an episode of *Punky Brewster*. At the library, I pulled each new Baby-Sitters Club book from the shelf as soon as it arrived. Sometimes I jumped double Dutch on the hot sidewalk with the Mexican American twins, Christina and Natalie, who lived two doors down. But mostly, I was a shadow. I was "eleven going on ten," and it felt like everyone else in my grade was twelve going on fifteen.

My shadowness followed me around the house. Gary's energy seemed to suck the air from anything around it like a goblin masked by an outward appearance of feebleness. The men in my mom's family were true WASPs who never raised their voices. Uncle Adam had walked through Grandma's house with gentle steps. The only time Dad had raised his voice to me was when I six and had jammed a whole pack of gum in my mouth, and wouldn't let him see what I was chewing. Nothing had prepared me for Gary.

"Get your elbows off the table!" he bellowed one night at dinner while he wrangled the gristle from his chicken bone with his teeth. No one in my family had cared about elbows on the table, but Mom didn't come to my rescue. Apparently now it was a rule. I ran to my room and hid on the top bunk. Gary's cat jumped up to join me and licked my fingers. My heart warmed, oblivious to the leftover chicken juice on my skin which had naturally caused his "affection." Another rule, made just for me, was to shower as quickly as possible. There was no set time limit, but if I didn't finish fast enough, Gary turned the water off from outside, and I was left with a head full of suds.

That night after Gary fell asleep on the couch, I crept back out and pulled cold chicken from the fridge.

In the spring, Mom and Gary sat me down at the kitchen table. "Shannon, we have something to tell you," Mom said.

I braced for the worst. "What's wrong?" I asked.

"Well, you're going to be a sister. I'm having a baby girl."

An indescribable love poured through me in seconds. In that moment I knew I was put in that house to be a big sister. Now it all made sense.

Mom was eight months pregnant when the earthquake hit.

Growing up near the San Andreas Fault, I'd been schooled on earthquake preparedness for as long as I could remember. We all knew a big one was coming—we just didn't know when. We were supposed to have bottles of water, flashlights, and canned food. And we were supposed to know where and how to hide.

The 1989 Loma Prieta quake hit in the late afternoon of an extra-still day, as I was searching through my box of baby photos for an eighth-grade school project. I heard the rumble first. As it grew in intensity, everything began to shudder around me. The house jerked back and forth as if it were trying to expel a poison. My dad popped up like a thought bubble in a cartoon. "Find a doorway," the cartoon said. I ran down the hall too fast to stop. I was about to bolt out the back door when Mom looked up at me from the kitchen floor. "Duck," she said. The telephone wire, visible through the back door window, bounced up and down in warning like a jump rope with no participants.

Mom held a kitchen knife in her hand as the cutting table rolled across the kitchen looking for its own place of safety. The freshly sliced carrots found a hideaway on the floor. Mom and I stayed crouched on the green linoleum tile until the house went quiet. What felt like minutes passed before we finally stood on our unsteady feet. A hesitant scan of the house showed us nothing much had changed. My stepdad's big seashell, which was usually perched on top of the tall bookcase, was now swinging back and forth from the chain of the hanging lamp. In the garage, a tall mirror rested in pieces on the concrete. The epicenter was closer to Santa Cruz, where the 6.9 quake demolished much of my childhood downtown.

Mom and I made our way out the front door. All our neighbors did the same. Adults and children emerged from their one-story ranch-style homes, all built in the 1950s. Two houses down, the twins stood with their grandparents and their little sister and brother.

The grandparents, the only Mexican American family on our street, stood out front with the rest of us. The Martinez family was known for their parties. Most holidays, their family's cars filled our street as everyone gathered in the backyard for a barbecue. Welcomed as an honorary Martinez, I often crashed the parties and inhaled Mrs. Martinez's tacos and burritos. Mexican music would blend with the dry summer sun, and I felt more at home there, with people who looked like me, than back home with my white family.

The day of the earthquake, everyone on the block became an honorary Martinez. The grandparents set up a grill in the front yard, and the neighbors brought what they could. Mexican music pierced the eerie stillness that follows a quake. We got through the aftershocks together, our bond increasing with each one. Each time, a hush rolled in, and we widened our stance a little farther. The aftershocks showed no sign of letting up as the night crept in. Many families planned to sleep in tents in the abandoned schoolyard across the street, but my mom and Gary didn't want to join in the fun.

"Can I sleep in your room tonight?" I asked Mom that night before bed.

"No," Gary said. "That's our room. You stay in yours."

Mom kept silent.

I cried myself to sleep on my top bunk, with audible wails that reached no one. That night more than any I wished my mom and I still shared the one-bedroom apartment and that her small frame still slept peacefully in the bottom bunk. I braced myself for aftershocks and pictured my wooden bed crumbling to pieces, or the too-close ceiling crashing down on my body. It was the last time I would cry with that innocence. After that night, almost all my tears were silent for twenty years.

———————

My sister Melanie was born on a school day, one month after the earth-quake and two weeks after her due date. My mom woke me that morning, gently rubbing my shoulder and placing her face close to mine.

"You're not going to school today. I'm going to have your sister," she said with a smile. I didn't know how she knew, but I believed her.

Within half an hour, Grandma, Uncle Adam, Aunt Deborah, Adria, and Elsie had all pulled up our driveway. We took Mom on a slow walk around the block in an attempt to help her water break. The crisp fall air filled our lungs and mist formed on our jackets. It felt like fairy dust.

I was in eighth grade now, and newly thirteen. The Christmas before, I had left a drugstore necklace for Soleil Moon Frye on the hearth of the fireplace, just like Punky had left a present for her mom who had abandoned her. On Christmas morning on the show, the present had magically disappeared and been replaced with Punky's childhood music box, which only her mother could have left, through Santa Claus's magic. When I woke up the next morning and saw the wrapped necklace just where I'd left it, I knew Punky wasn't real, Santa Claus wasn't real, and TV had tricked me. But my heart still yearned for magic. I was ready for someone flesh and blood to love. Someone whom I could be there for always, whose existence would clarify my own. I wouldn't just be the offspring of Mom's former relationship; I'd be genetically connected to a sibling. I yearned for her so much that it didn't matter that she shared Gary's genes too.

Melanie was born in a small hospital near my middle school. My mom had a difficult labor, and Melanie's umbilical cord was wrapped around her neck. The forceps used to remove her had left small indentations on the sides of her head. I loved my little nearly bald alien sister, whose sparse yellow fuzz was the softest thing I had ever touched.

That afternoon, I was in charge of making calls from the pay phone in the hall. "I have a baby sister. And she's pink."

———————

That same year, Dad moved to an apartment about twenty straight blocks up the main street from my house. I saw him more often now, but he was no longer Dad the Invincible, able to protect me from the ills of the world. I'd never be able to erase the image of him sprawled on the bed with dead eyes.

Dad had told me that he used to drink when he lived with Mom but that he had been sober for years now. Despite what had happened with the stranger, I believed him. I don't know how I reconciled his passing out, but my mind made some other excuse. Maybe because I knew he wasn't allowed to drink around me, and if I faced it, I might lose him. Or maybe it was because the image was just too upsetting. Still, his actions that day—or lack thereof—haunted me, and I found myself retreating from the closeness we once shared.

Dad was on edge with Mom's new marriage—not because he wanted her back, but because he didn't want to be replaced. "Which family do you really belong to?" he asked me on a phone call. His calls were never to simply to catch up and were rarely filled with small talk. He seemed incapable of shooting the breeze. Instead, he pontificated and interrogated, with not much in between.

"I belong to the Manuel family, the Luders family [my mom's side of the family], and the Hastings family," I answered.

Dad pushed back. "You belong to the Manuel family and the Luders family." He didn't say anything about the Hastings.

After our phone call, I wrote in my diary:

> *I live in a Hastings house, I live with Hastings people, I have a Hastings room, I'm lying on a Hastings rug, but these things are mine too. So I belong to the Hastings family as well.*

Gary, on the other hand, didn't see me that way. He had no desire to win me over or to consider me his child. Any generosity on Gary's part was just that—goodwill, not obligation.

Gary dismissed Dad just as Dad did him, saying he hoped Dad didn't hurt his current girlfriend, and once threatened to make me spend the night at Dad's house if I didn't do the dishes. As if being with my father were punishment.

One day Dad sent a cab to pick me up. I felt important, but I was also scared to be locked in a car with a stranger—a bald white man who could have been anyone and driven me anywhere. But he deposited me right in Dad's parking lot. I hadn't realized I was holding my breath until I stepped out. Dad opened the front door and called me up the steps.

"Excuse me for a moment, Daughter," he said as he made his way to the bedroom.

Inside the apartment, I opened the lid of a boiling pot to see a giant cow tongue staring back at me, so big that it protruded from the top of the water. The steam reached my hand and covered it with what felt like cow tongue cooties. I made a face as I walked over to the kitchen sink and washed my hands, then looked in vain for a towel. I grabbed a paper towel instead and opened the cupboard under the sink to throw it away. Next to the garbage was a tall bottle of vodka, opened but not empty. It was sort of similar to the smaller bottle of brandy that Grandma kept on a high shelf in the kitchen cupboard and brought down only to light the plum pudding on fire at Christmas. Grandma liked to tell the story of a distant cousin as a warning for all her progeny: "One night she decided to have a glass of wine. She liked the taste, so the next night she had another. Then the next night, another. Then she realized she had a problem and never touched alcohol again."

My thoughts were interrupted by a knock on the door. I opened it to find a Black man, slightly shorter and wider than Dad, with a black garbage bag in his hand.

"Hey, Frank," Dad said, emerging from the bedroom. Then he turned to me and said, "We've got some stuff to do. We're going to take my car," he said.

"Yeah," Frank said. "Damn DUI."

Dad and Frank carried bundles of laundry out to Dad's 1975 Plymouth Valiant—a long brown car Dad bought after someone stole his beloved Chrysler. One of the bundles was in a white basket, but the rest were in pillowcases and more black garbage bags. Dad stumbled as he walked down the stairs. Then he dropped a full pillowcase to grab hold of the railing.

I watched from a safe spot inside the doorway.

"Come on, Daughter," he said. "I can't leave you home alone." His voice sounded strange, like a recording in slow motion, and I felt a pain in the pit of my stomach. I grabbed the last bundle of laundry, shut the door firmly behind me, and then dragged the bundle down the stairs.

Dad and Frank waited for my load and then slammed the trunk shut. It popped back open and Dad tried harder this time.

"Shit," he said as it sprang back open. "We'll just have to drive this way."

I walked up to the trunk and arranged the bundles of laundry. I moved hangers toward the back and then slammed the hood down firmly. "Well, how about that," Dad said. "I've got a real-live Wonder Woman on my hands."

He walked over to the driver's side door, hanging onto the side of the car. He opened the door, sat down, and turned the ignition, revving it up loud like a sports car. I put my hands over my ears as I hopped into the backseat, and Frank opened the passenger seat and plopped down next to Dad.

Dad backed up but forgot to look over his shoulder, and he hit a post, hard. Then he put the car in drive and it swerved from side to side as it made its way to the street.

"Dad!" I screamed, as he turned the car left toward the oncoming traffic.

He swerved fast to the right and we made our way slowly down the center of the street as cars honked all around us. I put my hands back over my ears and the pain in my stomach was strong now. Dad looked back at me and smiled but I didn't smile back.

"When can we go home again?"

"Soon," he said.

When we returned from the laundromat, Dad went to his room and lay down on the bed. I opened the cabinet under the sink where I had seen the vodka and poured it down the drain.

The next day, back at Gary's, I heard the phone ring as I lay on my bottom bunk reading the latest installment of the Baby-Sitters Club.

"Shannon!" Mom yelled.

I walked down the hall and reluctantly took the phone. Something told me it was my dad. I hoped he wasn't about to yell at me for pouring out his vodka, even though I was sure I had done the right thing.

"Hello?" I asked.

Dad's steady voice sang through the receiver, serenading me with Stevie Wonder's "I Just Called to Say I Love You."

Dad scheduled our next visit but didn't come. I stared at the phone on the kitchen wall, but it didn't ring. I peered out the living room window, pulling back the thin white curtain, but there was no Plymouth in the driveway. Just oil stains on the concrete.

Mom walked in from down the hall. "No Dad yet, huh?"

I shook my head no and stared at my hands. A girl at school said the palms say everything, and the lines etched there tell your future. I looked at my lines but they led nowhere, just trails leading off in opposite directions. I walked to my bedroom and stopped at the bookcase at the end of the hall. I scanned the shelves for something to read and saw a thin, blue composition book at the end of the bottom shelf. I took it out and opened to the first page. It said "Journal" in my mother's handwriting. I read the first entry, back from when I was almost four.

> *Oct 13, 1980*
> *On Friday, R was drunk when he came to my house. I told him I was going inside, and he could send S in to me when he was ready to leave. S told him, "You smell like a Daddy." I was angry with R because he called me on the phone and jocularly threatened to blow me away or to burn down my house. L [Grandma] says for me to tell him that's not funny.*

I didn't want to picture my dad like the wolf in "The Three Little Pigs," but I knew my mom never lied.

I sat down cross-legged on the floor and kept reading.

Mom wrote about someone named Pauline she had talked to around the time we left Dad. When Pauline commented on Mom's getting through many difficulties, and then later didn't want to visit because she had just returned from a vacation, Mom was sure Pauline was prejudiced and didn't like that Mom had a mixed-race child. At the end of the entry, Mom wrote:

> *After a long, long time, I began to comprehend the basis for my resentful feelings. I realized that I felt ashamed, that it had been painful for me to admit to her that I had been living in a mentally and physically abusive situation.*

The book felt red hot, dispelling secrets my mom had hidden from me. She had always let me come to my own conclusions, to figure things out by myself. Now, on page after page, Mom spoke of her fears—of bad dreams, of bad memories. And she spoke of Dad's drinking in a way she'd only hinted at before when she'd asked me if he had stayed sober during our visits. Now I knew why he'd been passed out on the bed that day with the strange woman in the corner. I never told Mom about the drive to the laundromat, just like I never told her about Dad passed out. I had watched these things as if in slow motion, underwater, unable to make a noise—and when I surfaced, they remained below, indelible in my mind and yet, at the same time, erased.

I slipped the journal into my room and placed it on my own shelf. It was my map to the unknown, and one I would continue to visit, searching for missing puzzle pieces to a hazy past.

———————

Mom still attended Al-Anon religiously, even though she hadn't been with Dad for ten years. I often went with her, preferring the boredom to staying home with Gary. My stuffed dog, Dominic, and I usually played War in the back while the grown-ups talked about things I only slightly understood. I tried to pace how many sugar cubes I ate from the tray next to the coffee—the jolts of energy kept me awake until we all joined hands for the mantra at the end: "Keep coming back. It works."

I liked anniversary nights the best, when people received chips that corresponded with how long they'd been in Al-Anon, just like those in AA received chips for sobriety. One night, as I sat next to Mom, I asked why kids didn't get chips.

"You should ask Sandy," she said, referring to the group's representative.

When I believed in something strongly enough, I wasn't shy around adults. After the meeting I walked up to Sandy in the front of the room and repeated my question.

"You're right," she said. "Kids should get chips."

At the next anniversary meeting, Sandy presented me with a thirteen-year chip in front of everyone, as if I were an adult too, as if we were all in this together. I sat back down next to Mom and examined my prize. The bronze head side centered an engraved butterfly, with FREEDOM • GROWTH repeated around the circular edge. On the tail side of the chip was the Al-Anon pledge: "God, grant me the serenity to accept the things I cannot change, the courage to change the things I can, and the wisdom to know the difference."

I'd heard the pledge for as long as I could remember, but after opening Mom's journal, I knew it and the chip meant I had survived something. And that she had too. We were bonded by something we never talked about. I stopped attending Al-Anon soon after, immersing myself in my new teen life. But that chip would stay with me forever.

6

THE CATCHER IN THE RYE
1990

By SPRING OF EIGHTH GRADE, my obsession with *Punky Brewster* had been replaced by one with *Doogie Howser, M.D.*, a TV show about a child prodigy who becomes a doctor in his midteens. Except I didn't carry cutouts of Doogie in my pocket. Instead, I had a poster of him on my wall. And I didn't want to be Doogie like I wanted to be Punky. I wanted him—or the actor who played him, Neil Patrick Harris—to be my boyfriend.

In an episode in the first season, Raymond, a Black teen from Compton, holds up a convenience store and holds Doogie and his friend Vinnie hostage. Over the next few hours, Raymond takes off his sunglasses, do-rag, baseball cap, and gang jacket after forming an unlikely bond with his hostages—all of them just kids, dancing to Young MC and eating all the junk food they can stuff in their mouths. Raymond has to negotiate with the police to be tried as a juvenile, even though he's not an adult. By the end of the episode, typing a diary entry on his IBM computer, Doogie realizes he might be prejudiced because he doesn't have any Black friends. If that was true, I feared, I was prejudiced too. Aside from an acquaintance at school, Dad was the only Black person I knew.

Dad's bottles of vodka either didn't return to their place under the sink or were hidden elsewhere. I could almost pretend that I hadn't seen Dad unhinged, that it had all happened in some parallel universe. Still, each time Mom dropped me off now, each time I crossed the doorway into Dad's house, some unspoken danger permeated the air. I pushed it aside. I had to.

Dad began to teach me Black history during our visits. Or rather, he let the TV do so. He regularly turned on the PBS special *Eyes on the Prize*, a fourteen-part documentary that covered the civil rights movement. Burned in my brain were black-and-white video recordings of hoses turned on Black citizens. Of the Montgomery Bus Boycott, where most Black residents of Montgomery, Alabama, stayed off the city buses for thirteen months after Rosa Parks was jailed for refusing to give up her seat. Of the Greensboro sit-in, when college students protested the whites-only counter at Woolworth's in North Carolina. Of Martin Luther King orating during the March on Washington. Perhaps to counter the heaviness of this history, *Soul Train*, the largely Black musical variety show, was also part of the rotation. *Eyes on the Prize* elevated my Black history beyond slavery, but I still lacked a contemporary, tangible connection to my race—current events, a mentor, or a friend.

––––––––––

The summer before my freshman year of high school, Gary's son, Nick, moved in with us. He'd been acting up back home in Sacramento and came to us for a fresh start. My family became a living version of *The Simpsons*, which had recently premiered and which Nick and I watched religiously. Gary was socially awkward just like Homer; Mom was accommodating like Marge; Nick was wild like the young teen Bart (his blond hair with buzzed lines on the sides was even almost yellow); and Melanie was baby Maggie, often left to her own devices. I was Lisa Simpson, nerdy and musical.

Nick and I defied most stepsibling logic by becoming instant best friends. He had the second bedroom all to himself, while Melanie slept in her crib at the foot of my bunk bed. But Nick often preferred my bottom bunk to his own room. We'd talk until we fell asleep. Of what, it hardly mattered, as long we were together.

Nick was a year and half younger than me but was the leader, pushing me beyond my quiet routines. We spent our summer building forts in the backyard from wood Gary had piled up for the fireplace, careful not to disturb Gary's haphazard vegetable garden filled with tall stalks of corn and thick vines of zucchini. We hammered and stacked and then played until Gary tore our masterpiece down because he thought it wasn't safe. Then we'd build another one.

We guffawed at the boy down the street whose father made him a fort out of a set from the home improvement store. The perfect lines, painted wood, and easily accessible entrance lacked the originality of our piecemeal creations. Not only that, but the neighbor boy had to return home for dinner when his mom rang a bell on the porch. Just like a dog, we thought. We could stay out as long as we wanted. No one was waiting for us at home. Even if Mom or Gary were home, they seemed oblivious to our passing in and out of the house. Mom had mostly stopped cooking once she got married. Gary was never happy with what she made. Nick taught me how to make frozen pizza, and the newfound self-sufficiency meant I never went hungry while Mom got full on little snacks. Nick and I built dirt mounds in the giant lot of the abandoned school and rode up and down and around in circles until the sun set. Other days we'd play two-person baseball in the grassy area of the schoolyard, taking turns with the glove and bat, or play three-person with the neighbor boy until his dinner bell rang.

Our street teemed with seventeen kids, and Nick had a way of drawing them all out. He recruited the twins' little brother to be his "apprentice." He taught him how to build forts and made him smoke a cigarette so he'd cough and not try it himself. We called ourselves a gang, and I wore the label with pride, though the worst we did was try to jump fences like ninjas. The few times we attended Gary's Christian Science church, Nick and I—the only two members of youth group—did everything we could do annoy the leader. Nick because he didn't believe in anything, and I because I was a Congregationalist like my mom. Gary's church was sparsely filled with old people who believed the founder, Mary Baker Eddy, should be studied just as much as God and Jesus. She just seemed like a kook to me. Someone who believed only God could heal, not science, which seemed ironic given the name of the denomination.

Nick took up more space than most people, just like Gary. At home, Nick and Gary would yell at each other, Mom would yell at Nick to defend Gary, and I would yell at Gary to protect Nick.

Once, Gary came in from work and saw that Nick hadn't washed the dishes. He turned to me as I was sitting on the couch watching cartoons. "You're going to hell!" he bellowed, his face turning red. My ears burned at his declaration. Gary was more religious than I was. He read only Christian books and often did devotionals at the kitchen table. Hell wasn't an abstract concept for him. And he wanted to banish me over dishes—and not even mine.

"Kick him in the balls!" Nick often commanded me during arguments. I never listened, because I didn't want to go anywhere near Gary's private parts. Plus, I've never been that flexible.

Another day, Gary, Nick, and I squared off in the living room. "Kick him in the balls!" I bravely yelled to Nick.

Then I felt a big, grown-up palm collide with my face before I could take another breath. I stood stunned for a moment and then ran out the front door, taking solace two doors down at the twins' for the rest of the day.

The next morning, I walked into the kitchen to find Mom sitting at the table.

"I want to move," I said.

"Oh yeah? Where?" she asked, somewhat amused.

"Back home with Grandma." I missed my makeshift bed in the laundry room, the clean backyard, the comfortable silence. A couple hours and a phone call from my mother later, Grandma declined my offer. I felt too embarrassed to ask why, but later, as an adult, I knew. Grandma never saw the secret Gary—the one behind the closed door. She didn't see the pieces of wood he threw at me from next to the fireplace when he yelled at me to answer the door after Grandma knocked. She didn't see the oranges hurled at me for no reason.

"Then I want to live with Dad," I told Mom. I silently vowed to pour all his vodka down the drain, to not mind if he had lady callers, to be happy on the couch.

"Your dad can't take you," she said later that day. I was sure he had rejected me too. But looking back, I doubt my mom even asked him.

She knew living with Dad was not a viable option. It wouldn't fix our current situation.

Mom took our misfit family to counseling. We sat on folding chairs in a circle while Mom answered most of the questions. I was no stranger to therapy, but it was uncharted territory for Gary—a strict Christian Scientist—and Nick could not have cared less.

"Gary," the counselor asked, "how do you feel about having a biracial stepdaughter?"

"Well," Gary answered, "let me just say this. I don't like my job, but I do it anyway, for the money."

My body felt hot and the room spun briefly. I was surprised to find myself still sitting in the folding chair and not crumpled on the floor. Gary didn't want me. I was the tagalong to my mother. I was the income tax that comes with winning the lottery. The dead skin that crumbles off a sunburn before it turns golden.

Mom didn't say anything. When I was forty-seven, she told me her silence was her attempt to protect me. Gary and I were fighting over her affections, and if she didn't engage, she thought, things would sort themselves out. But if she stood up for her daughter, Gary would see me as a threat and might increase his verbal attacks. She said she wouldn't have married him if she'd known of his racism, but that divorce would mean failure—a second failure after my dad. She'd waited eight years for a relationship and needed it to succeed, both emotionally and financially. She was still in school and would be "up a creek without a paddle" if she left.

The conversation left me with a better understanding of why she hadn't stood up for me, but I still wished she had. Instead, she often retreated to her room and slammed the door or left the house to cool off—both of which meant I was left to face Gary alone.

———————

On hot days that summer, I walked Melanie over to the Leigh High School pool so we could cool off. I barely knew anyone, but I didn't care, because my best friend besides Nick was with me, in her waterproof diaper. One afternoon I dipped her, spun her, and watched her laugh like I had countless times before. Some of the kids from my middle school acted as lifeguards. The girls' hair was perfectly feathered, and the boys' legs looked longer than they had just a couple months prior. Girls tanned by the pool, some facing up, some down. I was quickly learning that it was considered more desirable to be a white girl with tan skin from the sun than a part-Black girl in her natural tan shade.

As I carried Melanie into the locker room to change, I noticed a makeshift sign on the wall next to the entrance: a piece of printer paper affixed with tape, with a handwritten message in Sharpie.

> *Shannon has hairy legs and armpits.*
> *—The Management*

My knees threatened to buckle beneath me. The world around me whooshed into the distance as the sign took center stage. Then it rushed back as if to expose my humiliation. I looked around. The lifeguards weren't paying attention, but they didn't need to be. Their message was out there, blazoned for everyone to see. In the locker room, I wiped away tears as I pulled my shorts over my hairy legs and covered my hairy armpits with my T-shirt.

I'd finally started wearing a bra the school year before, after a mandatory scoliosis exam. All the girls had taken turns bending over in the locker room. I was the only one whose breasts were exposed instead of being cupped in a lacy bra. Just like when Uncle Adam tickled me recently in Grandma's hallway, going up under the back of my shirt—never crossing to the front, but the front was inches away—I had no material to hide myself. I left that locker room with a mild scoliosis diagnosis and a resolve to make my mom take me to Target. Now, after today's humiliation, I knew I had to add a razor to my routine. And I had to do something to change my status.

I walked the halls of high school as the youngest student, as far as I knew. I was probably the only kid in the whole school to still be thirteen. Classmates towered above me and seemed to carry with them some secret maturity that I couldn't inhabit.

In eighth grade, I had eaten lunch with a best friend, Noel, whom I saw occasionally outside of school, and a couple deaf girls who taught us rudimentary sign language. I had been part of the teen chorus in the school production of *Bye Bye Birdie* and marched in the Christmas parade with choir. But, aside from my lunches with Noel, I had mostly been alone in the crowd, smiling with friendly acquaintances, wanting both to become invisible and to have a hand reach out and pull me into true connection. In that quintessential teenage way, I believed my new life in high school just *had* to be different.

Leigh High School was in San Jose—just a block and a half from my house. My first-period class was cooking, and the first semester of cooking was baking. My five-person team was made up of me, a Persian girl, two seniors, and a white girl from my middle school whose hands were always covered in warts. Farah, the Persian girl, looked like she had stepped out of a TV screen. Students seemed to part before her in the crowded hallways. She wore better clothes than just about anyone, her designer purse and patent leather shoes matching her seamless outfits. Her hair was perfectly feathered just like the girls in *Saved by the Bell*. (Even the Black character on the show, Lisa, had relaxed, wavy hair and flawless feathering; I still sported an Afro, which this year was quickly becoming a curly mullet.)

Farah's air of mystery was compounded by the fact that she had come from a private middle school as a straight-A student after convincing her parents to let her try public. I was astonished that her parents gave her forty-five dollars a week. One day in Foods, she brought a catalog and asked us which seventy-five-dollar watch she should buy. She became my first "girl crush," someone I wanted to emulate as strongly as I had Punky Brewster. Someone whose skin I wanted to crawl into. I pinched myself that she saw me worthy of attention. When she was around, the cheerleaders didn't kick my desk. No one threw gum for me to fetch. Some of the girls who were mean to me at the beginning of the year pulled back. I filled my book covers with the names of a rotation of boys I crushed on. I detailed the progress of my desired transformation in a homemade diary titled "Shannon's Book of Popularity and Boys."

Farah didn't like to run in PE, but I didn't let that stop me. In eighth grade, I had become the fastest runner in my PE class, and I won a trophy for running a hundred miles over the course of the year. Now, at Leigh, I was determined to improve my mile time and to join track and field in the spring. But by January, my resolve had waned. One hot afternoon doing laps, I looked around at those walking fast beside me. They were the ones with the good grades. The one whose parents came to parent-teacher night. The ones who followed the rules. I was done following the rules. Some nerdy kids had some secret veil of protection, but I was not one of them. Not trying so hard was going to be my ticket to acceptance—I just knew it. Plus, Farah was far behind me, and had actually dressed out instead of cutting like she often did. I slowed my pace and let my breathing become more regular. My arms flopped to my side. It wasn't long before Farah and her Mexican American friend, Tina, caught up to me.

"Hey, we were just talking about you," Farah said. "We think you're really nice."

I beamed. I had made it. I was officially cool. That night after PE, I wrote in my diary, "What I had been doing all my life, I suddenly changed in 15 minutes."

My transformation wasn't just about fitting in. It was also about becoming the person the school expected me to be. Leigh was a little more diverse than Union, and I saw the chasm between white and brown students. Farah, Tina, and I weren't expected to achieve anything but mediocrity. The expectations weren't in words but in glances, in auras, in things unsaid.

A couple weeks later, I finally convinced my mom to let me get my hair relaxed. She took me to Dad's part of town and set me up at a Black salon. In the room peppered with Black women, I felt both more connected to and more removed from Blackness than I ever had before. They used different words, spoke more directly, and laughed heartily. The lye in the whitish paste burned my scalp, but I resisted the urge to cry out. When it was all done, my hair stuck down and straight instead of out and curly—albeit almost stiff as a board, and my head was covered in blisters. I still wasn't Lisa from *Saved by the Bell*, but I was closer.

Tina claimed to be a member of the "Red Rags"—the Bloods. We were a ways from Los Angeles County but the popularity of the Bloods and the Crips had spread to the area. Students weren't allowed to wear the gang colors to school: red for Bloods and blue for Crips. I took Tina's declaration as truth, even though, like many of the tough kids, she wore a Raiders jacket, which was tied to the Crips, not the Bloods. Farah was inspired by her tough stance and started to prepare for a fight with a girl at her old school, doing push-ups under Tina's watch.

I knew Farah couldn't always be around to keep bullies from kicking my desk, so I decided to take matters into my own hands for a layer of added popularity protection. Somehow I got my mom to the mall to spend what was at the time for us an exorbitant amount of money. Only Nick got luxuries. We entered the sports store and I pointed out the sleek black jacket with a logo of a pirate with swords on the back and gray stripes around the wrists and collar. I'd never been to a game, but that didn't matter. It's what Tina wore. It's what everyone who wanted to be tough wore. My jacket became my armor. I was small. I smiled too much. And if I was honest, I couldn't throw a punch if my life depended on it. But at least I had the jacket.

Farah, Tina, and I walked the halls with an unspoken bond of melanin. But even when we thought we were creating our own rules, we were reminded of the rules that had already been made for us. We'd already been placed in boxes. A boy passed us during lunch one day in spring semester: "Go back to Iran, terrorist!" he yelled to Farah.

This was the year of the Gulf War, and Farah was the only Persian student at Leigh. Even her good looks and wealthy status didn't make her immune to becoming a scapegoat. A student running for homecoming court accused Farah of cheating to get her name in the ballot box. Then a boy she had been friends with started making fun of her family.

A few days later, a crowd of students stormed the cafeteria during lunch. I instinctively knew it was about Farah. I broke through the crowd and saw Tina in front. She was fighting a girl who was standing up for the boy who had called Farah's family terrorists. My hands shook as I looked on. Tina saw me but seemed to look right through me, as if she didn't know who I was. People scattered, and I followed suit. I wanted to be there for Farah, but I wasn't sure what to say. I later found her sitting outside with some friends. I overheard her say that the boy who harassed her was coming. I asked if I could stay, but she didn't hear me. She started crying.

After school, I stayed with Farah in the empty halls instead of going to track practice.

"Whites have never liked me," she said, confiding in me more than she ever had. "I can't deal with some of them."

"I know what you mean," I said. "My best friend's mom in sixth grade was prejudiced and wouldn't let me see her."

She seemed to half hear me, still embroiled in her own trauma. "I don't want you to get involved with what's going on with me. You might get hurt."

When Farah's mom came to pick her up later that afternoon, she met with the school counselor. Farah told me later that the counselor had asked why she was hanging around Mexicans. I assumed I was included in that bunch. No one ever knew what I was.

My mom met with the counselor that semester, just like she had when I was in sixth grade. She wanted to know why I was almost flunking out. The counselor said my grades were fine. My mom knew she meant "for a Black girl." But my mom didn't yell like Farah's had. She saw the injustice but let it go.

At the end of the year, I squeaked by with a 1.9 GPA, Farah went back to private school, Tina dropped out or moved away, and Nick returned to Sacramento.

7

HOW TO WIN FRIENDS AND INFLUENCE PEOPLE
1991

I FELT LOST THAT SUMMER WITHOUT FARAH. My Baby-Sitters Club books were no longer interesting, and the twins two doors down had each other to play with. So when Noel invited me to a youth group event at her church, I decided to go, never imagining that I was about to walk into what would feel like a new universe.

Crossroads Baptist Church was in the neighboring Los Gatos, the richer town that started a few blocks over from my house. Crossroads was a megachurch—about two thousand members—before megachurches became popular. It had two Sunday services plus separate services for middle and high school students.

The youth event, called Student Life, took place on a Friday night. Mom dropped me off in the parking lot, and I waited outside for Noel like she'd instructed. A group of girls who looked like cheerleaders came out from the large building and sprayed each other's hair orange to match the team color they'd been assigned. My green shirt, bought from the flea market to represent Noel's team color, hung unevenly from my too-small shoulders. I tried to tuck in the bottom corner to hide the hole made by bleach my mom used in the wash, and I ran my hands down the shirt to smooth out the stiffness from it having hung on the line in the backyard. There was nothing I could do about the unevenly sun-faded color.

The girls with the newly orange hair passed me as they made their way back into the church. "Are you here for Student Life?" one of the girls asked me.

"Yeah," I said. "I'm waiting for a friend."

Ten more minutes passed. I paced back and forth as tears welled in my eyes. If Noel was already inside, I'd be standing in the parking lot the entire night. I turned on my heel and made my way toward the building. When I peered inside, I saw a video camera and froze. Beads of sweat formed on my forehead. There were no video cameras at the congregational church youth group I'd been to, just five or ten high schoolers who did crafts to pass the time.

After forty-five minutes, I got the courage to sneak into the bathroom to compose myself. A short woman with short blonde hair came up to the sink next to me and asked if I was in the high school group. I tentatively said yes and that I was waiting for my friend. The woman led me to a large room where groups of teens stood mingling.

"Where were you?" Noel asked, with a braces-filled smile and blonde hair that feathered out haphazardly on each side.

"I was in the parking lot, waiting for you."

"But I was waiting there for you," she said. "You must have been in the wrong one."

The youth room was almost the size of the congregational church's main worship room. The girls with the orange hair performed a dance on the stage to a song I didn't recognize. Then a Snoopy cartoon played on a large projector. Once the cartoon ended, we were told to stand on our chairs and sing "Pharaoh, Pharaoh" to the tune of "Louie Louie" by the Kingsmen. After a couple rounds, I picked up the chorus and sang along, my body mimicking the twists and hand gestures.

A short, bouncy man who introduced himself as Eric McCrae—with a full, trimmed mustache—delivered a sermon about having a strong foundation. It was different from the sermons I'd heard at Mom's church about Jesus being a good man. Eric said we needed Jesus in order to avoid building our lives on quicksand. Instead of donning a black robe with a multicolored stole, Eric wore a casual polo shirt tucked into pleated khakis and blue tennis shoes.

Later that night we headed outside to a quad area and then into a large gym that had been transformed into a makeshift diner. Noel and I sat with some of her friends and ordered hamburgers, fries, and hot dogs. Someone at another table threw ice at us and, as though we were at the Max in *Saved by the Bell*, an ice fight ensued.

As scared as I had been to enter the building, I didn't want to go home once the night was over. My eyes had been opened to a world I never knew existed. One with music and silly dancing and people with smiles so wide I thought they would burst. When Noel later invited me to summer camp and said I could get a scholarship from the church, I didn't hesitate. Mom gave me forty dollars of spending money when she dropped me off in the church parking lot.

The camp, which the church dubbed Shore Break, took place at Point Loma Nazarene, a Christian college in San Diego set up against the ocean. Noel had also invited Jenna—a girl I first knew through Noel who was becoming a friend of mine as well. Jenna was tall, with no-nonsense straight brown hair that hung past her shoulders, no-nonsense clothes, and prominent front teeth that were the centerpiece of her warm smile. She was nerdy but not in a way that bullies cared about.

We all rode down in two large church buses that resembled upscale Greyhound buses, with CROSSROADS BAPTIST CHURCH emblazoned on the sides. It was my first time setting foot on a fancy college campus, with its wide-open space, perfectly manicured lawns, and beautiful white buildings. We bunked in the newly constructed dorm rooms, the paint so fresh we could smell it. I soaked in the clean, bright walls and the over-whelming sense of quiet that felt in opposition to my home life. During our days at camp, the leaders kept the energy going with games on the soccer field overlooking the ocean. Here, no one was being teased, and no one was trying not to participate. Instead, we all ran into each other while playing flag football with inner tubes around our waists. We wore our identical Shore Break tank tops. We sang songs about Jesus, led by an extremely good-looking guitarist with a flattop and a wide mullet. And we stopped for a day at Disneyland on our way home—my first time in the Magic Kingdom.

I'd heard about Jesus regularly at Mom's church. But Crossroads spoke of him differently. He wasn't just a wise man from history; he was a savior, and the only way to get to heaven was to ask him into your heart. If you didn't, you went to hell. I felt like Mom's church had left out some crucial information, and I wondered why Mom had never thought to impart that wisdom to me. When I asked her, she had her usual, unaffected response to just about everything: "I don't know." If I'd pressed further, I'm sure she would have said that wasn't the type of Jesus she believed in.

At the camp, Noel talked about her own salvation—of feeling Jesus come to her when she was a child and answering his call to live for him. That night, as I lay in the dorm bed, I was sure I saw a pale-skinned figure with long hair and a beard, in a white robe, come to me in the pristine dorm room. And I knew I needed to see him in order to fully join this group. But it wasn't just about belonging: A few weeks earlier, I'd been in a car with a reckless friend of Noel's on the way to a concert. I'd found myself praying for the first time—telling God I'd focus on him in exchange for safety. Maybe God had brought me here to make good on that promise.

The next morning during devotionals, when Noel, Jenna, and Noel's dormmate came together to pray and talk about God with our strikingly beautiful leader, I mentioned my experience from the previous night. "I want to accept Jesus into my heart," I said. Their faces lit up as they led me through the correct words. As easy as pie, I was one of them. Now that I had given my life over to God, he replaced the void left by Punky going off the air and became the new figure I entreated. And a father figure, no less. It was like killing two birds with one stone.

The following fall, at a Sunday evening service, Jenna and I were baptized in a baptismal pool built into the edge of the balcony along with a few other kids from youth group. When it was our turn, Jenna and I entered the pool together. I spoke as loud as I could about my life before the summer Shore Break event; Jenna talked about how we became Christians together on that trip. We both focused our eyes on our current crush, which changed often. After we spoke, Eric McCrae took turns gently lowering us into the water as we arched backward against his strong hand.

At the start of sophomore year, a neighboring school closed, and half the students came to Leigh High School. Fights broke out. Athletes who had played against our school didn't know how to flip the switch of their allegiance, and our own jocks weren't making it easy. The school called an emergency pep rally to try to bring unity. I laughed at their attempts. After all, they were the ones who had pitted us against other schools. But in the end, new friendships were formed across rival lines.

Leigh was in San Jose, but most kids from the youth group went to Los Gatos High. LGH looked like a college, with big columns, indoor hallways, and bright, green lawns. Its ambience and importance resembled the school in *Beverly Hills 90210*. In fact, it resembled just about every school I saw on TV. At Leigh, we walked from small, crowded classroom to small, crowded classroom in outdoor halls. I called it a ghetto school until Aunt Deborah sternly told me what a ghetto was really like.

Noel wasn't around as much that year, and Jenna and I became closer friends in our own right. She didn't mind that my head was in the clouds. She was more studious, more serious, and more practical, but she seemed to like my childlike innocence and the freedom to bring out her own. Jenna lived with her grandma and uncle—a family unit I could understand. Her mom, who had bipolar disorder, came in and out of her life much like my dad did mine. Jenna's mom had trouble supporting herself and was known for being recklessly impulsive.

In the afternoons, I had a remedial math class with Mr. Stevens, who liked to talk about his pet bird. A girl named Amy sat behind me. We often turned to each other as partners to go over practice questions. She was short and thin like me, with not the right clothes, also like me. Her brown hair frizzed out a little, unlike Jenna's, which fell straight.

"Do you want to join my babysitters club?" she asked one day. Finally a girl who spoke my language. The babysitting club never materialized, but our friendship did. In PE, she pushed me into a locker, but she had such nervous energy that I knew it was her way of being friendly. Amy went to a small Foursquare church, which, she told me, was just like Crossroads except they spoke in tongues. Up until eighth grade, she was homeschooled in the church basement. We were coming of age in the MTV generation, but we weren't part of it. Neither of us had cable, and even if we did, it might have been more worldly than we were ready for.

At lunch, Jenna, Amy, and I ate together, Amy and I subsisting on a daily slice of pizza and a Coke. Tuesdays were "McCrae Days," when our youth pastor, Eric McCrae, came to the campus during lunch to hang out, but the three of us rarely saw him. Eric loved to talk about how blessed he was to get such a beautiful wife when he himself had been such a nerd. He loved the cool kids, and the Leigh High boys were cool. But there was another reason he didn't sit with us. It would take me until adulthood to realize a middle-aged man couldn't easily sit with teenage girls on a high school campus, for fear of being labeled a predator.

Church, though, was another story. Jenna and I went to everything, and Amy often joined us since her own church was so small. Sundays were spent at youth group service, contemporary service, and evening service. Wednesdays had youth group once again, with Noel in the back, helping run the A/V. I was suddenly propelled into a world of cheerleaders, jocks, and intelligent pretty boys who were trained by the church to tolerate everyone, even shy nerds like me. By senior year, almost all the popular kids at school were Christians—some from Crossroads, and others from nearby churches. They landed on homecoming court, attended AP classes, and made up the student government. I had a new type of security now. My Raiders jacket never left the closet after freshman year.

For a while, a biracial teen came to youth group. He was part of the popular set, but our shared ethnicity put us on equal footing in his eyes. We talked about the challenges of being mixed race, broaching the subject carefully, tentatively—each of us not wanting to spook the other. After all, sightings of mixed-race people were still extremely rare in the early 1990s, especially in my world. He stopped coming to church after just a few weeks. Someone told me he had joined a gang after police had falsely accused him of doing something wrong. I understood sinking to the level one is expected to inhabit.

———————

Crossroads began to take me to far-off places for the first time. Spring was for mission trips to Mexicali, Mexico. Summers were for hitting the road with a musical tour. The summer after sophomore year landed us in Seattle, Washington, with Charlie Wedemeyer—a football coach and motivational speaker with Lou Gehrig's disease. He was paralyzed except for his face and toes. On a clear summer day, our tour bus came to a halt near Mercer Island, on I-90, along with everyone around us. We stepped out to see the Blue Angels flying overhead, dipping and swirling in their aerial display. Dozens of strangers held their heads up to the sky, standing idly by their vehicles. No one honked. No one seemed upset. It felt as if the whole world had paused, just for a little while.

When I was still new to the church, I joined an elderly woman leader to protest in front of Planned Parenthood. We sat against the wall near the entrance, holding signs about fetuses and death. Church answered difficult questions with ease. The world made sense within the boundaries of evangelical Christianity: Abortion was murder. God made "Adam and Eve," not "Adam and Steve." Divorce was a sin. Premarital sex led to destruction. Evolution was a conspiracy. Jesus walked on water. We followed the adage from our youth pastor: "Stand for something, or you'll fall for anything." I counted myself lucky that I hadn't fallen for anything. Not for Christian Science or gangs or even just the wrong crowd.

I held my sign in front of Planned Parenthood fully convinced of my rightness. I imagined internally confused mothers-to-be viewing my sign and being transformed, appreciative that someone had helped show them what God wanted for their lives. I imagined them sitting down with us, picking up an extra sign, and transforming the next woman, and the next. In my naïveté, I was stunned when a woman walked by, turned to the gray-haired leader, and yelled, "Bigot!" I didn't know what the word meant, but I wanted her to take it back. It was my first realization that my newfound beliefs might not be appreciated by everyone. My extended family bit their tongues, but I could tell they disapproved as well. Aunt Deborah hated Christianity as much as she hated television, with Uncle Adam not far behind her. Grandma was not as vehement, but she still didn't believe. Despite all that, I think they were happy that I was becoming more confident—and even my grades improved. That winter, I got everyone to come see me in the Christmas performance, which Crossroads called Carol Sing.

Carol Sing was the church's biggest yearly event and most likely their largest fundraiser. The performances took place in the gymnasium, which was transformed into a meticulous set, complete with painted scenes on the walls that began to appear in October. Children, middle schoolers, high schoolers, and adults all participated, and we began practicing not long after the walls started to transform. High schoolers and college students also served as waitstaff, filling glasses and serving dessert. Carol Sing had about ten performances leading up to Christmas. Ticket sales were so coveted that churchgoers actually camped out in line hours before the ticket window opened, as if they were trying to snag tickets to a Sting concert. I was part of the fervor, arriving in the early morning to snag tickets for my family.

Performance nights were imbued with backstage energy. I had grown up playing fast card games with my family; my youth group circle did the same, including while we waited for our scenes to start or our waitstaff rotations. Life as an only child had been lonely, playing War with my stuffed dog where no strategy was involved. Backstage at Carol Sing, in the unused side rooms with folding chairs and folding tables, my imaginative world was transformed into reality. Hands slapped the table and friends yelled in excitement.

Walking onto the set felt just as magical. I had been the best singer in my sixth-grade choir, but just like my mom's, my voice changed with puberty. I could hold a note but with no fanfare, and my vocal range diminished. In the talent show my eighth-grade year, my violin bow shook so vigorously that I could barely make it through the song. And I was so quiet that year with Noel and our deaf friend that the next year, when I said hi to one of the boys I used to eat lunch with, he looked stunned and said, "I thought you were deaf!" There was no backstage fun during my eighth-grade run of *Bye Bye Birdie* where I was in the teen chorus—at least not for me. But by the time I found Crossroads, my nerves had settled and I knew how to open my mouth. I was far from a social butterfly, but I wasn't a wallflower. Carol Sing gave me the opportunity to step onto a stage once again. I was never given a solo, but I loved harmonizing with my church family.

Almost all the most active youth group members had parents who were also part of the church. Crossroads printed a yearly member directory, complete with professional photos. I saw my peers standing next to their parents, looking like amalgamations of their mother and father and variants of their siblings. In that sense, I was still a person set apart. Someone who didn't quite belong.

The church had one other Black member, a worship team drummer named Darius. I decided he could become a surrogate father. I nervously approached him one day after worship as he was putting away his drumsticks. We'd never had a conversation, but we knew we were the only Black people in church. As I walked up the steps to the stage, I folded my hands in front of my body.

"Hi," I said. "I was wondering, would you ever consider being a sort of father . . . would you consider . . . I don't know my dad that well and he's not a Christian. Would you . . ."

Darius smiled. "You want me to be a father figure for you?"

"Yeah." I smiled with relief that he understood my request.

"Sure," he said. "Let me give you my phone number."

He motioned toward my church program. I ran down the steps, grabbed a pencil from one of the pews, and ran back up to the stage to get his phone number.

Darius wasn't quite old enough to be my father, but beggars couldn't be choosers. He was bald and a bit heavier set than my father. He dressed more leisurely, in a nice T-shirt and pleated, light brown slacks. We met twice in the home he shared with his white wife across the street from the church. We sat awkwardly on the couch, searching for some kind of connection. I'd imagined it differently somehow, that we would automatically have the father-daughter bond I saw on TV.

One afternoon after church, Darius and I ran into each other in the near-empty auditorium. "Hey, Shannon!" He wrapped his arms around me and lifted me off the floor, twirling me around in the aisle. In that moment I realized he was just a man, and I was just a girl. I ended our meetings. His skin was the skin of my father, but he was a stranger, and no amount of melanin could change that.

Aside from Darius, the only Black men I encountered in my part of town were the homeless men Mom and I passed in the car on our way here or there. Men stumbling from alcohol, asleep on benches, holding cardboard signs at traffic lights. Each man tugged at my heart as if he were my father. As if my father were one small shuffled step away from losing everything, of ending up with a similar fate. In my imagination, the eyes of the man who was also somehow my father would lock with mine as Mom and I sped past; I'd call out, we'd turn around, and I'd come fix it—somehow. Or I wouldn't, being only a child myself, and the small security I'd known, Dad always housed, would disappear completely.

Even with the limited knowledge of youth, I knew my dad lacked a term I would learn decades later—generational wealth, which has divided Black and white Americans unfairly all the way back to slavery, and continues through the prison pipeline and housing and job discrimination. I knew he had no one to fall back on, no safety net to catch him if he fell. And I knew I was half him. Who would catch me?

8

SISTER OUTSIDER
1991

THE SUMMER BEFORE MY SOPHOMORE YEAR of high school, around the time I first joined Crossroads, I took the Amtrak train for a three-hour ride through the fields and factories to get to Dad's new apartment in Sacramento. I don't remember his leaving. Likely because it didn't sting so much. I was used to his inability—or unwillingness—to stay in one place for too long. "Papa is a rolling stone," he'd say, quoting the Temptations. Perhaps this time his leaving was also just a bit of a relief—physical distance from the bad memories of the past two years, even though there had been some good ones.

That day wasn't my first time taking the train. When I was eleven, shortly before Mom met Gary, Dad took me, Mom, Aunt Deborah, Adria and Elsie, and their Spanish exchange student to the Martin Luther King Day celebration in San Francisco. Each year on the day, the Amtrak on that route was renamed the Freedom Train. In the somewhat packed Amtrak car, someone broke out singing "We Shall Overcome," a popular song of the civil rights movement. Almost everyone chimed in, including my family. I didn't notice that most of the riders were white; I felt a surge of pride and connection to my Black history.

This time, my Walkman provided a soundtrack to the rumbling of the wheels on the track and the landscape that passed out the window. As I glanced at houses that my eyes caught for seconds before they disappeared, I imagined the lives those homes held, and I imagined what freedom my own life could hold, once I had the freedom to choose. Someday I would leave Gary's decrepit home. Maybe then I'd no longer slink down toward the floor when I watched TV in the living room, scared that a high schooler would look in as they passed my house on their way to their own. It was bad enough that I wore hand-me-downs and didn't know how to do my hair. If they saw where I lived, with the peeling paint, the overgrown bushes, and the untreated wooden plank that acted as a pillar on the porch—that would be the end of any semblance of normalcy. I could just imagine what they'd think if they knew Gary kept a bag of garden snails in the freezer to kill them, or if they saw how the living room walls were slightly tainted with soot from the fireplace.

I stepped off the train to see Dad leaning against a wooden pillar like a man straight out of the Harlem Renaissance. He took off his newsboy cap to reveal a patchy head of hair made thin by discoid lupus. The hair that remained was grayer than just last year, and his face had faint red splotches, as if a child had painted it at a carnival with a small brush. Nonetheless, he was still the Black Prince—his self-appointed nickname.

As we ambled across the light-rail tracks to get to the car, Dad yelled, "Watch out!"

I screamed and ran as fast as I could to the other side of the street, certain that I was about to be crushed under an oncoming light-rail car. Dad hooted and hollered from the middle of the tracks.

"Got you!" he said. "Woo, you were so scared!"

I tried to look angry, but a grin escaped my face to copy his. There was my dad. Not lying drunk on a bed. He was alive, laughing, joking.

When we drove out of the parking lot, Dad took a left turn onto a one-way street headed in the opposite direction. I held my breath and prayed that the drunk dad who had swerved his way to the laundromat was far behind. As I yelled out, Dad quickly turned the car around to match the street signs. I slowly let my breath even out and relaxed my clenched fists. My back sank into the passenger seat as I took in the quiet streets and the gently manicured miniature lawns.

On the way home, we stopped at Woolworth's, passed the cash registers, and walked up to the lunch counter. My dad and I didn't have many traditions, but this was one we both had come to love. I felt important sitting next to Dad on a swivel chair as he ordered two cups of hot apple juice. The warmth of my cup relaxed my hands, my arms, my shoulders. The apple juice slid down my throat like a welcome friend. At the counter, it never mattered that Dad and I didn't have much to say to each other. We were buddies, sitting side by side at the counter of a department store chain that had once segregated patrons and incited a sit-in in 1960. At the counter, I always imagined us propelled into the *Eyes on the Prize* documentary.

"Did you have a segregated Woolworth's counter back during civil rights?" I asked.

"No," he chuckled. "We didn't have those laws in St. Louis."

My cheeks burned as I chided myself for not knowing the answer before I'd asked it. I should have known Jim Crow wasn't in the Midwest. But Dad didn't seem mad, just amused.

After I'd taken my last sip of apple juice, Dad led me to the checkout line to get a sheet of lollipops, another one of our traditions. The flat lollipops came in varying colors, and I always chose a sheet with the most red pops I could find. I was getting too old for apple juice and lollipops, but I liked our routine. Plus, it was something special that my dad could afford.

As we got up to the front of the line, Dad took his wallet from his back pocket. I pulled out his driver's license to see his bad photo, just like I did with my friends. The face looking back at me had deep circles under his eyes and a wry smile. My eyes ran over the details on his card—his height, his weight, the year he was born.

The year he was born.

It was there, plain as day: 1945. I wouldn't have given it a second glance if Dad hadn't told me the truth during our last phone call. He was sixty-two, born in 1930—nineteen years older than my mom, and a year younger than my grandma.

I wasn't mad at Dad for lying about his age, but I was a little mad that this false age appeared on my birth certificate. It felt as if this simple lie erased the validity of my existence. My birth certificate was the only thing that connected my parents to each other, and to the three of us as a unit. There was no marriage certificate. Not even a divorce decree. There was no shared home. There was no shared ethnicity. There were no siblings that carried both my parents' DNA. Dad's false age seemed the last straw, as if I myself were rendered a walking lie—a phony.

———————

Once home, Dad went over to the VCR and slipped in *Shaka Zulu*, which he had rented for my visit—a favorite of his that he wanted to pass on to his daughter.

Shaka Zulu was chief of the Zulus in southern Africa in the 1800s. The movie was about his rise to power, growing the existing fifteen-hundred-person tribe into a powerful force that conquered lands throughout the region. Dad watched the movie from his chair with intense pride. He leaned forward and slapped his leg whenever Zulu overcame hardship or thwarted his enemies. Toward the climax, Shaka Zulu's tribe crests a large hill, armed with weapons. They chant in formation as they descend on a British army. A young, pale Brit peed his pants as he stared at the tribe in wonder.

"Look at that white fool, shoot," Dad said.

I knew Dad played the movie to show me the power of my people. I knew he thought I'd be mesmerized by the sheer force of the African spirit. But violence had never appealed to me, and I saw the faces of my family in the white soldier who soiled his pants. I saw Uncle Adam. I saw my cousins. And I saw how completely my world with them didn't align with my dad's world. His eyes seemed filled with hatred and derision in a way I'd never seen before. It was as if he was laughing at my family's expense. I wondered how he could have ever loved my pale mother.

I knew I was making too much of his social commentary. After all, Shaka Zulu was triumphant against all odds. His makeshift army over-came the strong British forces, forces that had no place on African soil. But it wasn't my father's allegiance that upset me. It was the term "white fool," as if this soldier should be hated simply for the color of his skin.

I didn't say a word, but Dad knew his daughter well enough to know when I was upset. My pursed lips and lack of response spoke volumes.

———————

Dad won a worker's compensation lawsuit that year. He'd had a heart attack. He said it was caused by the physical stress of caring for an elderly patient along with the emotional distress of not getting paid on time, which caused him to become dependent on brandy. The lawsuit meant that I would get $200 a month from Social Security for child support, which I had never received before, and $3,000 in one lump sum when I turned eighteen. Mom and Gary set me up with my own bank account, and the money covered all my expenses, except groceries and shelter, which was Gary's domain. While technically the money came from my dad's efforts of winning the lawsuit for himself, it just felt like the government had finally righted a wrong, providing me the financial support that I'd never before received from either of my dads.

Once they married, Gary had Mom hand over her paychecks, and he gave her an allowance in return. While Nick got expensive haircuts and designer shoes, Mom and I weren't supposed to ask for anything. With the money from the government, suddenly I could pay for things like school class photos, shoes from Walgreens, and food out with friends at Denny's and McDonald's.

It couldn't, however, pay for more expensive items that I still went without. I came to my English teacher's class on cold mornings with no jacket, having nothing to replace my Raiders jacket, which felt like it belonged to a previous version of me, a version that at that time in the Bay Area was associated with gang affiliation, especially for teenagers, and especially for brown ones. Fear of gang paraphernalia was so strong that we were encouraged not to wear solid red or blue shirts or red, white, or black paisley bandannas.

One morning after class, my teacher handed me a blue paper bag with London Fog on the side.

"I don't wear this," she said. "I was thinking you could have it."

I peered into the bag and pulled out a light blue coat.

"Try it on," she said.

I slipped the coat on over my hand-me-down sweater from my step-aunt. It fit perfectly. I marveled at what felt like fancy fabric.

"Thank you," I said with a smile.

As I walked home from school, I heard hooting coming from a car as it passed me on the road. A couple popular girls pointed at the London

Fog bag and laughed. My embarrassment was tempered by the thoughtful-ness of my teacher. The coat may not have been cool, but it kept me warm.

———————

Dad sent mom a copy of the psychological evaluation that was used to win his case. He had carefully whited out parts he wanted to keep from us, like how old he and his relatives were, his relationship with Mom, and his drinking, all of which I'd later read in an unredacted copy found among his papers after he died—his ages true, but his drinking pared down in his favor. In those pages I learned a lot about my family. Grandpa Bennie, whom I had met three times before he died, worked as a Pullman porter, assisting passengers as they rode the trains. He left the family when Dad was young, and Dad would wander the streets looking for him. I learned that Dad struggled in school, and one teacher told him to stand up in front of the class and admit he was dumb, which he wouldn't do.

In that first redacted copy, I kept reading the twenty-four pages about my dad's life, searching for my history in the pages. He had dropped out of school at seventeen, joined the army, and took a test that said he had a high IQ. After driving a fire truck in the Korean War, he worked as delivery driver for a deli; a stocker for a bottling company; a die casting machine, punch press, and drill press operator; a janitor and school bus operator; and an orderly. After prison, where he got his GED and took correspondence courses, he worked for social services offices as a coun-selor, the director of community affairs, an interviewer, and a community specialist. Then he worked as a grant writer, an encyclopedia salesman, a paralegal, and a nursing assistant. I couldn't wrap my head around all these jobs and what they meant, except that it further proved he was, as he said, a rolling stone.

Three of his siblings and his mom all died young of cerebral hemor-rhages. Dad always said he was about to die. Maybe he thought he was cheating death somehow, outliving so many relatives. He got stomach cancer when I was in sixth grade, and then the heart attack at his job as a nursing assistant that got him the worker's compensation. As often as Dad said he was about to die, he also said he was going to come

into money. At least the money he did get was more realistic than the
$30 million he said he was going to receive the summer before I started
high school, most of which would go to me, I had written excitedly in
my journal.

But how could I believe anything from someone who said he was
going to receive $30 million. Maybe nothing in the report was true. I had
no way of parsing fact and fiction, and the unredacted version didn't help.
I knew he hadn't left Mom, as he stated, and also not because Grandma
was "manipulative" and "intrusive." I knew Mom hadn't prevented Dad
from seeing me and that she hadn't had an affair with his brother in Santa
Cruz during her attempt to connect me with that side of the family. The
truth was slippery for my dad, and he created a narrative that suited him,
that cast him in a perennially positive light. But his doing so cost me an
assurance of his life story, and thus of my own.

At the beginning of sophomore year, all the students gathered in the
cafeteria for statewide testing. Before I could even get to the test questions, I found a problem I didn't know how to solve. I had to check a
box for race, but only one. I always knew I was half and half, so either
answer felt wrong.

I took my form up to my friend Sara from church, who was Mexican
and white. "Which do I choose?" I asked.

"Black," she said, matter-of-factly. "And I choose Hispanic." It was
my first lesson in double consciousness. The world didn't allow for my
true identity. When my Blackness and whiteness were set side by side,
my Blackness was more important. Another incident that semester would
solidify that fact.

I walked to my locker one afternoon to deposit books and grab my
lunch. As I got closer, I noticed white writing across the locker and
thought maybe one of my friends was pulling a prank. Indeed, it was a
prank, but not by a friend and not for my amusement.

Across the locker in Wite-Out were the words WHITE POWER.

I stood stunned, unable to move. Noel walked up to me and, after
reading the words herself, hugged me tight, her long blonde hair rubbing

up against my cheek. I didn't want to react to the message, to give it the power it craved, but Noel's arms around me validated the feeling deep inside that I'd been violated, that whoever had written those words meant harm. I'd never been as aware of my Blackness, of my otherness, as I was in that moment. Someone had created a firm line between my identity and theirs. There was no room for my half whiteness.

I looked up to find a crowd gathered silently. Noel walked me to the principal's office with her arm draped over my shoulder. My eyes barely made out the concrete as they splattered it with tears. The school did nothing to respond besides clean off my locker. No assembly was called. No lectures were given in classrooms. The population of Black students at the two-thousand-person school was about 2 percent. And they cared two cents about a hate crime in 1991.

In April 1992, riots broke out in Los Angeles after police officers were acquitted for beating Rodney King. Right before I learned about the riots, Gary suggested I name my new hamster Rodney. At the time I appreciated his uncharacteristic involvement in my life and took him up on his suggestion. As the coverage of Rodney King widened, I realized Gary's suggestion was just a way to poke fun at my expense. Poor Rodney the Hamster didn't live long, his existence tainted.

Dad sent me a clipping from the *San Jose Mercury News*. In the center of the article was a picture of him at a community meeting. He looked pensive, thin but strong and, at the same time, feeble—his discoid lupus visible, including the bald patches on his head, which he hid underneath a cotton fedora. I couldn't believe that my own father had his picture in the newspaper. At the same time, it didn't mesh with the father I actually saw—the one who didn't say much when we were together. Yet every word he uttered seemed carefully chosen, not to seem smart but because he was smart.

But I didn't agree with him that Rodney King represented the plight of Black people. I knew he'd been under the influence and had led the officers in a chase. I knew from the news that Black people had looted stores and opened fire. Amy said these men were in the wrong, and

San Jose Mercury News • **Local** • Wednesday, May 6, 1992

Teach kids to say 'no' to racism, panel urges

■ MEET
from Page 1B

ple for the next generation.

"We can't change the whole country," said Samuel D. Henry, a forum panelist and assistant vice president of student affairs at San Jose State University. "But we can sure start here."

The approximately 90 people who attended the meeting at the First Christian Church on Fifth Street may have left with some doubts about specific solutions. The panelists and audience members who spoke, however, left no question about the depth of the problem.

The anger, fear and frustration in the county's minority communities were there long before Rodney King was beaten and long before the police officers accused of using too much force were acquitted, many speakers said.

Reginald Swiley of ARISE, a black advocacy group, sat on the 11-member forum panel. He said his daughter has told him she never wants to bear a black son. Life, she told him, is too hard for black men. His voice faltered as he related how his wife had cried the other night and suggested it might have been better if the entire black race had died, rather than endure the racism blacks face today. And Swiley explained that when his 13-year-old son goes out at night the father worries not that his son will encounter a criminal but rather a police officer.

Henry read an original poem, "I Can't Go Jogging in Woodland Hills," which questioned whether

a black man can jog in a predominantly white Southern California suburb without attracting police.

"I can't go jogging in Woodland Hills," the last line reads. "Can I go jogging in San Jose?"

Gloria Baxter, an audience member, told of returning home last week to find her 18-year-old son pacing, visibly upset.

"He said, 'Mom, I don't understand,'" said Baxter, a black woman and acting executive director of the Bill Wilson Center.

Robert Manuel, upset about L.A. riot coverage, attended forum Tuesday.
RICHARD WISOM — MERCURY NEWS

"'I don't understand why people don't like me, why they hate my people.'"

The Rev. Frank Selkirk, pastor of New Jerusalem Baptist Church, told of being pulled over by police late at night because he was a black man in a luxury car.

San Jose Assistant Police Chief William Lansdowne, another panelist, said after the meeting that the department is working to end the perception that blacks are often stopped by police for no good

reason.

The two-hour forum was sponsored by the Community Partnership of Santa Clara County, a federally funded project seeking to create new ways to deal with the county's major social problems.

The partnership set up a panel representing academia, law enforcement, minority communities, churches and the county human relations commission to present various views on the local effects of the Rodney King verdict.

It would not be realistic to expect such a forum to solve the complex problems surrounding race relations, said Andrea Schneider, the Community Partnership's director.

"What I heard today is that people are also tired of all the rhetoric," she said. "I expect to get some phone calls from . . . groups who were interested in moving this along."

Some started working before the meeting ended. Aminah Jahi, an audience member and executive director of the African American Community Service Agency, said her group would form a committee to discuss and propose more specific steps to improve race relations and life in the black community. By the end of the meeting she had collected a stack of business cards from people who wanted to help.

IF YOU'RE INTERESTED
Those interested in exploring ways to improve race relations can call the Community Partnership of Santa Clara County at (408) 452-4700.

without a firm opinion of my own, I adopted hers. I was most concerned that the youth group wouldn't be able to make its yearly pilgrimage to Disneyland. It didn't seem right that the seniors would never get this unique opportunity again.

During my adulthood, incidences of police brutality made a different impact, particularly during the string of video-captured aggressions that began in the mid-2010s. The amount of force—often lethal—for tiny infractions like selling untaxed cigarettes on the street, or for no infraction at all, left me enraged. I understood that racism and race-based fear led to these abuses of power.

———————

Sophomore year, I once again went out for track and field. I called Dad one evening for advice about my coach, who seemed to be playing favorites and ignoring Jenna and me. I had written the coach a letter and realized my writing voice sounded a lot like Dad's. It was the first time I'd noticed a connection between us, besides the physical. Our kinky hair, our long fingers and feet, and the way our big toes curved inward had always linked us, but this was artistic, cerebral. I read Dad the letter, then he asked me to read it again. He approved of my argument and asked me to send him a copy, then gushed about my good grades and encouraged me to keep it up. That was the dad I wanted, one I could come to for real guidance.

But at this time, Dad started calling every couple weeks to talk about his accomplishments—a random quote in a newspaper article about Jackie Kennedy, pictures in NAACP events—and then he'd hang up without letting me talk. During one phone call, he said, "The world is full of racist people who will never treat you as a human being. You'll be hated by the majority of Americans. What are you going to do about that? What are you going to do when the world turns its back on you?"

"I don't know," I answered softly, twisting the phone cord around my finger. I didn't think I could tell him about the locker incident. I didn't tell him that Jenna's grandma asked her why she was hanging around with "that Black girl." For one, it would mean the world he warned me of was true. His questions felt like a way to put fault lines in the life I lived without him even though he would never be there if the world cracked open.

One day Dad called to tell me he was taking a class about how to be a better father. "Not that I need a class," he said, "but I'm always trying to improve myself. I'm supposed to have my child write an essay about our relationship. I know our bond is strong. So, you just write that in your essay."

I was never at a loss for words when I put pen to paper, but the assignment seemed impossible. I realized he was living in a delusion about what constituted a father-daughter relationship. Or perhaps he did know, and this was his attempt to prove the world wrong. If he got an affirming essay from me and a good grade in the class, he'd have tangible proof that he hadn't messed up as a father. As an adult I'm more aware that in Dad's mind, maybe the act of conversation itself constituted a good relationship, particularly since I was the only one of his children he spoke to regularly, and the only one he saw in person except for one brother, one time. But at the time, as I compared him to other fathers, like my youth pastor and Uncle Eugene, his presence felt minuscule.

Telling my dad the truth felt like waking a giant who's already having bad dreams. I didn't trust what he would do or say. I didn't want to scare off what little amount of fathering he was willing to do. But at the same time, I couldn't lie.

I typed out a two-page allegorical essay called "The Comforting Cat," about a girl who doesn't have a "cat" at home.

> She had never had a cat that knew when she was sad. Her friend's cat always waited for her friend on the front porch and knew exactly what time she was supposed to be home every day. When her friend wasn't home in time, you could see the fear in the cat's eyes. But the girl had never experienced that. She had no idea what it felt like to have a comforting cat who was always there and cared about her.

"Dad," I typed at the end, "I hope that story makes sense to you. The only father I can truly have a close relationship with is my Heavenly Father. And even he is hard to trust at times."

Dad never responded to my essay, so one night on the phone, with a shaky voice, I asked him if he'd received it.

"Mm-hmm," he said.

"What did you think?"

"I like the way you said it, but I don't like what you said. We'll talk about it when you come for a visit."

But, just like always, we never did.

9

THE POISONWOOD BIBLE
1993

With Dad in Sacramento, my heavenly father became my soul focus. I never dodged Dad's calls, but they came less frequently. I never said no to a visit, but they rarely transpired. Probably never a day closed without thoughts of him—complicated thoughts about his absence and also about the discomfort of his presence. Every church song about God the Father imprinted fatherhood in my psyche. Every line about God's children reminded me that I was my father's child. At the same time, I sought to erase longing for my fallible father and replace it with the one I was told I could depend on.

I spent the summer after my junior year in Florida, Indonesia, and Russia with Teen Missions International—a missions organization that sent hundreds of teens around the world, my trip paid for by members of my church. I had wanted to sign up for the Kenya team, but two white friends at Crossroads, TMI veterans, said I wouldn't be able to handle Africa. So I chose Indonesia based on the picture of brown-skinned boys and girls in the brochure.

We boarded the TMI bus at the San Francisco airport and rode it all the way to Florida, picking up more teens as we ambled along. I marveled at the hot rain in Texas, and then at all the Black people working at the fast food joint in Georgia. It revealed a more pronounced racial divide than I'd seen back home.

"You're from California?" one employee asked with wide eyes as he handed us our food. "How many drive-by shootings have you seen?"

At boot camp in Florida, dozens of thirty-person teams slept in tents, bathed with buckets, and ate food on plastic trays that we carted in cloth bags. We climbed over giant cement "books of the Bible" and swung over marshes in the obstacle course—our mandatory brown leather construction boots flailing toward the finish line. Under the giant multicolored tent, made to evoke a backwoods revival, I and hundreds of other teens—mostly white, with the occasional brown or black face visible in the crowd—belted out a then-popular evangelical song, "Please Don't Send Me to Africa":

> I'll serve you here in suburbia
> In my comfortable middle class life
> But please don't send me out into the bush
> Where the natives are restless at night

Real Christians became missionaries, and the realest of them went to Africa, because what could be scarier than the heart of darkness? The song bothered me, but I didn't know why, so I sang with as much fervor as those standing beside me under the multicolored tent.

Real Christians also worried about the salvation of others, so my thoughts turned to Dad. I sent a letter from boot camp urging him to ask Jesus into his heart if he hadn't already.

In Indonesia, I received Dad's reply.

> Dear Daughter,
> I must assume that you already know that I understand the full meaning and scope of the profoundness of your letter. I use the preceding terms—as underlined—simply to illustrate the depth of my understanding. I do not intend upon a play of words. Your letter was certainly moving and insightful, which, as usual, makes me very proud to be your father! I do have a bible and will with haste read those passages that you suggest.

I did not know that you had pursued the Christian faith with such fervor. For reasons unknown to this date, you chose— obviously—to limit contact with me. I respect and never have chosen to combat that decision. I have a reservoir of memories from the day you were born up until approx 1990 that no father and daughter could be closer. That sustains me to this date. Whatever the reasons for your detachment pale with the relationship of father/daughter remaining within us that could and should still exist and be pursued. It's understood that children somehow believe that parents will always be around and there's no urgency to keep regular contact. Although I did keep regular and close contact with my mother, Carrie Olivia Brown, it was earth shattering to me when she died in the bathtub at age 57. I still have not recovered from that!

Again, I respect and appreciate your stance in life. Let's hope that we can recapture the closeness that has always existed between us.

With much love and pride, Robert C.

I have often said I love you more than life, and been told that's impossible, yet within my own psychic being, I know it is to be true.

In 1990, my father had moved three hours away, the year he said I had detached from him. Yet, I wondered if he could somehow sense a shift from me through the phone or in between the lines of my letter. Maybe the detachment *was* my fault, I thought. I couldn't forget the day I found him passed out drunk, the day he drove drunk to the laundromat, or the fear I'd read my mom express in her journal the year they'd broken up. I couldn't forget the way he'd laughed at the white soldier in *Shaka Zulu*—or the way he'd tried to make me question my relationship with my grandma and uncle Adam, telling me in a visit that they didn't have my best interests at heart. And I couldn't forget the uneasiness when he told me he was mentoring a Black girl in his apartment building, unsure if my unease came from jealousy or worry. I wouldn't rest easy until I knew he had accepted Jesus and had become some new version of himself that redemption was sure to create.

My team leaders that summer were a married couple, Susan and Ronald—who had two teenage, adopted Native American children—and a man and woman about college age. I had expected Susan and Ronald to be like my youth pastor Eric McCrae and his wife. The expectation didn't last long.

Our attire had to be approved by boot camp employees, and my required dress shoes didn't pass inspection. I didn't have enough money for another pair, so Susan handed me cash and walked me to the makeshift shoe station. I chose a pair and pulled the money out of my pocket, not realizing I hadn't grabbed it all. Susan sounded off like a clone of my stepdad, accusing me of pocketing her money for my own gain. It was an identity I'd be accused of for the rest of my life: a mooch, a trickster, a lazy thief.

"I'm sorry!" I said as I pulled the rest of the bills out of my pocket and placed them on the counter. "I thought I had grabbed it all."

Susan seemed to believe me in time, but I got no satisfaction from her change of heart. She and Ronald would terrorize us all summer.

My team was made up of a hodgepodge of white teens from across the United States: the thirteen-year-old boy who drank mouthwash for the alcohol; the boy who chose Teen Missions instead of juvenile hall, who insisted he was possessed by the devil; the girl from Appalachia with light brown hair kinkier than mine, who I surmised must have some hidden Black roots; the older man with cerebral palsy and learning disorders; two homeschooled girls from upstate New York; the girl from Alaska who would become a lifelong friend, whose parents would die in a plane crash a couple years later.

After boot camp, we spent two days flying across the world, the first flight for some, including me. Liz, my friend from Alaska, screamed in pain on the plane from what turned out to be a deviated septum. Susan chastised her for craving attention as I tried to comfort her. The team flew to Newfoundland, then to Ireland, then to Moscow, Russia, where many citizens looked displaced, presumably from the fall of the Soviet Union. We flew on to the United Arab Emirates, where we boarded a plane with guards holding machine guns at the top of the steps; then to Kuala Lumpur, Malaysia, where boys shined shoes and jumped into the pristine water to fetch coins; and then we took a ferry to Jakarta, Indonesia—our final destination.

Proselytizing was against the law in Indonesia, so we were to say we were a musical group on vacation. Indonesia was five years away from the May 1998 riots and the Asian financial crisis. As we rode through the streets with toilet paper inside our fanny packs, rows of shacks were interspersed with mansions. A local man ran up to one of the teens as we walked to our lodging in the attic of a church and ripped the necklace off her neck. We yelled "open sewer" to the person behind us as we walked single file in the city. At a volcano tourist stop, women surrounded us to try to sell wares, including a woman who offered her baby for five dollars, I guessed most likely hoping to give it a better life.

We sang in underground churches throughout the area, uplifting those who shared our faith. The churchgoers always laughed at one line of a song we sang in their language until we learned we were singing "Praise the spinach" and not "Praise the Lord." In an orphanage, we entertained dozens of young brown faces using racially stereotyped puppets that popped up in front of a bloodred curtain: a chanting Indian, bowing Asians, groovy rapping Black dancers, and a Western cowgirl and cowboy. "Red and yellow, black and white, they are precious in his sight, Jesus loves the little children of the world." My role was in the mime show, where we groped the sky unhappily until someone put a Bible in our hands.

Ronald, our leader, liked to scream at us in the mornings. Like Gary, he wouldn't stop until we started crying. His wife, Susan, was also on the receiving end, which further fueled her anger toward us and her two children. Ronald and Susan developed what they called "leader's restriction," wherein anyone who was deemed problematic could speak only to the leaders for the rest of the day, which I later learned was a tactic used in the Children of God cult. At night, the "bad" kids had to sleep in the front of the room, while the "good" kids got to sleep in the back. I didn't like being a good kid, because I knew the bad kids weren't bad.

But I also felt that somehow all the yelling was my fault. Leader's restriction was my fault. How else could I explain going from Gary's house to this, and first from Grandma's house, where something had happened but I didn't know what. I was the common denominator in all these scenarios. Maybe I attracted abuse, I thought. Maybe subconsciously

I had chosen these team leaders. Maybe it was my penance for not being able to make it in Africa.

Our team fractured, unable to stay unified as our leaders pitted us against each other. On the bus, a boy on leader's restriction who was never allowed to speak to the girlfriend he came with because pairing up was against the rules, sang to me from the seat behind, resting his head between the seat in front and the window. "Yesterday / all our troubles seemed so far away / Now it looks as though they're here to stay / Oh I believe in yesterday." I breathed deeper than I had in days, the warmth of his friendly voice filling me more than all our praise songs.

Our team remained fractured throughout our time in Jakarta and into our two weeks proselytizing in Bali, and persisted as we entered Moscow for debrief with the Kenya and Uganda teams. One of us heard a rumor that in a previous year, a team's flight home had been canceled and they couldn't find another for a week, until after they apologized to the leaders and God for their behavior, even though they hadn't done anything wrong. We feared God would test us the same way, though we knew apologies needed to come from our leaders, not from us. But the worry lingered.

In Moscow, we stayed in abandoned youth military barracks complete with brightly colored playground equipment. We visited Red Square and watched the tradition of newlyweds walking up and down the square. In the cafeteria-style building where we gathered during the day with the Kenya and Uganda teams, we noticed the stark difference between our team and theirs. We spread out over several tables, not wanting to eat together; the other teams laughed and joked as they sat side by side. We heard lectures and received literature about how to keep the high of Teen Missions and how to share our experience back home. But my team wasn't on a high. We were quick to tears and anger, and sad about leaving each other but eager to get back home.

On one of our last days, each team performed on the cafeteria stage. John, who had sung to me, was on leader's restriction, just like most days, and wasn't allowed to perform. Right before the event, some on our team hit Susan, the leader, with one of the harshest criticisms Christians can make of each other: she didn't possess the fruits of the spirit—love, joy, peace, patience, kindness, generosity, faithfulness, gentleness, and self-control. A few apologized after a rage from Ronald, but others didn't, including me. I wasn't one of the ones who had confronted her, but I believed the words of those who did. I couldn't stop picturing the way she yelled at me at boot camp, and how she screamed about wanting to punch one of the teens on the bus.

Onstage, those of us in the mime show hid our sadness under our painted faces—the hurt, the hopelessness, and even a lack of feeling altogether. After our performance, John was supposed to sing Prince's "The Cross" with two other boys, all on guitars. The boys were off-key without him, their voices tentative, subdued.

> *Black day, stormy night*
> *No love, no hope in sight*
> *Don't cry, he is coming*
> *Don't die without knowing the cross.*

One of our team members walked to the front of the stage and sang along, an encouraging smile breaking through her mime makeup. Soon, we all emerged from behind the curtain and joined in, many of us with painted faces and vacant eyes. After our performance, the same fights broke out and we were splintered once again. But for a moment, we had overcome the leaders' desire to divide us.

After that summer, parents began writing to the organization, asking for Susan and Ronald's resignation. Somehow the letters always ended up in Ronald's vengeful hands. As the next summer neared, the mom of a team member who had needed counseling after our summer worked on-site at the Florida headquarters. Because she could see the right people in person, Susan and Ronald were finally let go. Those who had sponsored them with donations received a slip of paper in the mail that read, "Due to unforeseen circumstances, Ronald and Susan Price had to terminate their work here at Teen Missions as of April 15, 1994."

Despite my unpleasant experience with Teen Missions, I started to see myself as a missionary. By senior year, I'd developed a firm identity at Crossroads, one that finally seemed to make Eric McCrae proud. During an icebreaker one Wednesday night, one of the students asked us to come up to the front if we fit random criteria.

"Who has foreign money?" the student asked.

I rushed to the front of the room and pulled out some Mexican coins from one of our spring trips. "Missionary!" students called from their seats. It wasn't an insult—it was one of the highest compliments a Christian in our church could receive.

But that wasn't my only new label. Frank, the pastor of the college group, appeared on my doorstep one Thanksgiving morning, as Mom, Melanie, and I prepared to head to Grandma's for our yearly feast. Frank was in his midthirties, tall, with curly brown hair. I had been to his house a few times for church events.

Frank handed me a big box.

"Here," he said. "It's a dead cat."

I held the box awkwardly, unsure what to say.

"Just kidding," he said. "It's from Petrini's grocery store, and I have no use for it."

"Thank you."

Once inside, I opened the box to find a full turkey dinner. My family had never not had food. I had never gone hungry. I tried to imagine what would make them treat me like charity. Was it my hand-me-down clothes? Or did I wear my few new clothes too often? Was it because I was Black? Was it because I didn't have a father? Later that night I noticed a piece of mail on the kitchen table addressed to Mr. and Mrs. Manuel. I opened it, since Mr. and Mrs. Manuel didn't exist. Inside was a check for $200. The next day I called the church in confusion.

"I don't know why you got it," the secretary said. "Maybe it's because of financial difficulty."

"I don't think we have any financial difficulty," I replied. We had become a charity case.

———————

That winter, Eric McCrae invited me to Urbana, a student missions conference at the University of Illinois Urbana-Champaign. The conference was for college students, and I was the one high school student from Crossroads who got to attend, for reasons I surmised must be because of my missionary interest.

Eight of us, most of whom I didn't know, made the journey from warm California to freezing Illinois for the few days between Christmas and New Year's, including Eric McCrae and Frank, who had brought me the turkey dinner.

I entered the expansive stadium for the first rally with Angela, a warm and soft-spoken college student. Strangers wearing college sweatshirts of every hue swarmed about the expanse. We couldn't find anyone else from Crossroads, so we chose a couple folding chairs on the main floor. Afterward, Frank ambled up to us in the hall outside two open double doors.

"I looked everywhere and couldn't find you!" I told him.

"That's because you didn't yell, 'Dad, Dad!'"

I knew better than to fully soak in his sentiment. I'd realized with Darius, the Black drummer, that my dad couldn't be replaced, but it still felt nice.

Urbana was my first college experience, and it was everything I imagined. Angela and I met some of the Crossroads guys for pizza in the dorm lobby. She and I gabbed into the night about Crossroads boys as we lay on our bunk beds. One night as we all trudged through the snow, Eric McCrae and a Crossroads guy slid back and forth on the ice. Strangers laughed heartily and called us crazy. We picked up the snow beneath us for an impromptu snowball fight. My life felt like a movie.

All the attendees spent New Year's Eve in the stadium, holding tiny candles as we belted out songs about God and our desire to become missionaries. But while I saw that as my future, the conference itself felt suffocating, pushing us into something instead of letting us figure it out on our own. If we were truly following God, they said, we would go overseas. And to prove our commitment, we each had to select a year and country for our journey, written on identical sheets of paper, before heading back home. I don't know what I wrote, likely Liberia, where some Black Americans had expatriated to, and likely 1998, the year I would presumably graduate college.

———

In spring of my senior year, the youth group prepared for a summer mission trip to Australia. Graduating seniors were allowed to go since the trip was only taken every four years. We did fundraising events like car washes, and we took on "jobs" for church sponsors, like cleaning houses and putting notebooks together for someone's NASA meeting at Moffett Field. As the date got closer, I was still nowhere close to my goal. My family wanted me to back out and get a summer job, now that Melanie was older and they didn't need me to care for her.

I met Eric McCrae in his second-floor office in the gym. The large building held an ever-familiar rubber smell that emanated from the pristine floor. As I walked toward the stairs leading up to the office, I took mental stock of everything these walls had held over the past three years. The Halloween cardboard box maze that led us, on hands and knees, through pitch-black tunnels for a full hour, as it weaved through thematic rooms and up and down those very stairs. The Christmas 'Round the Table Carol Sing. Movie nights, craft days.

Eric's door was open, so I walked in and sat in the chair across from his desk, fearful of what I had to say. After I'd listed my reasons for not going, he used a counterargument that no good Christian could ignore.

"Didn't you say God wanted you to go?"

"Yes," I said.

"So who changed? Did God change, or did you change? I feel that God wants you to go. I could have misinterpreted God, but I don't think so. I want you to know that not every trip is like what happened to you last summer."

Even though I still believed in God, I vowed to never be hedged in by him after this, or at least by what someone said of him. I wanted to go to Australia, but I didn't think Eric should speak for God or use him for what felt like manipulation. But I still appreciated Eric's desire to show me a different experience, especially, he said, because I'd had such a bad one in Indonesia. I leaned in for a hug, standard with Uncle Adam, and Eric pulled back. In my impulse, I had forgotten that he wasn't family, and I felt ashamed, as if his pulling away meant I had made a romantic move.

That summer, I did go to Australia, thanks to Gary paying the difference, and to a wealthy donor from the church. Gary liked to swoop in and pay for things with no expectation. Plus, he was religious too. In Australia, we stayed two people to a host family, and I was with a tall, leggy blonde. Boys looked at her constantly, but only I knew her secret.

She snored like a four-hundred-pound man. "Just hit me with a pillow," she said when I complained. But I could never hit her hard enough to stop the snoring.

Aside from the lack of sleep and feeling like our host parents preferred my roommate, I loved staying with the host family. The husband and wife treated us with a level of interest that I'd rarely experienced in a living situation. Each night, we'd sit together in the living room and watch TV—sometimes *Mr. Bean*, sometimes *Australia's Funniest Home Videos*—while we drank hot chocolate.

All the Crossroads crew took a trip to the UGG factory and watched a sheep get sheared. Everyone raided the shop to buy the finest products. I found a clearance bin up front, full of child-size slippers, and bought a pair for Melanie, carefully counting the money I had left. On a trip to the mall, where almost everyone bought Billabong sweatshirts, Jenna and I found off-brand tourist sweatshirts that read AUSTRALIA across the front. The neck was a strange split cowl, but I could afford it. I also bought a tourist pen—my one splurge in every country I visited.

Even more so than back home, the locals stared at me in wonder, or maybe just confusion. In Mexico I passed for Mexican; in Indonesia I passed for Indonesian. But in Australia, the locals asked, "What are you?" At a barbecue with another host family, while I stood in line for pavlova, a woman jokingly asked if I was sure I was American. The man next to her popped up with an unsolicited response: "Well, she sure doesn't look Australian." If I were older, wiser, better at comebacks, I would have reminded them that Indigenous Australians occupied the land before they did, and that America was built on the backs of people who looked like me. Instead, I smiled, feeling at once both highly conspicuous and completely invisible.

10

BETWEEN THE WORLD
AND ME
1994

SENIOR YEAR, AMY, JENNA, a sophomore named Heather, and I were
the four-person best friend group I'd always wanted. Heather lived with
her parents, just like Amy, and in a cookie-cutter home. The four of us
spent every weekend together. Sometimes we tried on clothes we couldn't
afford at Mervyn's and JCPenney. Heather could afford them, but she
played along, never purchasing items when we couldn't. After taking pictures of each other in the dressing room in matching black overalls and
form-fitting floral shirts, or fancy dresses, or denim shorts and flattering
T-shirts, we'd undress and re-don our daily attire—most of mine too-big
hand-me-downs in various shades of pink from my step-aunt; T-shirts
custom made for Crossroads youth group events; and the Georgetown
Hoyas sweatshirt Gary had found at the city park where he worked. The
clothes I tried on showed off my figure, but I only felt comfortable doing
so in the dressing room anyway. At less than one hundred pounds with
size D breasts, I worried form-fitting shirts would make me look like a
sex worker. I didn't want anyone looking at my body.

Amy's idea for a babysitters club sophomore year had never come
to fruition, but we toted around Melanie and Amy's toddler nephew in

Amy's baby blue 1979 Mustang as if they were our own children. We traded off filling up the tank for ninety-nine cents a gallon. McDonald's and Chuck E. Cheese were our hot spots with the kids. When we were on our own or with the foursome, we opted for the Denny's diner, where I always ordered french fries and a root beer float with my money from the government.

Toward the end of one Denny's night, two skater boys leaned over from the bar area toward our booth.

"Hey, I'm Dale," one said, pursing his lips against his lip ring and adjusting his black beanie.

"Hey," Heather answered nonchalantly, almost mockingly. Heather had a no-nonsense attitude and the most experience with boys, even though she was the youngest.

The second boy flipped the collar on his dark shirt. "What's goin' on."

"Nothing," Amy mumbled with a nervous giggle.

The first boy took a bite of his mostly eaten hamburger. "Hey, could you give us a ride home?"

"Sure," Amy said.

The three of us got up from our table and walked over to the front counter. Once we'd paid, we looked behind us for the boys, but they were gone.

"Must have gone to the bathroom," I said. "I don't want to have to sit next to them in the backseat."

"Well neither do I!" Heather said.

Amy unlocked all the doors just as the emergency exit sounded an alarm. The skater boys ran from the exit in a dine and dash and jumped in Amy's car.

"Drive!" the first boy said.

Too flummoxed to turn them away, Amy pulled the car out of the parking lot. The events of that night became a frequent topic of conversation, and the boy with the lip ring was inducted into our memory as "Lip Ring Dale."

The extra driving made me late for the curfew I had implemented for myself. Amy stayed over after we took Jenna and Heather home. The house was dark. Mom slept soundly. Amy slept on a mattress on the floor that we hauled in from the garage whenever someone spent the night.

We ate a late-night snack of Chewy Chips Ahoy, our favorite indulgence, and talked about the orphanage we planned to open in Africa. We didn't know where, or how we would fund it, or what children would come, but it was our dream.

———————

The next morning around 7:00 AM, I was startled awake by Gary pounding on my bedroom door.

"You have to do the dishes right now!" he bellowed with the usual baby inflection in his voice. Gary often decided things needed to be done "right now," with "right now" coming at any moment in time.

My heart raced at the sound of his booming voice that sucked all the oxygen in the house.

"We're sleeping," I yelled back through the door. I was slowly learning to fight back. It was the only way to communicate with Gary.

The banging continued. "Get up right now! Right now! Right now!" His voice was even more insistent, almost hysterical, as if the house were on fire and I was the only one who could put it out.

"Can I get dressed first?"

"No, there's no time!"

I groggily got out of bed and stepped over Amy, hoping she was sleeping through the ruckus, though I knew she must have woken up. When I stepped into the kitchen, I saw none of the dishes were mine. But that didn't matter to Gary. Our relationship had worsened over time. That year, I had free rein over the house until Gary came home with Melanie. Then she and I would retreat to my room for the rest of the night until he fell asleep. Sometimes when I happened to emerge from my room, Mom would tell Gary about a good grade I got on an essay, or a good math score. "You're such a good boy, Tigger," Gary would say in response, to the cat.

Years later, Mom mentioned something in a conversation that answered every question about Gary's behavior, like a fog clearing over turbulent waters to show the origin of the storm. "When we were first together," she said, "one day in bed he asked how big Robert was. I told him that was an inappropriate question that I wouldn't dignify with a response."

Gary was influenced by the myth of Black hypersexuality and insecure about his ability to compete for my mom's affections. And, intertwined with thoughts of virility, his knowledge that my Black father had hurt the woman he loved. I walked through his home as a constant reminder of Mom's past—a past that his mind likely embellished to fit white society's narrative. But living in his home, at seventeen, I didn't yet have that clarity. All I knew was that my stepdad didn't like me, even though he got along with his white ex-stepdaughter from his previous marriage.

When Mom got up that morning, I dreaded her retribution for coming home late. "I'm sorry I missed my curfew," I said.

"What curfew?" she responded. Somehow that felt worse than retribution. I took it as proof positive that she didn't care about where I was or what I did. I had to be my own guardian. She trusted me to be out late, trusted my friends, but I wanted her to worry, to ask herself "Where's Shannon?" if I didn't come home before she went to bed, instead of drifting off in a peaceful slumber.

In the spring, Amy and Heather joined me on a weekend trip to see my dad in Sacramento. I knew Dad's small one-bedroom would be a culture shock for Heather, who lived in a perfectly decorated two-story home, but not much different from the cramped apartment Amy shared with her parents and brother. Amy and Heather welcomed the adventure, and I didn't want to go up alone. I hadn't seen my dad in probably a year.

A boy our age with light skin, dark hair, and a mustache sat near us on the train. Heather, the only one of us who had dated even though she was youngest, bopped him on the head.

"Hey," she said.

Within a matter of minutes, the boy had a name (Josh), a nickname (Trainman Josh), and Heather and Amy on his lap. I didn't go on boys' laps. I didn't know why. The cells in my body wanted me to, but some force larger than them kept me away. "Danger," the force breathed into me. "Danger."

But Trainman Josh was not dangerous. He became immortalized in a photo and would remain a topic of conversation for years to come, to the point where it felt like we had always known him, and always would.

Dad met us at the train station. On this visit, there was no classic car. The four of us hopped on the bus. Dad approved of my friends right away, and they approved of him. He smiled at our nonsensical laughter. Amy and Heater poked each other. "Triple-T W!" Amy yelled. I felt my face turn red, but Dad didn't ask what the phrase meant. We'd picked it up from an anti-drug assembly at school, when a female character in the skit yelled, "Tits to the wind!" Afterward, we had exclaimed "Tits to the wind" while we threw our bodies forward, chests out, as we glided up and down the youth group room, until the elderly female leader chastised us. We didn't understand the reprimand, but we changed our exclamation to "Triple-T W."

When we reached Dad's apartment, at first awkward silence filled the empty spaces, just like when it was just Dad and me. But he came alive when he took us to the mall on the light-rail. His face lit up as he told random strangers that we were with him, proud that he had three young girls to protect. At one point he pretended to get off the light-rail, and then jumped back on at the last minute. "Gotcha!" he said. At our request, he took pictures of us throughout the mall. Like most of our mall experiences, we weren't there to shop. Instead we ran from here to there, rode the elevator up and down, and posed with giant Looney Tunes statues. That night on the pullout couch, we braided each other's hair before bed. My two worlds had never blended better.

For my senior class portrait, I got my hair done in braids by a professional who came to our house to give us a cheaper rate under the table. The pictures from my Indonesia trip, where my hair frizzed out of control, made me self-conscious. And since I looked ambiguously other, I hoped the braids would make it clear that my brown skin came from Black-ness. My experiment failed when my crush, Josh, asked, "What are you, anyway?" Josh was homecoming king, student body president, big man on campus, captain of the football team, and miraculously my friend. On Tuesday mornings, we and other Christians gathered around the Leigh High flagpole for "See you at the pole." We held hands and prayed for our school and our fellow students. The best mornings were those when Josh stood beside me. His large frame and floppy hairdo were inviting like a jovial cartoon character. His large, warm hand always squeezed mine before letting go. I passed him letters in the halls filled with angst about my family life and fraught relationship with my father. He received each letter with a smile and hug.

Josh wasn't my only crush. My mind had become consumed with boys. Ironically, it seemed the trick to getting a boyfriend was to not want one, but that proved impossible, given my lack of male attention in any form. It seemed guys wanted to feel like they had to get past a father to date a girl, and there was no father standing in the way for me. I was wide open and therefore completely undesirable. I knew I must reek of desperation.

Three months later, I took the braids out before school. I cut through the now-frizzy extensions and then unbraided them to let my own hair free. But what I thought would be a quick transformation devolved into a cat's cradle gone wrong. Over the past few weeks, my hair and the extensions had serpentined together in an indelible bond, unwilling to be broken. I put down the scissors and called Grandma, who was often free for emergencies. Together we wrestled and gently combed the stubborn strands until my hair broke free. We put in a fresh coat of relaxer, and she rinsed it out under the kitchen sink. Her warm hands massaged my scalp with motherly tenderness and skill. A few years later, a bit of relaxer would fly off my gloved hand and land on a painted metal closet, immediately stripping the paint right off.

No one talked to me about college. Not Leigh High counselors or teachers, not my mother, or Grandma, or Aunt Deborah. Whenever the subject did come up, it was always about my cousins Adria's and Elsie's future plans. The only people who mentioned college were the leaders at my church. They had big magazines full of Christian colleges for seniors to apply to. I flipped through the pages, letting the feeling I got from each ad guide me. I finally settled on a little college in Iowa called Northwestern. The ad had a picture of a man pulling a canoe to shore. His eyes looked directly at me. He looked a little like Frank, the college leader who had brought me the turkey and said I should call him Dad.

I planned to fund my private school experience with a scholarship given to a Crossroads senior each year. I felt confident in my chances until I saw a certain girl was applying too. She was my nemesis, though she didn't know. I measured my life against hers, frustrated that she always seemed one step ahead. Her parents attended Crossroads. She went to Los Gatos High. She had perfect, shiny hair. She was pretty without trying. She didn't date, but guys respected her. Last winter the girls in my prayer group had a contest to see who could get their leg hair the longest, and even though my legs got stubbly by the evening if I'd shaved that morning, she even beat me there.

When I stepped in for the interview, about six adults I knew were on the committee. Seated around a large table, they started the questions within what seemed like seconds. Only one question had me completely stumped: "If you get this scholarship, how do you plan to fund the rest of tuition?" Right then, I knew it wasn't mine.

At the end of the interview, I walked out and immediately started to cry. Because someone was always better than me—and because I was always around white people, a white person was always better than me. Though it often wasn't, their one-upmanship felt racial, that I could never viewed as the best because I didn't match the skin of what they believed the best to be. I sat down next to the girl and started laughing in embarrassment from my tears. Then I was back to crying, and then we both laughed together. She got the scholarship.

———————

Grandma and Mom were impressed when I got my acceptance letter to Northwestern. I was pretty impressed myself, even though I'd later learn that anyone who met the minimum requirements was let in.

"Where did you get all that gumption?" Grandma asked. I had no idea what gumption meant, but I was glad I'd finally done something to make her proud.

I sat at the kitchen table one afternoon to fill out the FAFSA—my ticket to federal aid. I quickly learned I'd have to include Gary on the paperwork. The form asked for his income bracket.

"Mom?"

"Yes," she answered as she came into the kitchen.

"Which box do I check for Gary's income?"

My mom pointed to the second largest option.

"Are you sure?"

"Yes," she said.

"How can I get aid then?"

"I don't know," Mom said nonchalantly.

"How did you?"

"I got pregnant."

"So you think I should get pregnant?"

"No, of course not. I just don't know what to tell you."

I called Dad. He told me to call the United Negro College Fund. The man on the other end sounded confused by my inquiry and hung up the phone.

Gary's income didn't make sense. I didn't know why I had to wear hand-me-downs, why Mom never had enough money for anything, why Gary dumpster dived for cans. I had assumed his asceticism came from his own lack of money, but he would soon purchase land in Oregon, near his sisters. I finished filling out the FAFSA and hoped for the best.

———————

That spring, Dad called me with updates, as always, self-focused and in almost rapid fire.

"Last December, a white man came into my apartment and started beating me up. We fought for a long time on the porch. He had a screwdriver and tried to stab me with it. He finally ran off and an ambulance came and took me to the hospital.

"But you know what else?" he continued. "Two white lesbian women live next door. Once, I mentioned that I didn't have any money to buy food. They gave me thirty dollars. Some white people are trash, and others are generous. You never know.

"And there's something I need to tell you," he said, not stopping for my response. "I might have lung cancer. If I get an operation, I'll be fine, but if I don't come out fine, and they have to put me on a respirator, I don't want to be kept alive. You understand?"

"Yes," I said. I wasn't sure that I would want to be kept alive either in that circumstance, but I hoped I wouldn't have to be responsible for killing my dad.

"I'm ready to die whenever my time comes," he continued. "I've lived much longer than I expected. So many of my relatives died of cancer at an early age." In their forties. I remembered. The same age Mom was now.

The greeting card section of any store taunted me each June for Father's Day, almost violent in its insistence on being seen—rows of cardstock in bright colors, designs peeking up from each slot against crisp white envelopes. I used to look for the perfect card, but each sentiment left a larger pit inside me. "You're the best." "Thank you for always being there." "You've taught me so much." There was no card to describe my dad's role in my life. But after the phone call, I decided it might be time to send one.

Dad called again the next day.

"They say I have a 97 percent chance of having cancer. They're having me come in for testing over the next two weeks. I don't think the operation will kill me. I came close when I had stomach cancer. My heart stopped beating. I saw myself from the corner of the room. Did I tell you that?" I nodded, though he couldn't see me. "But God saved me," he continued. "It just wasn't time for me to go yet."

"Do you think you're going anywhere after you die?" I asked tentatively. Maybe this was the moment I could begin the scripted salvation talk we had learned in youth group. I'd led a stranger to Christ this way when we went door-to-door, as well as a girl who came to our performance in Australia. Two checkmarks that helped me feel worthy of Crossroads, like I was pulling my weight.

"Yes," Dad said. "I've known since I was twenty-five. We have to sit down and talk about it soon. And about a lot of other things."

The talk would have to wait. The next week, I called to check in.

"What did the tests say?"

"Great googly moogly," he said, one of his favorite phrases. "Now they say I have a 99 percent chance of *not* having cancer."

I felt the pit in my stomach rise and fall, rise and fall. Dad had been "dying" my whole life, at least according to him. These last two phone calls seemed to usher us into a new level of urgency. Or would they fall off, like most of Dad's declarations? Could I really be sure he was safe?

As the semester progressed, I began to feel untethered. Jenna and Amy decided to join me at Northwestern College, and we proudly wore our college sweatshirts. But it was looking less and less likely that I could go. Gary offered to help pay the first year's tuition, but I didn't know how I'd manage the second year. Mom thought I could take a year off in Iowa and then count myself as independent. I wasn't so sure. And then, everything crumbled.

My mom asked Aunt Deborah for advice, as she often did. Deborah was sure I wasn't mature enough for college, and Mom backed her, as she always did. In a letter, Mom said I shouldn't have student loan debt. She said she was still paying hers off. She said she had wanted me to have a social life instead of studying like Adria, and that Adria's studiousness had given her tendinitis. She said if she got a full-time job to help, she wouldn't be able to be around for Melanie, the way she hadn't been around for me.

> *Don't be too critical of your old mom or of yourself. We have both begun life with disadvantages, as did your dad. Use your hardships as a means to build your strength and character. You will achieve your dreams. I feel like I have achieved mine, and it has taken a lot of time and work and struggle for me to do it. I think your father just gave up, although I don't think he'd admit it.*

There were no answers, only barriers. Mom had achieved her dreams by going to school, and she wanted me to achieve mine, but she didn't want me to go to school. No one knew what to do with me. No one told me what I could do. No one mentioned state school. It was decided— through Grandma, Mom, and Aunt Deborah—that I'd move in with Grandma and go to Cabrillo, the community college Mom had attended when I was little. I resigned myself to the idea, glad at least to be going back to the house I still thought of as home.

Aside from the church scholarship, I had applied for one other, through my school's Home and School Club, a parent volunteer organization that supported students. It felt almost too easy to be true—a list of essay questions, a letter of recommendation, and a decent GPA. I got an invitation to the awards ceremony. No one got an invitation unless they were winning an award.

I uncharacteristically wore a dress: my nine-dollar, black floral dress from the flea market. Mom sat beside me in the small auditorium. So many of the students I admired were in that room. Smart students. Students with AP classes and good grades. My crush. I couldn't believe I was part of their circle. As I sat waiting for my award to be called, my heart beat so fast and hard I was sure everyone could hear it. When they called my name, I somehow made it to the table without fainting. Everyone clapped. My mom's face glowed. I decided, in exactly that moment, that I was smart.

I took Dad up on his latest offer to come visit that spring before graduation, and this time I went alone. For the first time maybe ever, we had real conversations. But they still felt accusatory in tone.

"Gary doesn't have any authority over you," he said. "He can't make college decisions for you."

I agreed, but there wasn't anything I could do to change the situation.

"I'm going to send you six or seven thousand dollars," he continued. "Maybe that will cover it. But Cabrillo does sound good too."

I never knew whether to believe anything Dad said. His promises almost never came true. He was going to make a million dollars. We were going to have a cat. We were going to have a dog. He was going to marry the girlfriend he had when I was in middle school. But nothing ever changed. It was always just me and him and his crummy apartments. Regardless of my knowing he probably wouldn't have the money, I knew Cabrillo was the best option, paid for with the lump sum I'd get from the government.

Dad gave me some handouts from the church he'd been attending down the street about grieving a family member by reaching out to God. I must have looked depressed, because he said, "I'm not doing this because I think I'm going to die." After his last proclamation of having a 99 percent chance of not having cancer, his possible death had left my mind. But now that he had brought it up, it came back full force.

That spring, I graduated from Leigh. Heather's mom, always mothering to Amy and me, gave us each money to buy jeans—our first store-bought pairs in years instead of the hand-me-downs we were used to. My extended family came over after the ceremony to celebrate. For all Dad's absences, I thought he would have seen me graduate, but he didn't make it. On my last night of youth group, I stayed after everyone had left, my back up against the back wall, legs crisscrossed. I crossed my arms in a self-hug as tears welled in my eyes. Youth group had been my family for the last three years, and I couldn't fathom life without it. The senior class transitioned to the college group, but most of us were leaving for college out of town, and I knew things would never be the same.

11

ROOM WITH A VIEW
1994

When I returned from Australia in late summer, Uncle Adam, now twenty-six, picked me up from the airport and drove me straight to Grandma's house, just as planned.

I didn't want to step foot in Gary's house, and I wouldn't for another three years.

That night, Mom and Melanie joined us for dinner and a VHS of *Mrs. Doubtfire*. I excused myself halfway through the movie to take a nap, and I woke up fourteen hours later, my mom and Melanie long gone. I had slept heavily through the jet lag and through the peacefulness of returning home. No one pounded on my door in the morning to wash their dishes.

My bedroom was no longer the laundry room, as it had been when I was young. I had moved to Mom's old room, between Grandma's and Uncle Adam's, and directly across from the hall bathroom. Grandma and I replaced the bright-orange chandelier from the 1970s with a white one, and the forest-green curtains with a softer blue. We replaced the well-worn sheets with a crisp set with a blue floral design. For the first time, I had a double bed. A large wooden desk sat in the corner, waiting for me to fill it with homework and, as my idol Anne Shirley would say, delightful imaginations. My paperback copies of the Anne of Green Gables series sat on my cedar chest—inherited from my great grandmother—along with my full set of the Chronicles of Narnia. My stuffed Piglet kept them company, a reminder of my high school friends who each had their own stuffed representative from Winnie-the-Pooh's Hundred Acre Wood. No one was Pooh. We were a democracy with no leader.

"Dinner!" Grandma said in a singsong voice that first full night home. I couldn't fathom her call. It wasn't a holiday, just a Tuesday night. Dinner at Gary's had long ago devolved into solo meals at arbitrary times. "Breakfast," "lunch," and "dinner" held no meaning. If I was hungry, I ate. My staples at Gary's had been frozen pizza, spaghetti, and grilled cheese sandwiches—the latter two being easy re-creations from my first time living at Grandma's house. When Melanie was little, I had fed her a steady diet of toddler biscuits, which she called "cooqua," for cookie. On weekends, I made us pancakes. When I was bored, I baked us ginger cookies from an old family recipe. Dinners at a table were for families in sitcoms. Then I remembered I'd left the Hastings family behind.

I walked into the kitchen and saw napkins in the middle of the table in a holder Adam had made in high school shop class. Fresh salad sat in its own wooden salad bowl with matching wooden spoons, which we always ate after the meal instead of before. Adam had made spaghetti in a pasta maker that rolled out uniform pieces with a simple hand crank.

Grandma reached a hand out to me as I sat down. "Pass me a fork, lover?" It was her pet name for me, akin to "one who loves." I sighed deeply, sinking into the familiar kitchen chair. After nine years away, I was home.

As the days went by, Uncle Adam's girlfriend, Stephanie, often joined us for dinner—and stayed the night. Premarital sex occurred on the regular just down the hall, pushing my conservative buttons. My consolation prize at not moving away for school had been returning to my former life, with Grandma and Adam as my stand-in parents who had shrouded me in love and tradition. Stephanie, who was short and plump with long blonde hair, lived with her mother. But she walked through the house as if it were her second home, upsetting my balance. I had lived there longer, but it seemed intimacy trumped—or at least equaled—blood ties. It wouldn't be long before she moved in. For the first time, I realized it's never possible to return to something that once was. The past remains in the ethers, close enough to be tantalizing, but too far to be touched. Not that I wouldn't try.

My return to the house also carried with it a feeling of danger I hadn't expected. Seemingly out of nowhere, I remembered that child protective services had come to the house when I was young for something having to do with Uncle Adam. I was sure this memory was new, and sure I had no memory of what had happened, if anything. I brought it up to Grandma one evening when we were alone. I leaned against the doorway between the kitchen and the dining room in case I needed to make a quick escape. From what, I wasn't sure.

"Did something happen with me and Uncle Adam when I was little?" I asked tentatively.

Grandma put down her magazine. "What do you mean?"

"I don't know . . ." My voice grew soft. "Something happening that shouldn't have happened?"

Grandma looked in my direction, yet her gaze landed just above me. Squaring her shoulders, she answered, "If anything happened between you two, it was your fault for being a flirt."

I never brought it up again, but those words stayed with me forever.

A few days before the beginning of the semester, Dad called.

"I'm having surgery for lung cancer in a couple weeks," he said. "I want you to come up."

The familiar rock dropped in my stomach each time *cancer* made it into conversation. "Of course I'll come," I said.

"I have 95 percent chance of making it, but I want to be prepared," Dad continued. "You know I'm ready to die when the time comes. I'm going to buy that house I told you about and make sure everything is in your name. I want you to be taken care of. You're my baby girl."

"OK," I said. "Keep me posted and I'll come up." I imagined what it would be like to have my own home. To have my dad leave me a legacy. I'd feel him in the walls, in the financial freedom, in the care I was sure dads take of their children every day that would now be within my grasp. I'd be able to say, "My father gave this to me." Only, I'd have to lose my father to get it. Why couldn't I have both?

Dad didn't call back until October—the cancer scare now passed. "Now they're saying I don't have it." But I went up on my own anyway.

My father walked me up the steps to his second-floor apartment. He walked a little slower than the last time I'd seen him. Everything was just how I'd remembered it in every other apartment where he'd lived. He still had the Smokey Bear sheet set—a hand-me-down from Uncle Adam. He still had the particleboard set of drawers from my laundry room days. Artifacts lifted from a life that wasn't his. There was no more talk of houses in my name, just a senior man still sleeping between the sheets of Smokey, cradling a daily reminder to not start fires.

It was only six o'clock, but Dad was losing energy. He put me to the task of setting the clock on his VCR and entering receipts in his checkbook. His handwriting was no longer steady enough to do this on his own. "Arthritis," he explained. As Dad changed into his pajamas in the bedroom, I grabbed the receipts and saw a letter from Pacific Gas and Electric made out to "Jose Manuel," as if he were hiding his identity. Dad was becoming more and more of a mystery, and one that I would never entirely solve.

I diligently entered each receipt. Toward the middle of the pile, I picked up a receipt for a handgun, purchased just before he met me at the train station.

"Dad, is this a receipt for a gun?"

"Mm-hm, an air pistol," he said from the bedroom. "A guy broke into my house last year, and I had to beat him to the ground. I'm not letting that happen again."

Panic rose in my chest. *So this is how I will die*, I thought. *Why buy a gun the day before I arrived?* It didn't occur to me that he bought it to protect me.

I felt guilty for mentally accusing my dad of planned murder, and I knew I must be crazy, but I couldn't shake my paranoia. I remembered a connection with my dad and guns, but for the life of me, I couldn't think what it was. In what would become a common occurrence, I had blocked out Dad threatening to shoot his girlfriend Naomi with the BB gun when I was little. All that remained was the fight-or-flight response pounding in my body. Just like I didn't know BB guns weren't lethal when I was a little, I didn't know air pistols weren't lethal now.

Dad emerged from the bedroom and sat down at the foot of the foldout couch, slinging one leg over the other. We sat in silence for a moment, both examining the floor. He seemed to pick up on my silence. Maybe he could see my panic. I was never good at hiding my emotions.

"You know," he said slowly. "Your grandma is the reason your mom and I split up."

"What?" I asked, confused.

"She was always meddling. Your mom was a grown woman, but your grandma still wanted her to be a child."

The image of my mom's old journal, tucked away in my room back home, blazed before my eyes. The red ink told of Mom's nightmares, and of the way Mom's confidence was slowly being put back together after leaving my dad.

I didn't respond to Dad. There was no point. But he knew I didn't believe him.

"I swear on my mother's grave," he said.

She must not have one then, I thought. I felt my head pound, the way it always did at Dad's house. Visits were meant for deprogramming instead of connection. Except I was quickly learning that Dad wanted me to deprogram from everyone but him. In middle school, when Mom married, Dad had said I was just as much a Luders as a Manuel, but now he seemed threatened by my allegiance to a dual identity, perhaps unsure what secrets I would uncover that might make me choose sides. He didn't know that my mom's family never tried to pit me against him. No one but Gary, whom I didn't consider family.

I didn't answer Dad. I had come to learn that the only responses he would accept were agreement and silence, so I chose silence. But in my silence, he knew I didn't agree.

"You know, you don't need to protect your grandma. Or your uncle Adam, for that matter. When you were little, I protected *you* from *them*. Or at least I tried to. Adam was always put before you. They don't have your best interests in mind."

I thought about Adam's master bedroom, but then I thought about my new room. About Adam teaching me how to use a computer, and Grandma editing my English papers. Adam and I flew kites at UC Santa

Cruz. We rollerbladed on West Cliff Drive—the winding road that followed the ocean. There were the nights playing Pounce on the living room
floor with our decks of cards. His girlfriend Stephanie and me resting
our heads on Adam as he lay on the floor after a match.

Dad thought he was losing me, I could tell.

That night I fought against sleep as I lay on the couch under a thin
blanket. I felt like I'd walked straight into the clutches of the enemy,
armed with a gun bought upon my arrival. If I stayed awake, my dad
couldn't shoot me. If I closed my eyes, who knew what fate lurked just
beyond that open bedroom door. And then I felt shame wash over me
for thinking my father was a monster. Or the gun a monster that Dad
would unwittingly use to remove me, to remove my Ludersness. Maybe
to start over with a new daughter, to rid himself of an experiment that
had failed. That night, I hadn't considered that alcohol was part of what
scared me. He hadn't been drinking, but he could at any moment. I
resolved to never come back on my own.

———————

At Grandma's, each morning I took a one-hour trip to Cabrillo Community College. I left the house as the sun was slowly rising over the city,
at first masked by the height of our hill and the trees peppered between
houses. I walked down High Street—aptly named—with my backpack on
my back, my earbuds in my ears, and my portable CD player churning
out the Christian music of Amy Grant and Michael W. Smith.

The stillness of the morning made the city feel like it existed just
for me. I slowly made my descent until I could see the tops of the
Mission- and Spanish-style downtown buildings and a peek of the ocean
beyond. Sometimes the clock tower acknowledged my arrival with its
dong as it ushered me past the Catholic church and CathoLICK Girls
etched on the sidewalk. I entered the single-street downtown strip as
merchants slowly opened their doors, and I stopped at Noah's Bagels
when time allowed.

The bus stop was at the far end of the single downtown street. The
rumble of the buses always conjured up overnights in the Crossroads
Church bus as we made our way south to Disneyland and Mexico. The

Pavlovian effect was one of both sleepiness and adventure. I rode the city bus to class in the mornings with excitement at what each day's lessons would bring. But every day, I pictured a different me. I wanted to be Anne Shirley, brave enough to break a slate over a boy's head. Brave enough to stand before an audience and recite a poem from memory. But instead, I sometimes used the back exit from the bus just to avoid saying "thank you" to the driver. That semester, I barely ever opened my mouth on campus. If I did, it was out of necessity. Thoughts constantly filled my mind, but a heavy lock kept me from expressing even the most mundane sentiments. As a freshman in college, I was much like the freshman I had been in high school: a fish out of water, with the sense that I was an impostor who would soon be found out. I was a seventeen-year-old in an adult world, traversing the city without the people who already knew me. So instead, the city itself became my companion, ushering me into activities that forced me out of my shell.

I filled my evenings with as much as possible in an attempt to pretend I had made it to a four-year Christian college. I took classes at Bible Study Fellowship, an international program with roots dating back to the Billy Graham crusades. And I immersed myself in Santa Cruz Bible Church with almost as many weekly events as I had at Crossroads, which was now cut off from me. Gary hadn't wanted to spend the hundred dollars for the behind-the-wheel training in high school that was separate from driver's ed class. Without my license or wheels to borrow, I couldn't make it the forty-five minutes over the Santa Cruz Mountains to my old stomping grounds.

I decided my time in Santa Cruz was meant to infuse my "garden," to turn me into a godly woman, worthy of my future spouse and my inevitable immersion into the ministry. Vines, and fruit, and flowers, and seeds—common analogies for women's godliness in the church—were growing inside me. Stephanie took me to see the *Secret Garden* musical, based on my most beloved children's book given to me by my mom. I became obsessed with the sullen orphan girl who is transformed by tending to her deceased mother's overgrown garden.

When I was home, I read. Back when Grandma had bought her house, the year I was born, she had installed bookshelves fashioned into the entryway wall. In libraries, I never knew what to pull from the shelves. Rows and rows of books held too many choices, and many of them not my style. I had no interest in Agatha Christie mysteries or romance novels, now especially if the romance novels weren't about Christians. But my grandma's bookshelves held what, in my mind, denoted true literature. After all, each book had been vetted by her, or it wouldn't have been put there in the first place. The spines and pages themselves even smelled like her.

My grandma possessed a distinctive scent that remained unchanged. Opening the linen in the hallway released it tenfold, like dozens of Grandmas lying neatly folded on top of one another. It was a sweet smell—perhaps roses mixed with cedar. Her soap, shampoo, and laundry detergent might change, but she and her linens remained unaffected. Her books carried that same scent. Each page was Grandma. Each page was a fuzzy robe, a cup of coffee, and a free spirit.

As I lounged on the living room sofa in front of the wide corner windows, or rode the bus to and from classes, I delved into worlds of Jane Austen, Louisa May Alcott, and Alex Haley. These worlds differed from anything I had experienced inside the confines of fundamental Christianity. Books were my portals into other realities. Guilty pleasures in between line-by-line studies of Moses for Bible Study Fellowship. Grandma, who had always bragged about Adria and Elsie, brought up my reading at a family gathering at Aunt Deborah and Uncle Eugene's. "Did you know Shannon is an avid reader?" she mentioned to the group. They were the sweetest words I had ever heard, spoken from the woman I had most wanted to see me, to see the special person I was becoming. The conversation soon shifted to other topics. Nonetheless, I held on to what she'd said.

One book threatened to alter the truth as I had come to believe it. My English instructor, Nancy, was a thirtysomething white woman with a bright smile and a passion for literature that matched my own. In our very personal essays, she wrote encouraging notes on the margins: "Yes!" "Wow!" "I can see why you felt that way!" But The Color Purple would come to complicate my pure love for her.

We sat at tables that formed a rectangle. Our purple books peppered the table as we looked to Nancy for her daily nuggets of wisdom. "Class," she said, "love comes in many forms. We have read here the transformational love between Celie and Shrug Avery. This kind of love doesn't just exist in pages of fiction. I know this love intimately, because I also love a woman. My partner and I have been together for six years now."

I stifled a gasp as I peered at Nancy, attempting to pinpoint some part of her being that would explain her sinfulness and her confusion over same-sex love. She had shortish, wavy hair and wore comfortable clothes and a bright smile. I quickly looked down at the desk, unsure if my loving gaze would be taken the wrong way. No part of me wanted to see her naked, to kiss her, to even hold her hand. But how could I reconcile even platonic emotion for someone I believed was so determined to live in sin? Nancy's declaration broke through the barricade of my belief system, adding a caveat to what was interpreted to me as God's word. Ten years later, a best friend would come out to me before anyone else—a friend who would struggle with self-acceptance. Seeing his anguish would help rid me of my prejudices and make me an ally. But back then, my world was still black and white.

In the midst of what felt like a hotbed of secularism, I found a Christian at Cabrillo in October. Brian was tiny, under one hundred pounds, just like me. He sat next to me in beginning piano, with hands even more delicate than mine—made manly only by the faint tufts of hair on his knuckles. He wore polo-style shirts just like Uncle Adam, with the same thick brown hair peeping out from the V of the shirt's neck. On the cover of his piano book was a classic cross, hand-drawn in fine black ink.

The day I turned eighteen, we finally struck up a conversation.

"Have a good day," Brian said on his way out the classroom door.

The adrenaline of the icebreaker busted the proverbial lock from my lips. On no other day but today could I have had the perfect reply.

"Thanks," I said, before I could freeze back up. "It's my birthday."

Brian and I found a spot on the grass and sat cross-legged, facing the sun. For the first time since I'd moved to Santa Cruz, I relaxed into conversation with someone other than family. Brian and I both had a lazy eye. We were both lactose intolerant. We were both shy. The lunch hour flew by just like they had with my high school foursome, but even more enjoyably so. I took furtive glances at Brian's Bambi-like eyelashes and watched his hands nervously pick the blades of grass. As I shared, I felt as if I were going to pass out. I had never even talked to Josh—my high school crush—this way, with my mouth instead of my pen. Now I had a new crush.

We spent the next two months traversing Brian's church grounds and exchanging emails. In my room, we sat on my bed and looked through my album of childhood photos. An amateur photographer, Brian peered into my third-grade eyes behind the protective plastic on the page and told me what lens had been used for the photo. It felt like no one had ever gazed that closely at me before—had cared so much about little Shannon.

We discussed his broken heart and my broken father.

"I don't know when I'll be able to love again," he said about his recent girlfriend dumping him for another guy.

"I don't know if I can trust that someone won't disappear," I said.

One afternoon we drove in his BMW up into the hills of Scotts Valley to the home he shared with his mother. Inside, every piece of dark, heavy, wood furniture was placed in perfect harmony. Each knickknack had a purpose. Nothing was askew. On the coffee table in the living room was a nicely arranged pile of hardbound green leather books. I hunched over to read the top one: *Shannon.*

"What's this book about?" I asked.

"I have no idea," Brian answered. "It's just for decoration." I marveled at someone collecting books just because they looked good in the space, and a novel called *Shannon* felt like a sign that he and I were meant to be together.

I excused myself to the bathroom, locked the door behind me, and stared at Brian's framed baby shoes above the toilet. That one simple item separated his house from mine, though his was no more grandiose than Grandma's. The simple fact was, it was *his* home. A roof that his mother had created for him, infinitely held behind the glass of the shadow box. The two little shoes a reassurance for his mother that he would never outgrow her.

———

Grandma worked long days from home at her button, badge, and name plate shop in the converted garage. Uncle Adam helped her, while Stephanie worked downtown in a daycare, utilizing her bachelor's in early childhood education. I liked to help Grandma when I could, pushing the button machine, entering unique names of immigrants from all over the world into our database of Dominican Hospital employees. I dreamed of working from home like Grandma, being my own boss and using my smarts to bring home cash. I wanted to start my day in my robe, sipping coffee, and then retreat to another part of the house for work.

Grandma liked to go dancing on big band nights at the Dream Inn, a large hotel that sat on a hill above the beach. Then one night, she met a man.

"He asked me to dance," Grandma said at the dinner table, now fitted with the new occupant. "Then he wouldn't let me dance with anyone else."

Dennis smiled, put his hand on Grandma's leg, and patted it gently. "I know a good thing when I see it. I didn't want her to get away."

Dennis was a doughy man in ill-fitting pants and an extra-large polo shirt. He wore a complacent smile and a blue cap that read SPECIAL AGENT DEPARTMENT OF JUSTICE CALIFORNIA. His black, pleated pants looked like those on one of my egg-shaped dolls, staying in place by sheer magic.

"Dennis is coming here for Christmas," Grandma said. Stephanie, Adam, and I looked at one another with raised eyebrows.

Adam quickly got up from the table. "I see," he said, as he opened the refrigerator and pulled out a milk carton.

I'd heard stories of Grandma's impulsiveness. How she and my grandpa got engaged after two weeks and married two months later. How when he died, she'd traveled around Europe for a year in her VW camper with Aunt Deborah and Uncle Adam. How when they returned she sold the house in San Anselmo and bought this one, during Deborah's senior year in high school, and told Deborah—in a note—that she could finish out the school year with a neighbor. So Dennis's quick ascension up the ranks of our family wasn't a total surprise. (And my mom's lax parenting had roots.)

Dennis began to stand up, holding onto the kitchen table for support. "I'm going to get a glass of water."

Grandma gestured for him to sit back down. "I got it, lover," she said, using her term of endearment for me on this near stranger. It felt like a punch in the gut.

When Christmas came, I introduced Brian to Jenna and Amy, who were home for break from Northwestern College; Amy's college friend Dellie, an exchange student from Bahrain; and Heather, who was in her junior year at Leigh.

Everyone came over to my house to meet in person and open presents on the living room floor. I had no frame of reference at this time—no way of comparing it with the lives of secular girls—but the purity culture my friends and I had been raised in had stunted our maturity levels when it came to the opposite sex. To my surprise and dismay, my friends flirted with Brian, and he flirted back in a way he never had with me. As we opened our small gifts, Brian kissed each girl on the cheek and fell on top of her in laughter, including me after he unwrapped the small brown teddy bear I had gifted him. Hyperness and hormones filled the room as girls and the boy continued to fall on one another, and pushed me into the fray. Brian tickled me in response, just like Uncle Adam used to.

Later that night, we watched *Anne of Green Gables* at my request—a favorite of both mine and Jenna's, both of us idolizing our fictional hero, whom Jenna now emulated by avoiding the chaos. Through the movie, I attempted to re-create our high school tradition and initiate Brian into what felt like a most sacred space. But my other friends were still falling on each other, and still pushing Brian and me together while simultaneously pulling us apart. They talked of hand jobs and blow jobs and masturbation—all things we were prohibited from doing before marriage. *Anne of Green Gables* was my escape to a world where men acted like gentlemen and imaginative heroines spoke in poetry. I recoiled at it being tainted by hormones and talks of sex.

"I masturbate," Brian said.

"So does Shannon," Amy said. In three words, she revealed my secret shame, the biggest sin I felt I needed to atone for, and to the boy she knew I liked.

While they continued rolling around the floor, Brian grabbed Heather and almost kissed her. The shock of it felt like slow motion, and I found myself running down the hall to my bedroom. I took out the locked diary I kept for my future husband and turned the tiny key. "Men are scum," I wrote. "I'll never marry." My husband diary had no doubt been suggested at the purity seminar Jenna and I had attended at another church in high school. I had taken on the assignment with sincerity.

I sat on my bed, looking through my Bible for comfort and direction, when Brian came in holding the small teddy bear. He sat against the closed door so the others couldn't follow.

"Should I leave?" he asked.

"No," I said, and started to cry. "Things have changed so much," I said, my voice breaking. "I've heard more about sex the past few days than I ever wanted to know." Amy had gotten her first boyfriend the past semester at Northwestern, whom she broke up with before Christmas break. That experience seemed to change her, to make her a stranger with a new sensuality that I couldn't understand. She hadn't had sex, but she had become a woman. I still felt like a girl.

Brian nodded his head. "Amy and I talked about it and apologized to each other," he said. "I'm sorry."

"It's OK." But I was still hurt, torn between crying on him for comfort and kicking him out for what felt like betrayal. This was not how my one true romance was supposed to go. I had imagined our love story: friends becoming more, holding hands, stealing soft kisses. I had imagined him liking my friends as extensions of me, not as sexual beings in their own right.

My husband diary lay open on the bed, spine side up, with the box beside it. Brian stood up from the carpet and reached across me to grab the plastic decorative key inside the box. He knew of the husband diary and the key, which Jenna and I had each been given at the purity seminar. He put the key in his jeans pocket and tried to run out the door, but I grabbed his arm and demanded it back. He placed it in my hand with a look that said he understood its significance. I mentally kicked myself for opening the sacred box in Brian's presence, for failing as a godly woman.

Still standing in the doorway, Brian took my other hand. "You get a real kiss," he said. He leaned down and placed a gentle kiss on my hand before letting it go. His hormones had gotten the better of him with my friends, but I got the deliberate fairy-tale moment. Maybe I had won after all.

———————

Between Christmas and the New Year, Brian, Amy, Dellie, and I took a road trip to Disneyland in Amy's parents' van and stayed in her cousin's spare room near the Magic Kingdom.

"Are you two together?" Amy's cousin asked Brian and me during dinner. I didn't know what had given her that impression but was glad for it.

"As you can see, we're very quiet on that subject," Brian said. His not saying no felt like he might be saying yes.

That night I slept on the floor between Amy and Brian—his feet aligned with my head. I had never shared air with a boy I liked before, in that intimate space of slumber. I attempted to mentally erase Amy and Dellie from the room and focus only on the steady inhale and exhale of Brian's body.

"I don't like that mirror," Dellie said of the mirrored closet door.

"Mirror, mirror, on the wall," Brian recited.

"I hate that movie," I said before I could stop myself.

"What do you mean?" Brian asked.

"Well," I answered, choosing my words carefully. "The rest of that line goes: 'Who's the fairest of them all?' I don't think she should be considered the most beautiful just because she's fair-skinned." I surprised myself with candidness.

After a moment of silence, Brian replied, "Shannon, I think you're prettier than a lot of white girls I know."

I swelled at the compliment.

Rain drenched Riverside throughout the night and didn't let up the next morning. At Disneyland, the ticket agent handed us each a yellow rain poncho and a bookmark-sized apology for the inclement weather with a note from Jiminy Cricket: "Into each life a little rain must fall . . . and it looks like today is our day." The wise cricket wasn't kidding.

With most of the rides closed, the four of us rode Space Mountain repeatedly. Each time in line, I was forced to watch Brian and Amy flirt. Dellie stood by as an unfazed observer.

"I can't flirt," I said quietly as my eyes welled up.

"Sure you can," Brian said.

He took my chin in his hand and brought it inches from his face. My heart leapt. Then he pulled away.

"That's how you flirt," he said.

At the end of the day, back in the car, Amy was afraid to drive through the flooded parking lot. Brian took the driver's seat and pulled out while Amy crouched in between the two seats. As we drove away, Brian put his arm around her. I gripped the sentimentality of my tears matching the rain as it fell in torrents around us.

12

PRIDE AND PREJUDICE
1995

In January, I took the train to see Dad. I wondered why I made the journey again, alone, after I'd promised myself that the one before had been my last. I hadn't even gotten to Sacramento yet, and already things weren't going right. I forgot my deodorant. I forgot the adapter for Grandma's Walkman, so it only played music in one ear. I forgot my official "train song," Christian singer Phil Keaggy's "I Will Be There." I dropped five dollars at the metro, so I was short on cash for food, and all I'd brought was a Koala drink, gum, and two Tootsie Pops. But then I opened my Bible Study Fellowship homework and read about the Israelites who, despite their little faith, were protected by God with a "cloud" that showed them the way. I began to forget that my music was only reaching one ear, and when I stuck my hand in my pocket for ChapStick, I found the five dollars.

A boxing match played on Dad's little TV, a rerun in the background, simulating a level of enthrallment absent on our side of the screen. A man called out the play-by-play in a technical language I couldn't understand. Someone named Foreman sometimes swung at Moorer. Someone named Moorer sometimes swung at Foreman. The little ring, the little shorts, and the little movements back and forth seemed inconsistent with the boxers' bulging muscles and apparent hatred for each other. Each blow felt like a sucker punch to my Anne of Green Gables and Winnie-the-Pooh world. I looked away and tried to tune out the forceful contact.

With each visit, I hoped to uncover my dad's many layers and learn about who he really was. I knew almost nothing about him—or at least nothing that stuck. But I'd learned by now not to trust his stories anyway. I was sure even he didn't know where his reality and fantasy began and ended. My dad had been saying he was about to die for ten years—at least. Each weekend with him felt like a ticking clock with an alarm that never rang. It was a suspended urgency turned into numbness, brought on by the fruitlessness of attaching oneself to a ship that insists it's about to sink.

———————————

Back home, Brian came over for a visit. I sat at the foot of the bed and he at the head. "I have something to tell you," he said.

"OK," I said, unnerved by his serious expression.

"Amy and I kissed on Space Mountain," he said. "And we kissed some more on a night you weren't around."

I stared blankly at my white wall.

"Are you OK?" Brian asked.

I was annoyed by the question. Of course I wasn't OK. Why had he kissed my hand, told Amy's cousin we were quiet about the subject of dating instead of just no, and told me I was prettier than most white girls?

They weren't dating, he said. She had returned to Iowa. He had returned to Cabrillo. But they talked. In some of our Christian circles, even kissing was sacred and not to be consummated until the wedding day. When Brian and I had first met, he showed me the book *Passion and Purity: Learning to Bring Your Love Life Under Christ's Control*. The author, Elisabeth Elliot, was a former missionary to Ecuador whose husband was martyred there. To die for Christ was the most holy honor. His death elevated her words to the evangelical equivalent of a saint. Elliot warned against kissing with no commitment.

After Brian left, I called Jenna and cried. Then I called Amy and cried some more. To complicate things further, Amy thought they were in love—that if she hadn't returned to college, they'd be together. Amy had left for college that previous summer with no experience, and now I hardly recognized her. Over Christmas break, she hadn't come alive unless Brian was there. She didn't seem to have missed me at all.

In emails, Jenna and I decided not to kiss our future boyfriends until we got engaged, following the example of Anne Shirley in *Anne of Avonlea*. Jenna had already kissed boys, but she pictured a perfect future. For me, my resolve didn't matter anyway. No boy, including Brian, wanted to kiss me. Unless this was just a test. Unless he'd come around. "I wish we could all stay innocent forever," I told Brian in an email.

Santa Cruz's rainy season matched my mood perfectly, as if it were created as my own personal backdrop. I caught buses in the rain, went to school in the rain, cried at home in the rain. At night, in bed, I tried to silence the feeling that my best friend and my crush had laughed at me as they grew closer.

My head hurt. My stomach hurt and wouldn't let up. I'd had stomach problems for as long as I could remember, but the pain usually came and went. This time, its persistence was as strong as the gloomy weather. Stephanie thought it might be appendicitis. Grandma said it was only a virus and would go away on its own. I secretly wished it were appendicitis. I had always thought it would be romantic to be deathly ill and have an unknown lover confess his passion at my bedside. Then, of course, I would recover and we would marry.

After a couple more days of pain, Grandma took me to the doctor. On the exam table, the doctor felt my stomach, pressing here and there.

"Are you sexually active?" she asked.

"No," I said with an embarrassed smile.

"Are you sure you're not sexually active?"

My lips trembled slightly. My smile grew bigger to mask my anger at her audacity at not believing me. Not only did no boy want me, but this doctor was adamant that I had already experienced what I knew would be the biggest event of my life.

"Yes," I said. "I'm sure."

The doctor sent me home with the unromantic BRAT diet: bananas, rice, apples, and toast.

After a couple more days, the stomachache went away. But I still felt miserable.

———————

That spring, I took a women's history class for one of my history fulfillments. Learning about women felt more meaningful than memorizing dates of wars and insurrections. But I didn't expect the class to be feminist instead of just feminine. I wasn't against women's liberation, but I didn't want to be liberated. Instead I planned to go to school for the knowledge, graduate with high scores, and then marry the perfect man whom I was sure to meet at a Christian school, which I'd get to somehow. While I wanted the ideal of working from home in my robe just like Grandma, I had no way of making my ideal materialize. What would I work on? Who would pay me for it? What could my fingers, pen, and paper possibly do to generate income? I knew most strong, caring, wise Christian women became homemakers and stay-at-home mothers, and I was sure that was my ticket to a peaceful, fulfilling life. I'd have kids and support my husband. Maybe I'd graduate from a deaf ministries program and translate on the side. Maybe I'd sit down at my desk while my children were asleep or at school, and I'd write something inspirational for other mothers who understood the importance of being there for their children—more than my mom was there for either Melanie or me. I'd help my kids with their homework. Maybe even homeschool. I'd learn how to cook, and learn the best cleaners for countertops and linoleum floors. Maybe we'd live in a very small house, filled with books and laughter. My husband would be the pastor of the local church, and I'd have the ladies over for tea. These white ladies would look to me for guidance, and as the wife of a skilled pastor, I'd have that guidance to give them.

The third day of February felt like the first day of spring. I sat on the section of lawn where Brian and I had first talked after piano class on my birthday. I took in the sun on my face with my backpack beside me. The reprieve from the rain bolstered my mood, but my lack of "kindred spirits," as Anne Shirley called them, colored the moment. There would be no more McDonald's moments with Amy, no more hill walks with

Jenna, no more lusting after boys with Heather. The spring sun brought to mind McCrae Days on the senior lawn, and Josh's laughter booming from his friend group from his church. I wished he were here now, singing "Pray for Me" by Michael W. Smith, walking around me in circles, and holding my hand at the flagpole.

Two days later, I wrote an essay for my English class about how I defined home. "Home" was an ephemeral concept with no tangible roots. I thought Grandma's house was home when I first moved back, but no matter how much I tried to soak in the shelter, I felt like an outsider. Home would have to be what I made it, somewhere else.

In a letter, Josh invited me to Ozark Christian College, a small Bible college in Missouri, where I imagined us falling in love. But he had a new girlfriend, and when the college pamphlets arrived in the mail, they looked cheaply made. "Don't you want to go somewhere that values the arts?" Grandma had asked when I showed her the materials. She always seemed to know where I shouldn't go, but not where I should. Stephanie thought I should stay at Cabrillo for another year and get an associate's degree. It made sense, but only acquiring an associate's wasn't the big future I knew God had planned for me. I was meant for more. My family valued status, but it seemed no one cared about mine or expected me to amount to anything. And in the meantime, Adria got her acceptance letter to the Rhode Island School of Design.

"Hi, little one," Grandma's boyfriend, Dennis, said as he entered the dining room, now as always with a mesh cap that sat precariously atop his head. He stuck a giant grocery store pastry under my nose, hoping I'd bite. Grandma sat at table, polishing silver.

"No thanks," I said, and stepped away.

Dennis had barely left the house since Christmas. In fact, he practically lived here now. He was big for a man, but he felt even bigger—an elephant, or maybe a lion, ready to devour me at any moment. My fear didn't match his actions, though. He never tried to pounce. Instead he just took up space—space that seemed infused with danger just because he was in it. If he was in the living room, I avoided it. If I passed him in the hall, I looked down. I couldn't look in his eyes. My fear came from Gary, I knew.

Dennis moved on to the kitchen after I rejected his pastry.

"I think I need counseling," I told Grandma.

"Why?" she asked skeptically.

I leaned against the dining room chair and slowly rocked it back and forth. "I'm having a hard time with Dennis, and I think it's because of Gary. I don't know if I ever told you, but Gary and I literally didn't talk for the last year I lived there. Anything he said was negative." My voice got soft. "He said I was ugly."

Grandma put down the spoon and rag. "Gary doesn't seem like the type of person to call someone ugly. You must have done something to provoke him."

My lips pursed and I wondered if I would ever open my mouth again. Instead, I wrote a letter to Mom—about Gary, about Ozark Christian College and Josh's invitation, about Amy and Brian. I kept writing until I'd filled up five pages of binder paper, both sides.

That spring I took beginning and intermediate violin. I hadn't played since middle school, and picking it back up again made me feel like a Luders, connected to my family through the strings. Beginning strings was too easy, but intermediate violin was hard. My teacher often said she couldn't hear me, even though I felt like I was playing at top volume. "I can't hear you. Make some noise!" she'd say.

On an afternoon in February, I sat at the Cabrillo bus stop with a violin at my side. It wasn't *my* violin, but Uncle Eugene's, and the underside of the case was charred and malformed. Back when Adria was a baby, the Murphys' truck had caught fire. They safely got Adria from the covered truck bed, but the violin case was near the flame, on the floor of the passenger side. The violin was unharmed, but the scars on the case remained. Bits of black bubbled and exposed a flesh-colored undercoat. I connected with my musical family through the violin—but just like my rain boots in the snow, my cotton sleeping bag in the forest, my starchy shirt at middle school violin recitals, and my high-top sneakers at cross-country practice, the violin case was my not-quite-right accoutrement, an embodiment of poverty that I had learned to embrace. Literally wearing my scars on the outside. Even so, I looked at the cases of my peers with envy, wishing for their smaller, sleeker, and untainted designs.

Out of the corner of my eye, I saw someone amble toward me and then lean against the far side of the post that displayed the bus stop sign. And in a second, I recognized him. I had held the bus open for him the first time I went to the college group at Santa Cruz Bible—his arm in a sling—and then I saw him in the worship service, raising his good arm as he sang along. He wasn't wearing a sling anymore. He was strikingly handsome: tall, with a Roman nose, and his brown hair curlicued with mild rebellion. His eyes sparkled with humor and his skin matched mine. I peeked around the post at him; he peeked around at me. I wanted to ask if he was the sling man, but my mouth wouldn't open, no matter how many times I willed it to.

"Did you go to the Christian club meeting on campus today?" he asked.

My heart pounded. I didn't know he'd seen me there before. "No, I have a class during the meetings this semester."

He came over and sat beside me on the bench. "What's your name?"

"Shannon," I said.

"I'm Eddie." His downturned eyes were warm and playful, setting off a slightly crooked nose. "Is that a violin?" he asked.

"No, it's a machine gun," I replied, and then blushed at the corny joke.

"I bet you're good, aren't you."

"I'm not great. I'm out of practice."

"But you'll be great again."

I looked down at my feet. "Do you play anything?" I asked, desperate to change the conversation.

"The bongos. But just for fun." He tapped the base of his palms against the wooden bench in demonstration.

A bus came up to the stop, and Eddie hopped on. He rummaged through his pants pockets and pulled out his bus pass. "See you later, Shannon," he said with a smile.

In late February, Amy called. Brian had started dating a new girl, and we could either be there for each other to lean on, or suffer through the rejection alone. "CC said that she cherished each of Hillary's letters even before she opened them," I said of the characters in our favorite movie,

Beaches. "Well, I felt the same way about you," I continued, "and that's why it hurt me that your letters were so reserved and that you weren't sharing your heart with me. I really value our friendship."

"Shannon," she said, "I have thirty pictures of you on my wall, at least. I cherish our friendship too and like getting messages from you. You know, I think you're more like CC than Hillary. You probably think you're Hillary because CC is the more outgoing one, but CC has more of an imagination and Hillary must be pretty outgoing to be a lawyer." I smiled. I wanted to be like CC—a poor, scrawny underdog who makes her artistic dreams come true (in her case, as a famous singer).

Amy's resolve to be good friends again didn't last long. On another phone call, she tried to make me jealous, maybe feeling vulnerable at being so far away.

"Brian and I talked for an hour today and he told me all about his problems and all about Jen, and totally confided in me!" she said. "I probably shouldn't be telling you this, huh?"

"Probably not," I said.

"He told me all these secrets, and I can't tell anyone."

I did feel jealous, until Brian called a couple days later.

"I need to work on humbleness," I said. "Amy told me you told her all your secrets."

"I don't remember telling her any secrets," he said earnestly. "I wonder what they were."

I didn't know who to believe, but it was more comforting to believe Brian, even though that meant Amy would still be trying to come between us.

My extended family had a history of getting together as if we were homesteaders and not bumping up against the twenty-first century in Silicon Valley. When I was in middle school, we often had workdays at each other's houses, with the adults fixing up this and that while the children played. My first year of college, Aunt Deborah and Uncle Eugene started a family book club. Each month, someone got to pick a book, and the first month was Deborah and Eugene's pick: *Makes Me*

Wanna Holler, a memoir about a Black man who found his way out of gang life. I squirmed as we discussed the book, which I hadn't been able to finish in the midst of my schoolwork. My aunt and uncle sat cross-legged on the living room floor, explaining what inner-city life was like based on what they had read in the pages. I felt uninformed about my own culture, but I also felt something else: though I hadn't lived in an inner city, my skin afforded me more insight into the struggles of being Black than anything one could read. I looked around at the modest home, with the walls of books, the musical instruments in their cases, and the carefree looks on all the white faces. My own felt red hot, indignant, set apart.

After the discussion, I joined Mom on the brown plaid knitted wool loveseat and asked her about the letter I had sent her a couple weeks earlier.

"I know how hard it was on you, the way Gary talked to you," Mom said. She rubbed her hand along her arm, up and down and up and down. A frequent act of unconscious self-soothing. "I don't think you caused Gary to call you ugly. You didn't make him say it; he said it all on his own."

I smiled and looked down at my hands, my thumbs and forefingers intertwined.

Mom continued. "We probably haven't talked that much because we are both shy and reserved. But I'm glad that now that we're apart, we're finally able to." Mom and I talked for what must have been an hour, catching each other up on this and that, cautiously broaching the alienation I had felt in their home and the love my mom felt for me but had rarely expressed over the past few years. Melanie, now five, came wandering over and sat on my lap. I drew her into a hug and smelled her sweet hair. The rest of the family purposefully dispersed, understanding the importance, and rarity, of Mom's and my conversation.

As the gathering came to a close, I took Melanie's hand and walked her to the car with Mom, who gave me a hug before getting Melanie in. "You're turning out just fine," she said, gently patting me on the back before letting go. I took that as a benediction. "It seems like you have really grown up a lot his past year," she continued. I wasn't sure she was right, but I hoped so. My thoughts were still consumed by my need to be loved by a man—to be fulfilled by marriage—when I longed to just think about school and a career, the way I was sure my cousins did.

––––––––––––––

One Saturday in the middle of March, I decided to make chocolate chip cookies. I was happy to discover we didn't have sugar. That meant I would have to walk up the street a mile to the 7-Eleven. Then I found more sugar and decided to abandon the cookies altogether. Instead, I walked up Spring Street, a steep street two blocks from my house that led to an undeveloped section of UC Santa Cruz. I didn't get far before I remembered that someone on the radio said the following Monday was the first day of spring. My walk felt meant to be.

I passed a driveway full of young, bare-chested men sitting in lawn chairs, soaking up the sun. I looked down at my sweats and boots and felt ridiculous. I wanted to feel the warmth of the sun and the breeze on my legs. I took the next right I could and passed our old minister's house to avoid walking by the men again so soon. I went home, changed, and then passed the minister's house again in a T-shirt and black shorts with a sweatshirt tied around my waist. I had almost forgotten I had legs.

I got to the top of Spring Street and walked through the open gate into the grassy expanse of the Pogonip preserve. The hillside felt like Ireland, and up here, the wind blew gently in that way it only can above the fray. My favorite spot was up another unpaved path from this one, up another hill, with a bench at the top. Sitting on the bench, I could see all of Santa Cruz in front of me and, beyond the city, the pristine blue ocean that shimmered as it moved. I only meant to be out for half an hour at most. But when I came down the hill, I found another little trail that was just begging me for company. I hadn't walked very far before I saw a little ten-foot trail that led to a cluster of trees. I followed the trail and found myself in the middle of what felt like a dense forest. Everything was so still that the forest felt just like Anne Shirley's haunted wood. Right next to me sat a hollow tree trunk that looked like the perfect hideaway for imaginative children. I imagined that Leslie and Jess from *Bridge to Terabithia* spent many hours in that tree, talking of their magic kingdom.

I felt God even more out here than I did in church. In nature, God felt like less of a man and more of a being beyond what any human could fathom. He was in the grass, in the wind, in the stillness of the forest. And when he was less of a man, I felt more like an empowered woman. In my women's history textbook, a woman wrote about how boys learn how to "do," and girls are just supposed to "be." In the twice-weekly class, I learned about suffragettes and pioneers. I learned of the "cult of true womanhood," which emerged in the nineteenth century as what the ideal women should follow. It was everything I had learned in the church: serve your husband, serve your children, don't serve yourself. Through that class, my eyes were opened to the way my desire to be a housewife was based not on my own thoughts but on what men taught me to think. Since I couldn't control when I could become a wife and mother, I now wanted to pursue a career so I could have some control over my future. I thought about social work, just like Mom had majored in. I didn't know what kind, but I liked psychology and loved reading my mom's old papers.

I was a Manuel, and that meant I had to claw my way to something more than Manuels had been before me, and be a whole person without a whole dad, just like my dad had tried to be. As far as I knew, no Manuel had gone to college. Not my grandma and grandpa, not my dad, not my aunts and uncles who died before I was born. If I knew anything about Blackness, it was conformity—that your only hope was to conform to the best version of what white people thought you should be. But I was also a Luders, and that should count for something. Luderses went to college. My mom went to college. Somehow, in her mind, that didn't translate to me, though later she would say she always expected me to go. She felt like her schooling was almost a fluke, something she didn't deserve.

My tiptoe into female empowerment popped up in other areas. Stephanie, Adam, and I listened to *The Sound of Music* soundtrack one night as we played Pounce on the living room floor. I heard "Sixteen Going on Seventeen" for what felt like the first time. When Rolf sings to Liesl about how she needs someone older and wiser to care for her and tell her what to do, I wanted to scream to the recording: "You don't need someone to tell you what to do! You don't need someone to *tame* you!"

As expected, on the phone later that night, Brian thought I was being indoctrinated by bra-burning, hairy-legged feminists. But I wasn't deterred. That Sunday, I studied psychology instead of going to church.

"I want to get straight As next semester," I told Grandma and Adam over breakfast. My fall report card had been all As and Bs, and I was set to get a 3.0 spring semester.

"Well," Grandma said, looking skeptical. "You're going to have to work a lot harder."

"No more phone calls and emails," Adam said, shaking his head.

My ears burned. I was on the phone for less than half an hour that day. I hadn't sent an email in weeks. Adam had decided that he would go back to Cabrillo and pick up the education he had started a couple years before—that if it wasn't too hard for me, it shouldn't be too hard for him. Grandma and Adam were always telling me to work harder, but if I set a goal, they made it seem as if I would never reach it.

Terms like implicit bias weren't in the social conversation in 1995. If they had been, it would have better shaped my understanding of our family dynamic. My grandma would never have intentionally placed my part-Japanese cousins on a pedestal while assuming her part-Black grandchild couldn't succeed, but implicit bias rears its head without awareness. It's reinforced by the things we read, the things we watch on TV, and the discrepancy we see between races that doesn't take into account systemic racism and generational wealth. My grandma had grown up in a time when blackface was normalized, when affirmative action didn't exist. She was born less than one hundred years after the end of slavery. Grandma cherished her granddaughter and chastised anyone who showed prejudice against her. But it's more difficult to see one's own blind spots.

In the middle of May, I dreamt that I was back at Gary's house—a place I had only dreamt about twice before. In my dream, I was in the garage doing laundry. Like usual, the garage was cluttered with Gary's junk, with just enough space for Mom's car to squeeze in. Gary walked in while I loaded the washer. He and I began to yell, the tension in my sleeping body taking the place of actual words. Suddenly, we stopped yelling and started to laugh—hearty belly laughs with tears streaming down our faces.

The next day, Gary sent his monthly hundred-dollar check to cover the utilities my presence required at Grandma's house. Inside the envelope was a note that read, "Dear Shannon, I am enclosing a bookmark for you with a beautiful prayer. I wish you well. Love, Gary." I opened the note to find the bookmark, which contained the popular Irish prayer:

> *May the road rise up to meet you.*
> *May the wind be always at your back.*
> *May the sun shine warm upon your face;*
> *The rains fall soft upon your fields and until we meet again,*
> *May God hold you in the palm of His hand.*

Gary had never said "Dear" or "Love." I placed the bookmark alongside my other knickknacks on my bookshelf and wondered if he was finally accepting me as a member of his family.

———————

Brian suggested that Amy, Jenna, and I apply to work at Trinity Hills that summer, a Christian camp and conference center in the Santa Cruz Mountains. College students were hired every summer to work full time for one hundred dollars a week. They worked in childcare, the dining room, and housekeeping, and stayed in dorm rooms just like a college. The three of us applied, but only Jenna and I got hired. Through Brian, I learned that Amy called him and cried on the phone. We were supposed to be friends now, but if we had been as close as we were before, I thought, she would have called me, not Brian. When Brian told me Amy didn't get the job, I said, "That's too bad," but I'm not sure he believed my sentiment. The truth is, the summer would be much easier without having to watch Amy and Brian flirt.

13

THE AWAKENING

1995

THAT SUMMER, Jenna came back from Iowa and moved in with me at Grandma's house. Northwestern College was too expensive, so she decided to trade her four-year college experience for a year with me at Cabrillo. Amy stayed in Iowa with her new boyfriend and would enroll in community college there in the fall.

Uncle Adam dropped Jenna and me off at Trinity Hills for our summer jobs, me as a housekeeper and her as a waitress. The area was a veritable Christian paradise—an unincorporated community with its own post office and private homes, a conference center with a hotel, dozens of cabins, an expansive dining hall, and a giant field for concerts and other events. The center hired about fifty college students—about forty-five of them white—for their busy summer months for a weekly hundred-dollar paycheck plus food and lodging. We worked five and a half days per week—by day, not per hour. It didn't occur to me that in the guise of serving the Lord, the bigwigs were running a center by exploiting cheap labor.

On the first day, three boys plopped down at the small table in the mess hall where Jenna and I were eating lunch. I looked up to see one of the boys was Eddie—the same boy I had helped off the bus to get to church, and the same boy whom I had run into while waiting for the bus at Cabrillo. Only he wasn't a boy. At twenty-six, he was eight years my senior, just one year younger than Uncle Adam. The other two boys prattled on about mundane topics while Eddie sat silently in his white dishwashing uniform. I had almost forgotten how striking he was, even with slightly disheveled curls. I could tell that, like me, he didn't know how to participate in small talk, or just didn't want to. I was sure when he opened his mouth, deep thoughts must pour forth.

After we ate, Jenna and I settled into our two-story wood-cabin dorm. Finally, my life felt collegiate, where young adults ate, slept, and made memories in tight quarters—unlike at Cabrillo, where everyone sat in classrooms and then went their separate ways. All Trinity Hills needed were professors, backpacks, and actual classes—a Bible college in the woods.

I heard footsteps and peered out of our dorm room to see a tall blonde girl with perfectly feathered hair walking down the hall. I popped out of the room to greet her.

"Hi, I'm Shannon," I said.

"I'm Crystal." Her smile was radiant and she resembled a life-size Barbie doll.

"We're going to be great friends!" I said, surprising myself with my declaration. But somehow, I knew.

Crystal laughed. "I look forward to it!"

I wasn't wrong. Crystal was part of the handful of girls who made up the student housekeeping crew. We worked alongside two "linen men"— boys who kept our pantry shelves stocked with sheets and towels—as well as middle-aged, Spanish-speaking Mexican women who worked hourly and then went home to their families. I and the other housekeepers lugged buckets of cleaning supplies and vacuum cleaners up and down hills as we darted to cabins, hotel rooms, and guest dorms. In each room, I peeked at the tabletops to see what books the campers had bought from the on-site bookstore. Their choices provided a glimpse into their world, and I felt close to these strangers through a shared love of literature. I scrubbed their toilets with fervor, as if the paper sanitary wraps that we looped around the toilet lids came from God himself—SANITIZED FOR YOUR PROTECTION. When time permitted, Crystal and I speed-walked between the end of the workday and dinner. We shared the earbuds for her portable CD player and sang along to "Walking on Sunshine" by Katrina and the Waves.

Surrounded by Christians, I was once again swept into the evangelical world. Our days were filled with morning devotions, evening worship services, and daily prayer partners. I came to the conclusion that it was God who had made me so secure in myself that past spring, and that it was he who had mended my heart after the Amy and Brian incident. After one prayer service, I asked a counselor how to reconcile being a Christian with having a positive self-image, without feeling the need for constant apology, as is taught in the church. He said we should have a positive self-image while at the same time asking God to change us in any needed ways.

Brian was often busy as the camp photographer, immortalizing the goings-on of the summer staff, but I still saw him on occasion. One warm night, Brian, Jenna, and I went to Victory Circle—a semicircle of wooden bleachers built into a clearing in the woods where summer workers united for events. As we talked about relationships, Jenna's head rested on Brian's shoulder, and, on his other side, he gently draped his arm around me.

"I'm afraid I really hurt Jen," Brian said of his spring relationship. "She was really upset when we broke up."

"She'll be OK, I'm sure," I answered. "It really hurt when you and Amy got together, but I got over it."

"I'm glad you got over it," Brian said with a smile. He removed his arm from around me and took Jenna's hand. Jenna lifted her head and looked up at him, and the two stayed with eyes locked for too long. It was déjà vu. I bolted up and ran back to the dorms, depositing myself in Crystal's room until she got home from a date, and then poured out my saga.

"You're beautifully exotic," she said. "I know you feel like guys don't see you and don't like you as more than a friend, but I think they're just intimidated by your intelligence. And that's not a bad thing."

The next day was my one full day off a week. Jenna and I lounged at the edge of the conference center pool, soaking in the sun that shone through the opening in the trees. Jenna turned to me and spoke hesitantly. "Brian wonders if you would mind if we date," she said. I had sensed it coming, but it still felt like a sucker punch. In that moment, all I could do was laugh. God *must* have a sense of humor, like lightning striking twice.

At camp, I grew a reputation as a wise one. I gave advice to new friends, and even counselors with personal problems, like the hot male counselor with low self-esteem who claimed I was the only one who really saw him, yet ignored me in public whenever he had an attractive girl on his arm. At first I reveled in this role. I was living up to my name, which means "little old wise one." But I eventually grew weary of helping others when it didn't lead to reciprocity. Especially with Jenna now preoccupied with Brian, I began to retreat into my silent self, taking up residence in the laundry room that served my group of cabins, folding clothes and even running wet clothes through the dryer as a secret helper. One afternoon, a summer custodian stopped in with a smile: "Someone came into my room and said, 'A nice girl folded my laundry for no reason!' That must have been you!" I beamed at being called a nice girl.

Another afternoon I entered the laundry room to check on my own clothes. Eddie was seated in a folding chair, one leg across the other, with a notebook open on his lap.

"Hi," I said, and smiled.

"Hi." He smiled back. His left eyelid slightly drooped over his brown eye as if in a perpetual near wink.

I leaned against the washing machine.

"How's the violin?" he asked.

"It's good."

"Are you a music major?"

"No," I answered sheepishly. "I don't know what I want to major in. Maybe social work."

"I've been watching you," he said. "I think you'd make a great social worker. You really know how to listen to people."

I felt a wash of lightheadedness, just as I'd felt the first time I talked to Brian on the lawn at Cabrillo. It also happened with girls when we crossed the threshold from strangers to friends. It was as if my brain had to recalibrate to the new connection.

"What do you want to be?" I asked, intent on steering the conversation away from myself.

"Well, I want to be a pastor. Or maybe a mentor. Right now I'm a dishwasher." He looked down at his hands, and my eyes followed. They were the most beautiful hands I had ever seen, the kind of hands that cradle newborns in close-ups for cards and wall art. Palms that were large but soft; fingers that exuded both delicateness and strength.

I forced myself to break my gaze. "What are you majoring in?" I asked.

"I didn't finish my classes last semester," he said. "I had to stop so I could work." After a pause, he continued. "Are you Black and white?"

"Yeah." I was surprised he could tell. Usually only Black people knew I was Black. Other people mostly guessed Mexican.

As we kept talking, I learned Eddie was Mexican, white, and Native American. His mom had died of cancer and he didn't know his dad. His grandma's house was home, just like mine. Eddie seemed more like me than Brian did—both of us brown-skinned people just trying to make it. And he was magnetic in a mysterious way, maybe even a dangerous way, though I couldn't pinpoint exactly why. I had been watching him as well; aside from that first day in the mess hall, he was always alone. He almost never joined in summer events and never seemed to converse with anyone. He sat on the sidelines, in his own world, reading his Bible or a devotional, or just relaxed in his own company. That is, until we started spending time together.

Eddie taught me how to suck pollen from flowers and to taste leaves of different spices. We hiked the many trails through the forest with Sarah, a short, squat summer cook with witchlike hair and teeth with a mind of their own. She had an aura of inexperience like me, maybe because she had moved from Weed—a tiny town of less than three thousand people just south of Oregon. Despite her visible crush on him, Eddie treated her with the same respect as he did everyone else. At the same time, he didn't seem to have a flirty bone in his body. Our conversations were purely philosophical, almost completely about God. He touched me only when he bopped me on the forehead, something that cracked him up every time.

On a Thursday night, I walked to the Youth Memorial Building to meet Eddie and Sarah. They were improvising on the piano in the empty building with its big windows, stone-filled back wall behind the pulpit area, and high, sloped, wooden ceiling. Eddie's outfit was one of his usual mismatches that didn't quite work: a white turtleneck, deep-blue shorts that resembled swim trunks and hit mid-calf and showed off his naturally toned thighs, and the scuffed brown loafers he wore everywhere.

Eddie looked up at me. "Come play with us," he said.

I sat down on a corner of the bench and plunked out some low notes, trying to match the tempo of Eddie's and Sarah's music.

"Look at us," Eddie said with a smile. "God is working through us to make a perfect melody."

Once Sarah left around midnight, Eddie asked, "Do you want to go to Dogwood?"

I followed him to the one-room cabin he stayed in by himself. On the way, his ankle provided a soundtrack—*click, click, click*, with each step. Occasionally he flung his neck to the side, and the resounding *CRACK* seemed to provide relief. His failing body intensified the age difference between us. Though at twenty-six, his cracking and clicking likely spoke to a hard life, not age.

His cabin was down from the courtyard, on the way to the camp daycare. He opened the door without a key. It was unfurnished, with a mattress on the floor and little piles of clothes and papers in corners. I heard a preacher delivering a sermon, and my eyes followed the sound to a transistor radio that sat on the windowsill next to his bed. I had never been alone with Eddie before, but it felt surprisingly normal, like I had known him for years. He sat on his mattress and I on the floor, throwing grapes at each other from a bowl left nearby. I snorted a laugh and he snorted in imitation, back and forth until we couldn't control our laughter. I couldn't picture Brian ever doing such a thing. He was far too poised.

Eventually, Eddie stood up and went into the bathroom, and then returned with floss wrapped around his fingers.

"I shouldn't be watching you floss!" I joked, holding my stomach as it shook, with tears streaming from my eyes. "It's sinful!"

He bounced his eyebrows up and down as he ran the floss through his teeth.

Once he'd thrown it away in the kitchen trash, he returned and grabbed a brochure from his windowsill, and then sat beside me on the floor.

"I really want to go to this college," he said, pointing to information about a school called Burnside Bible College in Portland, Oregon. It didn't look too interesting to me. Too city, when I longed to be surrounded by nature, somehow going back in time to what I believed to be a simpler era. Somewhere in the Midwest, perhaps, where I just knew men must treat women with respect, and where my own innocence—the way I moved through the world—wouldn't stand out.

"I can tell God wants me at Burnside," Eddie said, still looking at the brochure. "I need to learn how to serve him better, to be a good disciple. He keeps giving me all these tests, and Burnside is a test too. He wants to see if I'll do it. If I don't, I don't know what will happen to me."

I was quickly learning that Eddie viewed God a little differently than I did and wondered if my own thoughts were too self-centered in comparison. I believed God would get me where he wanted me to go, but I didn't see it as a test. Rather, I saw him guiding me as if I were a miniature in the palm of his hand. He would pick me up and gently place me in the right location. Eddie's view of God was rougher.

A few days later, I invited Eddie and two housekeeper friends over for dinner at Grandma's. Eddie and I sat squished in the back of one friend's compact car while she blasted Cake, an alternative band she and the other friend had introduced me to. "If you want to have cities, you've got to build roads," sang Cake, with their perpetual upbeat tempo. I looked nervously over at Eddie, but he didn't seem to mind our secular immaturity for finding joy in non-Christian songs, and silly ones at that.

Twenty-five minutes later, we pulled up to my house. It was surreal to watch Eddie amble up my walkway and enter my home, which after only a few weeks away already felt so foreign. Eddie and my friends passed the pristine living room on the right that was bigger than Eddie's whole cabin. We made our way down the white-carpeted hallway, past the family memorabilia in glass cabinets on the wall, and into my rather light-blue bedroom. My bed had been replaced by Adam's bunk bed to accommodate Jenna, and, despite her more adult sensibilities, the room still looked like it was inhabited by much younger girls. I watched Eddie sheepishly as he eyed my *Lion King* poster, my stuffed animals on the top bunk, and my cedar chest with the pink floral blanket, both passed down from my great-grandma on my white grandpa's side.

"Can I get some water?" Eddie asked.

"Sure," I said.

I left Eddie and the girls in my room and then walked into the kitchen, where Grandma sat at the table balancing her checkbook before she and the rest of the family headed out for dinner.

"You've brought home a good-looking group of friends," Grandma said, beaming. I smiled.

The family stayed scarce until they left for their own dinner. Eddie used the pasta maker, my housekeeping friends made a salad, and I spread garlic salt and margarine on an open French bread baguette and toasted it in the oven. As we all sat down, I asked Eddie to pray. I wanted to ask him to hold hands but couldn't get the courage. Eddie asked for me. The hand that I had admired in the laundry room, and every day since, gripped mine tightly.

"Dear Heavenly Father, let us enjoy your bounty," Eddie prayed. "Let us come together in pure fellowship, shedding our earthly selves. We come to you as your humble servants, your children, asking you to make us whole. We dedicate this meal to you and pray that you will guide us in the way of salvation, keeping us holy vessels for your word."

Eddie waited a few seconds before releasing my hand.

We left home in time for the staff meeting at camp, and listened to Cake again on the way. This time the girls and I got up the courage to do our hand gestures for Cake's "You Part the Waters," playing invisible pianos and trumpets, and parting invisible waters with our hands. Even Eddie joined in.

Eddie and I continued our hangout at the conference center. His eyes, his smile, his big hands when he held mine for prayer, all told me he was interested. It wasn't the same as holding Josh's hand at the flagpole in high school. At least I was pretty sure it wasn't. But I had been wrong so many times before, I didn't want to jinx it. And something seemed to hold him away from me, a sense of mystery or danger that equated him with Dad, though there was no evidence of addiction. Despite the successful dinner at Grandma's house, I couldn't picture Eddie actually being part of my world any more than I could imagine Dad doing so. They were used to sparseness, to lives that didn't involve white picket fences and 2.5 children, to survival being their ultimate accomplishment. And yet, I was drawn to him as a male mirror to my own unmoored existence.

One evening after work, I took a bucket of cleaning supplies from the linen room and carted them through the conference center to Eddie's cabin. I knew he was working in the kitchen that night. I snuck in the unlocked door and deep-cleaned his bathroom. Weeks of built-up grime came off the sink, shower, and toilet. I swirled the toilet brush until the inside of the bowl sparkled. As I cleaned, I imagined love pouring out of my being and into his. This tangible act would surely show love in a way he hadn't experienced it before—a selfless act that required no reciprocation. To domesticity in action. Maybe if I could ease his rough life, he wouldn't be so afraid to let people in.

Toward the end of the summer, the staff got together for a talent show in the Youth Memorial Building. Two staff boys came out in boxers, sheets, and baseball hats and danced to excerpts of various songs. When their backs were turned, their shoulder blades arched like mini Greek gods, and their spines hinted at the spread of their hips below their shorts. While they performed, I was ensconced in a corner of the room, bent over, brushing my hair until it shot out from my head in all directions. When it was my turn to perform, I walked onstage with my giant hair and conveniently stood in front of the mural of a bright sun, which framed my do perfectly. I lifted my violin and played "Boil the Cabbages," deftly gliding my bow over two strings at once, back and forth with fervor. The song was one of the few fast ones I had mastered during weekends at the Land. I received a standing ovation. For the first time in my life, my hair was an asset, and for the first time, I wasn't nervous playing a solo onstage. I wasn't the high school kid whose desk got kicked anymore. No one threw gum for me to chase after. No longer did I retreat to the laundry room. In this setting, much like at Crossroads, I felt like I belonged. For the rest of the summer, staffers came up to me and asked to see my hair. I'd take it out of my thick French braid or let loose the bun that secured the top half of my hair. They'd ooh and aah as my hair spread out like Medusa's, seemingly defying the gravity that kept their own hair pointed toward the ground.

My last night at camp before the start of fall semester, I joined Eddie and Sarah after the camp banquet, which they didn't attend. We walked the winding, two-lane road into town to Safeway and then headed to the covered bridge. Partway there, I got up the courage to hop on Eddie's back. I squealed as he ran me through sprinklers and felt the warmth of his cheek on mine. His body was strong, like a fortress. He had the ability to lift me up as if I were a small animal.

Later that night, Eddie took us to his cabin. When I walked out of the bathroom, he was on the bed, and Sarah was seated in front of him on the floor. He was giving her a back rub. She had often complained of her bad back, but this was the first time I had seen Eddie touch her this way. My mind spun and I contemplated running out the door just as I had run from Brian and Jenna earlier that summer. But Eddie and Sarah as a couple just didn't seem possible. He had never flirted with her like Brian had with both Jenna and Amy. So I decided to stand my ground.

"I wish my back was messed up so I could get a back rub," I said.

"Just ask and I will," Eddie replied.

At about three in the morning, Eddie and I convinced Sarah to drive us to the Garden of Eden, a small secluded swimming hole in the mountains. It wasn't our first time there, but it was the first time at night and with just three of us instead of a bigger group. Eddie grabbed his kitchen staff sweatshirt for me to cover my perpetually cold, ninety-seven-pound frame. I pulled it on over my thin Northwestern College sweatshirt, wrapping myself in Eddie's scent, faint body odor mixed with a natural sweetness. After taking the car as far as we could, we hiked through the forest with only the moon to guide us until we reached the clearing. Sarah and I sat on either side of Eddie on the sand. Eddie turned to me and opened up about a meeting he'd had with his camp counselor.

"I kind of have a hard time with older people in charge," he said. "I take my anger out on them because I can't take it out on my parents, since they're gone."

I drew a squiggly line with a twig in the sand and thought of my father. "Yeah, if a kid doesn't have one of those parents, it's like they can't develop properly."

Eddie nodded and looked out at the softly flowing water in front of us. "Once," he said, "I saw a dad and daughter together and I just had so much emotion. But then I remembered God is my father."

Sarah got up and wandered off by herself, as if I had manifested my ideal scenario. Eddie and I talked a little bit more, about God and eternity and the pettiness of worldly problems. I thought of the events in Eddie's cabin from earlier that night and steeled myself for the scariest question I had ever asked. "Will you give me a back rub?"

"Sure," Eddie said.

I moved in front of him on the sand and sat cross-legged. His hands began moving across my back but found resistance from the double layering of sweatshirts.

"Why don't you take off my sweatshirt?" he asked.

I took it off and his hands got to work.

"Where's your scoliosis?"

I was surprised he remembered. I reached behind me and placed my hand on my mid-back. Eddie massaged all up and down my back with hands that never wandered, unlike a boy I volunteered with in my high school library, who had offered to massage my shoulders and then had reached down toward my breasts. "You're so skinny," the boy had said. In that instance, I jumped up and made sure we were never alone again. But I didn't want to jump up tonight. Instead, I was so relaxed that I almost fell asleep.

Eventually Eddie stopped and began stuttering, showing nervousness I had never seen. "Can I ask you a question? Would it be OK if I held you?"

I had secretly hoped for weeks that he would hold me. The fact that he asked made it better because it was courteous and I could tell he was nervous.

"Yes," I answered.

He took his sweatshirt from my lap and threw it over my head. I questioned his need to hide me but quickly dismissed it as he put his arms around me and drew me close to him. My body went slack and I almost cried from the intimacy, of reaching this "epoch" in my life, as Anne Shirley would say—though she would never let a suitor hold her in the woods in the middle of the night, especially if he hadn't declared his intentions. But in the real world, in the world of Grandma and Dennis, Adam and Stephanie, Jenna and Brian, finally I didn't feel alone. I matched my breath to the rise and fall of Eddie's chest; since I could feel his, I couldn't control my own anymore.

No one had held me since my mom had given me "lovies" as a kid, when I would sit on her lap when the world felt overwhelming. Though my mom often seemed preoccupied with her own feelings of overwhelm, her lap was always open, and her mothering always came through the most when I was hurting. My dad, on the other hand, always kept a distance, perhaps because his father had abused little girls at the school where he had worked as a janitor, which I had read in Dad's psychological evaluation. My mom once recalled placing baby me, naked, on my naked father's back on the bed. Dad had recoiled and rebuked her for the impropriety. As I grew up, I had no father's strong arms to lean against for comfort. Now, under Eddie's sweatshirt, my body melted as it used to when Mom would rub my back as I fell asleep.

Sarah came back a little while later. I was afraid she would be upset and thought Eddie might let go. Instead, he drew me in tighter and gave me a big bear hug. He made sure to keep talking to Sarah so as not to ignore her. I thought of Amy; I was in her place, the "bad guy" this time. Now I understood her better. I was sure Eddie would never date Sarah, just the way Amy knew Brian would never date me. Amy didn't steal Brian from me; he was never going to be my boyfriend.

After a while, Eddie let go and decided to swim, fully clothed. I lay down on the sand with his backpack as a pillow, and tried to stifle a smile. Sarah and I sat next to each other in silence while Eddie jumped in the water. "Hallelujah!" he yelled into the silent forest.

14

BLACK, WHITE, OTHER
1995

I HAD GIVEN UP MY DREAM of opening an orphanage in Africa. In its place, my ideas kept changing. First I wanted to major in women's studies and open a hope house for teenage mothers; then I wanted to major in English at a Black college and be an English teacher; then I wanted to go to Pitzer, a private college in Southern California. Most important, in my mind, I knew who I wanted to meet: He would be mixed like me, quiet, and intellectual. He'd be three inches taller than me, five foot seven, with glasses, a buttoned-up plaid shirt, and curls a little tighter than mine. His name would be Brian Scott and he would fit into my WASPy world.

My desire for a certain type of spouse went beyond merely wanting him to be accepted into my family. It would also mean I was accepted, more than I currently felt myself to be. He could be a link between who I was and who they were. Someone like Gilbert Blythe in *Anne of Green Gables*, who said things like "All pioneers are considered to be afflicted with moonstruck madness." No matter what path my life would take, I knew it would lead me to this mystery man, and that marrying him would be the most important event of my life. If I were truly following God's plan, God would bring us together, would reward us with each other. I knew he was out there, somewhere, praying to find me.

That fall, I continued to work at Trinity Hills part time, while jug-gling two music classes, algebra, career planning, and African American history. I had expected the history instructor to be the one older Black man I saw walking around campus the year before. Instead, I entered the room to find a few Black people, more white people, and a tall, pale, doughy, white instructor. After my initial letdown, he proved to be a capable teacher, but it wasn't the same as being taught my history by someone of my race—and to have an instructor who looked like me for *any* class.

My junior year of high school, my white history teacher had spent a few weeks teaching us Black history. With permission slips in hand, which our parents had signed the day before, she instructed us to lie on the floor of the classroom. She bound our hands and feet with rope and read us a portion of *Roots* while seated in a folding chair in the middle of the classroom. The class grew silent. As I sat, bound, between my white classmates, hearing the story of Kunta Kinte from my white teacher's lips, I felt more seen at Leigh than I ever had before. It was a dangerous experiment, but, at least through my eyes, she had succeeded. I thought of the "White Power" warning on my locker from the year before and of the silence that had followed. I thought of my white English teacher from freshman and sophomore year, who, while she had been my favorite, had changed "Juneteenth" to "June tenth" in my paper, assuming I had made a typo. I thought of the one Black girl in my grade, a cheerleader who teased me along with her white friends. Now, on the floor, I looked over at the two other Black students, both boys, one mixed race, and the silent understanding between us. The mixed boy, though popular, made an exception for me, smiling at me across the divide of social rank. The African American history class was more cerebral—there was no tying of hands and feet. My knowledge of history swelled, but my personal connections remained the same.

That semester, my intermediate orchestra instructor named me concertmaster—a position I had secretly hoped for. I told Adam of my triumph that night at the kitchen table. Adam guffawed. "That's not real orchestra," he said. "It's only intermediate."

My lips trembled. Music felt like my strongest connection to my fam-ily, my surest path toward acceptance. Uncle Adam's dismissal felt like an indication that I would never hit that mark. I wanted to prove that I was one of them, that I could also be the best; only, no one ever really expected it of me. I was the marked one, the literal black sheep among a white flock. Playing the white man's tune—Mozart, Vivaldi, Bach—and once given a seat at the table, told the table was second rate.

On October 3, during intermediate orchestra, the percussionist didn't play when she was supposed to. The twenty-odd white heads, and my head, turned toward her as we stopped playing. The woman took one headphone from her ear and gasped. "OJ Simpson just got acquitted!"

I hadn't been following the OJ Simpson trial. We didn't watch news at Grandma's house, preferring magazines and the *Santa Cruz Sentinel* newspaper. I wasn't into organized sports, and neither was anyone else in the whole extended family, not even Gary or my stepbrother Nick. But the look on the percussionist's face said all I needed to know about the trial. Her eyes popped, her mouth formed an *o*, and the fear in her eyes was so strong that it was as if she thought OJ would come murder her in her bed that night. It was the first time, in my very white world, that I'd ever seen fear of a Black man in a white woman's eyes. My mom had feared my dad in her diaries, but with good reason. The percussionist's intense fear was so fully rooted in her own imagination that the moment became etched in my mind.

Over the course of the school year, Grandma and Adam continued to squash my spirits with their praise for other members of the family, often around the dinner table. Adam and Stephanie bragged about how late Adam stayed up studying, unlike me who went to bed at a decent hour. Grandma relayed a story from Aunt Deborah about how my cousin Elsie, who would soon transfer to a private girls' high school, was disappointed with her 97 percent on a paper since she was used to getting 100 percent. Adam complained about his workload and said, "You're happy getting As, Bs, and Cs, but I have to have perfection or failure. I can't have a social life like you."

My family wasn't wrong about our differences: I was more social, but only because everyone else was so *unsocial* by comparison. For most of us, the family stood in as our friendships, and no one veered much from that circle. But I had the college group at Santa Cruz Bible, where I sometimes played violin in the band, and Trinity Hills, which increasingly felt like home.

Over time, Eddie provided little slivers of insight into his rather closed-off existence, which exuded from his aura even as he sought connection. Losing his mother, never knowing his father, made him unable to express or receive love, he said. I longed to be the safe refuge he deserved—to hold him while he cried on my shoulder from past hurts. But it didn't seem possible for little me to tear down the walls of a twenty-six-year-old. And I had my own past hurts to contend with, including never receiving the romantic love I felt *I* deserved. On one hand, Eddie and I both wandered through the world with brown skin and no father. On the other hand, he was twenty-six and lacked a stable job or direction, and I was eighteen and could be anything, even despite my family's reluctance to help set the course.

One afternoon, Eddie and I joined Sarah in the bakery, where she'd just been promoted to the coveted position. We made brownies and then headed to listen to a speaker at the open-air conference room. From our bench in the back, we heard the speaker say God doesn't require us to be perfect. I wiped tears away, hoping no one noticed.

That night, instead of going home, I stayed at Eddie's new cabin—even smaller than the last—which sat behind and under one for conference center guests on a sloped road. I slept on Eddie's air mattress in the kitchen. I imagined being married to him in this hundred-square-foot cabin. The walls would enclose us in a protective shroud. There would be no grandmothers or uncles to appease. I could place anything anywhere I wanted, give it my own touch and expand beyond the walls of a bedroom in someone else's home. In the morning, as a mouse scurried by, Eddie's alarm blared incessantly. I didn't dare touch it without his permission. He slept as if unconscious, unaware of the noise, until the guests above him came around to the back, opened the unlocked door, and turned it off.

Sarah and I often met Eddie at the cabin for prayer, or at the small chapel right in the center of the courtyard. The chapel, used mostly for weddings, had an indescribable stillness, and a wood scent sweeter than any I'd known. Two large closets were at either side of the chapel entrance, with labels for BRIDE and GROOM. Light filtered in through the stained glass mural of wheat stalks behind the pulpit. Sometimes, Sarah couldn't join us, and Eddie and I held hands as we prayed in what felt like a holy room.

Few outright insisted anymore than men were closer to God, but we were still trained to believe they somehow had closer access to their creator. After all, wives were to submit to their husbands, and husbands to the Lord, and in our conservative denominations, only men could pastor a church. Eddie guided Sarah and me in prayer as a spiritual leader, older and wiser and more in tune with God. Our sessions were also unspoken competitions for Eddie's attention: if one of us got more time alone than the other, she could develop intimacy with Eddie that the other would not, tipping the scale of who would become his partner. I didn't think Sarah had a chance, but I also didn't want to test my theory.

Eddie's prayers often felt circuitous, winding from here to there and back again as the minutes ticked on. Sometimes there were tears, sometimes outbursts of praise. God seemed so close to him, so intimate, and yet, as I had noticed before, so much more demanding than how I viewed him. When it was my turn to pray, I tried to match Eddie in length and feeling but found myself lacking. It didn't occur to me then that something else might be driving Eddie's fervor, or at least increasing its intensity. After all, my assigned prayer partner on the housekeeping staff droned on and on too. It was a way to "prove" our spirituality—in the guise of God, but really to each other.

Eddie started making the hour-long trek to my house on occasion, walking twenty minutes from Mount Hermon to the bus stop and taking it through the hills and on the freeway into Santa Cruz. It was the route I took the other direction to get to work—and to him. We were still often with Sarah, much to my chagrin, but sometimes we got time alone. Eddie and I got closer and closer physically over the next few months, taking a nap on his bed back-to-back, and sometimes praying so close that we felt each other's breath on our faces. In those moments, every part of me wanted to be even closer, to know what it would feel like to kiss him, and to be held by him again like I had at the Garden of Eden that past summer. But when we were apart, I feared the intimacy and wanted to keep myself set apart.

Sometimes Eddie led me outside on adventures I wouldn't have otherwise taken. One night near dusk, we took the bus from Grandma's house to the ocean and then walked to Natural Bridges—the northernmost beach along West Cliff Drive. We walked on the sand until we got to the rocky shoreline. Eddie stepped up first, carefully placing his foot in each naturally formed indentation, and then looked back to guide me up with his hand. Up on the rocks, against the cliff behind us, we peeked into small pools of water that dotted the rocks and at the sea anemones and starfish that made their homes inside. Their colors were vibrant and their tentacles stretched out in scary yet wonderful ways. Every so often we crouched down to touch a tentacle, watching the sea anemone retreat and then open itself up again.

We continued our trek on the rocks until we reached a large, sandy break in between them that filled with water at high tide. The sun had fully set now. We walked up the sandy area, listening to the waves, until we reached a small pond that sat between the beach and somewhat secluded houses near the road. The air was misty, gently covering the soft streetlights that shone from the road, illuminating swans that floated in the shallow pond. It was perhaps the most beautiful sight I had ever beheld, and I never would have seen it, especially in the moonlight, without Eddie.

"The Bible doesn't support feminism," Eddie had said one day at the chapel.

"How do you know?" I asked.

"In Ephesians, it says, 'Wives, submit to your husbands as to the Lord. For the husband is the head of the wife as Christ is the head of the church.'"

"But being a feminist doesn't mean you can't be submissive," I said. "It just means you know you're a person separate from your husband and have the same rights as he does."

"When you get married," he answered, "you give away your rights."

I sat up a little taller and squared my shoulders. "So the husband can just make you do whatever he wants?"

"Well, he's supposed to guide you on the right path. You're supposed to trust that he knows what's best for you, because he's in touch with God."

"But what if I marry someone who I think is in touch with God, and then he just ends up doing something ungodly?"

"It doesn't matter," Eddie said. "You still have to go along with him."

I was glad I hadn't kissed Eddie. I felt it would have given him a power over me. I had learned in my women's history class about suffragettes and about the profound inequality that women had endured in the past. I couldn't turn my back on what my ancestors had achieved, and yet, Eddie was right, the Bible did say that women were supposed to submit to their husbands. Two worldviews fought in my mind. To let women's equality win would be to quell the words of the book that guided my life and those I trusted to interpret it. So instead, I tucked feminism inside my breast and carried it with me like a baby I nourished in secret.

I still often felt Eddie was keeping something from me. Something related him to my dad, carrying around a private burden that he wouldn't share with those he loved—whether to protect me or him, I wasn't sure. I had a vision of Eddie as an older adult, drunk and beating his wife. He once said he planned to go to a twelve-step meeting at Santa Cruz Bible, and I wondered which one but didn't think I could ask. Was it for alcohol? Drugs? Something else? Whatever it was, it solidified for me that he was struggling with an addiction that felt out of his control.

———

One evening I picked up Grandma's copy of *Time* magazine. I flipped through the pages and found an ad for a book called *Black, White, Other: Biracial Americans Talk About Race and Identity*, edited by Lise Funderburg. On the cover were black-and-white headshots of six mixed-race adults, all of whom looked like versions of me with a different smile, or different eyes, or a different nose. I knew I had to have the book. Uncle Adam and I sat at the shared computer in the garage and placed the order on the brand-new website Amazon. It was my first online purchase. When it arrived in the mail, I sat on my bed and scoured the book repeatedly. Over the next few days, I read and reread each of the dozen or so oral histories and peered into each author's eyes.

The only people I had ever seen before who looked anything like me were the two mixed-race boys in junior-year history and church. In commercials, in billboards, in poster ads in stores, white men were always with white women, Asian men were always with Asian women, Hispanic men were always with Hispanic women, Black men were always with Black women. Their children always matched them perfectly. The media treated mixed kids and interracial families as Snuffleupaguses, believed in but not seen.

Finally, here was the beginning of a community. Finally, I could hear my thoughts and experiences mirrored back to me in others' stories. Feelings that I had suppressed or not been able to find the words for, and experiences similar to mine that I thought no one shared, were expressed in the pages. *Black, White, Other* would change my life, and twenty years later, I'd learn it changed countless lives of those of us peppered across the United States who hadn't yet come in contact with one another. But it didn't make me feel more at home—not then. I was still a brown person among white family.

Through reading the book, I once again felt my singleness was due to my predominantly white surroundings. Though I didn't think boys saw me as ugly, perhaps my difference made me unapproachable, just like Crystal had said. I remember a male summer counselor telling me not to worry, that guys don't always judge on appearance. His intended words of support were an affront. "I just see you as white," Amy had said last year. That didn't sit right with me either. But only once in a while did I notice I was a different shade from all my friends—and from all my crushes except Eddie. My attraction to him felt destined. He wasn't so white that I felt an unspoken barrier, and he didn't seem as enigmatic to me as Black men did. And perhaps I was more attractive to him as well because my skin matched his.

One day that fall at Cabrillo, a Black student walked past me and said, "Hey, how you doin'." I knew it was Black code, a version of the Black nod. It felt like an initiation into a world that always felt separate from me. He saw me as one of his people.

A couple days later, I called Dad to catch up, perhaps bolstered by the nod from the Black student. Instead of being happy I reached out, Dad rebuked me for not calling sooner.

"You obviously don't care about your father," Dad said.

I hung up the phone and cried. Nothing I did seemed to bring us closer together. It was almost as if Dad preferred the distance while blaming me for it, or maybe he still felt I was slipping away from him. My phone call was too little too late—but he hadn't called in months either. It didn't seem fair. At the same time, part of me took it to heart as if I had failed him.

On Thanksgiving, the family came together at Grandma's house, except Adria who was across the country at the Rhode Island School of Design. We pulled out our china handed down from generations. Grandma had been cooking since the night before. We went for our usual walk around the neighborhood pond after eating. When we returned, we ate our yearly pumpkin and mincemeat pies. We sang songs together around the table. I felt that I'd taken my family for granted and wondered if I'd be there next year, or if this would be my final year before going away to college. But when Christmas came, all of that closeness felt gone. My feelings about my family—and what I thought they felt about me—waxed and waned repeatedly. Mom and Melanie didn't make it because Melanie had strep throat. Adam and I talked about how Christmas would never be the same now that we were adults. I didn't think it would be the same anymore until I got a family of my own.

Eddie had dropped all his classes before November—not because he had to work, but just because he no longer wanted to go. After Thanksgiving, he went home to Hollister—a small farm town an hour away—to visit his grandmother. Each day he was supposed to return, he didn't. Sarah said he might never come back. I longed to call but I didn't have his number. I was sure I must have driven him away, either because he knew how I felt about him or because he didn't. Or, I thought, maybe he left because he could tell I had a wall up. It wouldn't be the first time a man had moved away while I lived at Grandma's house. My dad had done the same thing.

After a week, I got his grandmother's number from Sarah.

"You didn't drive me away," Eddie said on the phone. "I was reading through my old diary from 1991, before problems started taking over my life, and I've been living in a daze since then. Now I know the steps I need to take to get out of it."

"What problems?" I asked.

"I can't tell you," he said. "But you probably know. I know what I need to do. I want people to see me, not my problem."

I didn't know what problem he could be referring to, but if I was supposed to have known, perhaps it was about me, I thought.

"Does it have anything to do with us?" I asked.

"We should talk about it in person."

"OK," I said nervously. And with uncharacteristic determination, I added, "I'll give you forty-eight hours."

Eddie returned but didn't continue the conversation. When I ran into him at work, he seemed distant, aloof. After two days, I went to work only to find I had the day off. I was determined to get to the root of whatever was causing this changed behavior. It wasn't the first time by a long shot that Eddie had turned hot and cold, but this time felt different.

I found Eddie swimming at the conference center pool, bobbing up and down and moving through the water much the same way I did—without proper form. I was determined to make Eddie come to me, not the other way around, even though I was hanging on by a thread. Sometimes I thought about life without Eddie, but on my terms, and I never actually did anything to sever our relationship, whatever that relationship actually was. The thought that he might leave me filled me with anxiety. I walked up to the giant cross on the hill and cried against the concrete base. The cross was meant for contemplation and prayer. Eddie and I had prayed there on occasion, as had the house-keeping crew last summer. Being there alone amplified my fear that things had changed forever. When I walked back down to the pool, Eddie was getting out.

"You have to say something, even if it's that you hate me and never want to see me again."

"No," Eddie replied, drying himself off with a bath towel. "I'm not going to say anything."

I eventually turned on my heel and walked toward the bus for home. The trip felt extra long, taking me away from my place of refuge.

Two nights later, Eddie knocked on my door wearing a black garbage bag as a poncho against the rain. He had come all the way from Trinity Hills with only an hour and a half to catch the last bus home. When the rain let up to a soft mist, we walked around the pond, arm in arm, watching the ducks float this way and that.

"The rain is awful when you're homeless," Eddie said. "Last year I used to walk around the grocery store all night because I had nowhere to go." It wasn't the first time Eddie had mentioned his time being homeless, but hearing him talk about it drew me to him even more. I could be the home he needed, if only he'd let me. We both didn't have one. Not in the traditional sense. We could make a home together, filling the void in each of our lives.

I had never talked to Uncle Adam about boys, but at Stephanie's suggestion, I got up the courage after Eddie left. I knocked on Adam's bedroom door. He opened it and stood in the doorway.

"Um, I don't know what to do about Eddie," I said timidly.

"What's going on?" he asked with genuine concern.

"Well, something is bothering him and he won't tell me what. And instead of telling me, he keeps ignoring me. At first I gave him forty-eight hours, but now it's been longer than that, and I don't know whether I should wait for him to come around or if I should just leave him alone. I think he likes me, and I think that's what he wants to tell me, but I'm not totally sure. He seems to but then he pulls away."

Adam leaned against his open door. "He probably isn't exactly sure what he wants, so he figures if he doesn't address the issue, he'll save himself from both rejection and commitment." It made sense.

Three days later, on a Sunday night, Eddie and I joined Jenna and her friend at Carol Sing, Crossroads' yearly Christmas celebration; then we headed to the Chart House restaurant for mud pie, which had been a special outing in our senior girls' prayer group; and finally to the lighthouse along Highway 1. Eddie was silent for all of it. Just as he was about to leave Grandma's to catch the bus, I asked if he wanted to come in to look over the spring class schedule for Cabrillo. He'd dropped all his fall classes on the last add/drop day but wanted to start anew in spring.

"Let's pray over the courses," he said.

I grabbed the course catalog from my bedroom and joined Eddie on the living room couch. He bowed his head and began praying.

"Lord, I wasn't following your spirit today when I looked at pornography in the bookstore. I'm so furious with myself." Eddie often used prayer to speak to me. Sometimes to criticize me, and sometimes confessional, like today. At the time, I didn't realize the manipulation. His secret seemed serious, but not as destructive as alcohol. Not like Dad. "Father," he continued. "Let me live by Luke 11: 'Your eye is the lamp of your body. When your eye is healthy, your whole body is full of light, but when it is bad, your body is full of darkness. Therefore be careful lest the light in you be darkness.'"

After the prayer, Eddie raised his head to me. "I do care for you beyond friendship," he blurted out. "I just want to see where things go."

I nodded. "I understand. Just don't hold back in talking about it. Then we don't have to worry about things getting misinterpreted."

He left for the bus an hour later, and I went to bed relieved that I hadn't imagined his interest. And relieved that he had come back to me.

Eddie started spending more time with me at Grandma's house. Her approval of him had diminished since that first day, when I had brought him and my two girlfriends home for dinner. Eddie was socially awkward, still not fond of small talk, and spoke mostly of God. I took her disapproval as judgment of this awkwardness, and of his poverty, which didn't fit into our middle-class home. I judged him too, mostly when I wanted my family's approval.

Near the end of fall semester, Eddie offered to stay up all night with me to help with my math test. We sat at the kitchen table for hours, me doing math and him picking his college classes. It didn't alarm me that it took him hours to pick classes. Instead, his simple act of staying up with me for school felt especially significant, especially at my kitchen table. He was my champion, supporting me like Stephanie supported Adam. I wasn't the odd one out. I was one of a pair—had successfully brought someone into my life, just as both Adam and Grandma had.

———————

My pick for family book club was easy: *Black, White, Other.* The mixed men and women within those pages spoke my truth louder and clearer than I could speak it myself. I didn't yet know about *unconscious bias,* the term that would grow in popularity in my forties. When the term took off, family and I discussed the concept and my grandma's attitude toward me. But without the language at nineteen, all I knew was that the family—and especially my grandma—treated me differently, and my only difference was my skin color and my absent father.

After our book club discussion, Mom and I sat in a corner of the dining room table while the rest of the family ate cheese and crackers. I took a sip of tea and told her about my latest conversation with Dad.

"That's sad," Mom said. "He's acting the same way with you that he did with me."

"How do you mean?" I asked, leaning in.

"He used to be jealous all the time, afraid that I was cheating on him, and he was afraid of losing me. He always threatened to leave me when he thought I was going to leave him. I think he's shying away from you because he's afraid of you pushing him out of your life."

He did love me, I thought. It made perfect sense. I just had to prove that I wouldn't leave. Just like I had to prove to Eddie.

One night Eddie and I walked from Grandma's to Casa Nova, the local lesbian café—one of just two cafés downtown. He hadn't told me where we were going until we reached our destination. I was glad for the secrecy or I probably would have objected, sure that I would be entering a place full of debauchery, still believing in "Adam and Eve, not Adam and Steve."

The café was a converted house on a side street that paralleled the main downtown strip. When I walked in, I was taken aback by the normalcy of what I saw. Eddie walked us to a table, each of which was spread out with miniature lamps for cozy privacy. Eddie sat across from me looking exceptionally handsome in the soft red light. His blue collared shirt was unbuttoned at the neck, and his sleeves were rolled up past the veins gently protruding from his arms.

A waitress came by, and Eddie ordered two cups of chai tea. He told me about his study of Romans 1, in which the apostle Paul presents the gospel of Jesus Christ to the Christians in Rome. Eddie's eyes sparkled as he spoke. His face was radiant. I took in his crooked smile, his extremely white teeth, and his big, expressive hands. A friend who had met Eddie recently said he had a ruggedness like the men on the cover of romance novels.

"You need to become a pastor," I said, after Eddie finished speaking.

"Well," Eddie said, "I wanted to get into the air force to get a skill and get school paid for, but when they offered me the position I really wanted, I admitted to lying on the medical papers. Then they refused me." Eddie took a breath. "I was depressed and in a mental institution for a while. Then I got more depressed and saw secular counselors, and they messed me up even more. I'm not good enough to be a pastor."

"But that's a good attitude to have," I said. "You'll be humble instead of arrogant. It's good you want to improve, but your imperfections shouldn't keep you from teaching. All things are possible with God."

I saw Christ in Eddie as I looked across the table. It would be just like Christ to associate with lesbians and sit in their café. And it would be just like Christ to have a burden for these people, I thought, and to be talking to a friend about Christ in a place that didn't accept his teachings about who we can—and can't—love.

We continued talking until the last buses left the metro two hours later, and we walked the two miles in the near dark back up to Grandma's house.

A couple days later, Eddie and I wandered through the large and busy bookstore, Bookshop Santa Cruz, in the heart of downtown. In the psychology section, Eddie took a book off the shelf about mental illness.

"The psychologist I saw a couple years ago diagnosed me with schizoaffective disorder," he said.

I looked at him, my heart racing with fear and intrigue.

"They put me on medication that messed up my brain so much that I couldn't even decide whether to turn left or right at a corner," he said. "I'm just now coming out of it."

The diagnosis answered a lot of questions. I understood why he signed up for and dropped classes, and why he sometimes stayed up all night and other times could barely function. It answered why he sometimes prayed with such fervor and for such long stretches of time. In my mind, it also answered why he was hot and cold, why he had a hard time with commitment. It was easy to believe that the schizo-affective disorder was responsible for everything that came between us.

That night, Eddie stayed over. He had his own toothbrush in my holder—a spare one from Grandma's pantry. As we brushed our teeth together in the bathroom, Eddie turned to me. "I love you," he said with a mouth full of toothpaste. I didn't respond. He spit in the sink and said it again, more mellow this time, as if he were sinking into the idea. I still didn't respond, afraid it wasn't real, that he might take it back. I remembered a dream I had my freshman year of high school, in which a crush asked me on a date. When I said yes to the crush, with the intensity of a dream's camera lens, his face laughed down at me as I gazed up from the ground.

I brought myself back to the bathroom, the dream fresh in my mind, and with a faint uneasiness about Eddie's declaration in the bookstore.

Through a mouthful of toothpaste, I simply answered, "Thanks."

———

After the New Year, Jenna moved to France to be an au pair. With her gone, Eddie offered to visit my dad with me. With him there, I wouldn't be afraid of Dad's gun or have to hear his tall tales. With a buffer, he wouldn't insist that my family was against me.

I called Dad to let him know I was coming. It was the first time we had spoken in a while.

"You're changing," Dad said. "I can hear it in your voice. You're becoming a Luders and drifting away."

I wanted to hang up, but instead I finally confronted him.

"Dad, you're the one who's never there. You never visit even though you say you will. You never came to any of my performances." My voice

broke as I began crying. "You didn't even come to my high school graduation, or my middle school one."

"Daughter," he said, his voice breaking also, "you're my life." I didn't
believe him, but I still planned to visit.

15

OTHER VOICES, OTHER ROOMS
1996

THE TRAIN RIDE WOULD HAVE BEEN PEACEFUL, if not for the destination at the other end. True, it wasn't like I was traveling to meet a stranger. This was, after all, my father. Yet he was a stranger now nonetheless, or at least a mostly warm acquaintance.

This time I was not alone; Eddie sat beside me. I was glad for the male companion but nervous at how my father would behave toward this man who appeared to have some sort of intentions with his daughter.

It was late afternoon when we approached Sacramento. I hurried in vain to gather my things. I was ready to get off the train, but I was coming to learn that Eddie's slowness was a given, as if he were determined to be the last one out the door. I watched fretfully as person after person passed me on their way off.

Finally, we deboarded. I found my father waiting close by. He was as tall as ever, towering over me like a giant, with his brown pleather jacket covering his thin frame. I was taken aback by my eagerness to see him; the stranger suddenly became familiar as I remembered scenes from our past: drinking apple juice at the booth inside Woolworth's; doing push-ups and lifting weights before bed; wrestling over the hidden words on

Wheel of Fortune; me marveling at how tall he was as I held his hand on the way to the bus; marching in San Francisco for Martin Luther King Day, and his arms sheltering his little girl from the mob of people rushing to board the Amtrak. My dad's arms had provided me safety against the ward of strangers that day.

Now Dad approached, and I was forced to return to the present. To my relief, he seemed to welcome Eddie and me warmly. If he were wary, he tried not to let it show. The visit proceeded as they usually did. Dad's earlier declaration on the phone that we "*must* sit down and have a talk" never materialized, and words of much significance were scarce. I wanted to experience that deep conversation that he always appeared to desire himself, but time after time it was replaced by the blaring of the television and intellectual conversation lacking in feeling.

As the sun set, the three of us headed out to the porch.

"Look at that girl over there," Dad said, nodding his head to the right. "She's always standing out there, eyeing me. She should be inside. I don't want a relationship with her; she's just a child."

I looked down the road and saw a girl standing outside her house. She appeared to be my age, while my dad was in his midsixties. The girl didn't seem to be eyeing my father. I thought about the young girls he claimed to have mentored in his home and wondered if he had the same thoughts about them.

The next morning, Eddie convinced Dad to take us to a local church down the street. The one-room church had two small rows of well-worn pews separated by an aisle in the middle. Parishioners eyed us cautiously. Dad had the right skin, but Eddie and I clearly didn't belong, not just because of our relative paleness, but also our preppy (albeit cheap) clothes. The three of us took our seats on the left and settled in. Middle-aged women sat fanning themselves with cardboard fans with small wooden handles like Popsicle sticks. They adjusted their colorful hats adorned with tulle on top, while men in loose-fitting suits shook each other's hands.

After worship—livelier than any I had seen—the minister, draped in a black robe, spoke of the Valley of the Dry Bones from the book of Ezekiel. "Ezekiel saw that valley full of dry bones," the minister bellowed from the small pulpit. "Bones of God's people."

"Hmhm!" came voices from the congregation.

"Ezekiel heard God say, 'Dry bones, hear the word of the LORD!'"

"Amen!"

"Dry bones. 'My people,' God said, 'I am going to open your graves and bring you up from them.'"

Women stood up from their pews and raised their hands high. "Hallelujah!"

"Dry bones. 'I will bring you back to the land of Israel,' God said. 'Then you, my people, will know that I am the LORD'!"

Eddie and I had stepped into a Christian sphere completely alien to us, with foreign dress and foreign repetition and foreign ways to worship God. I squirmed in my seat and looked over to find him wiping away tears of quiet laughter. I chastised myself for letting Eddie bring me here, of thinking he would see God in this place. And if I looked a little deeper into my own consciousness, I was aware that I didn't see God either. How could the God I knew be in these words that I had never before heard, about dry bones in a valley, by a minister who didn't speak with what I believed to be the eloquence and quiet analogies of my pastors back home?

I wasn't necessarily taught that there was anything wrong with the Black church, or with other churches in general, but conservative Christianity naturally instilled an in-group/out-group mentality that easily led congregants to believe that anything outside their church's door was inferior. I judged everything in relation to Crossroads from my youth group days as if it were a gold standard.

The next day, Dad, Eddie, and I headed home after buying groceries at the local market. As we waited at a stoplight across the street from Dad's car, another girl my age walked up and stood near him. I didn't notice her at first, but Dad turned to me and whispered, "Look at how that girl is watching me. She acts like she doesn't see me, but I'm no fool."

The girl was tall, like my father, with matted, overprocessed hair, or maybe a weave past its prime. Her vacant eyes looked in the direction of the street and she seemed confused about whether to cross.

"What's your name?" Dad asked her.

"Denise."

"Do you need a place to go, Denise?"

Denise looked at my father with helpless intensity and began to issue forth of a list of grievances. "I don't got no place to go. I just got evicted from my apartment. I don't got no place to go." The words came out quickly, frantically, broken.

"Do you want to come to our place for dinner?" Dad asked. Denise nodded.

The four of us crossed the street together. Dad put the groceries in the trunk and then opened the passenger-side door for Denise, waving her in. The familiar headache crept up, but I stayed silent in the backseat.

Back at the house, Eddie and I cooked for four instead of three. Spaghetti. French bread. Vegetables. But Dad didn't want it. He wanted chicken. Into the oven went the chicken, as Eddie and I struggled frantically in the kitchen. Eddie was eager to show off his cooking expertise.

Dad and Denise were getting drunk in the living room, violating Dad's court order not to drink during my visits. It was the first time he had done it so brazenly, perhaps because I was now nineteen. Dad's words began to slur and his temper grew shorter. After dinner, he issued the sleeping arrangement.

"Denise will sleep on the bed. I'll sleep on the floor. You, Shannon, will sleep on the pullout bed in the living room and your friend will sleep on the floor. Got it?" Eddie's and my sleeping arrangement was the same as it had been the night before, but now it was a command.

Eddie and I settled into a movie in the living room while Dad and Denise retreated to the bedroom. We lay on the foldout couch, trying to ignore what was most likely going on close by. After a while, Denise came out of the bedroom in a hospital gown that Dad had no doubt asked her to wear. Her behind peeped through as she turned to the bathroom.

Eddie flipped the channels on the television until he settled on PBS. Mammals of ancient lands fought one another and devoured those below them on the food chain. Eddie was mesmerized, but I was disgusted.

At one point during the feast and famines, Dad emerged from the bedroom. "Get off that bed, boy!"

Eddie hopped off and took his place on the floor. I felt protected, as I had that day boarding the Freedom Train, even though in this case, his protection wasn't necessary. Plus, Dad seemed to be trying to make up for his own bad actions. Eddie was forced to retreat to the floor, yet my father was in the bedroom with a girl my age.

The television show proceeded and all was quiet. Eventually, Denise came out of the bedroom. I don't know whether she had changed back into her clothes, because her words took up all the space in the room.

"Can I use your phone? He touched me. He touched my breasts. I'm gon' call my mom."

Her voice sounded as scattered as it had been that afternoon. I doubt she'd known Dad was going to touch her, even though she'd gone into his bedroom and put on his hospital gown. She was too spacey to know what she was doing, to be able to consent to Dad, whom I imagined she had probably seen as a father figure who would sing to her sweet lullabies and gently move her hair away from her face as she drifted off into a deep slumber.

Eddie silently handed her the corded phone from the coffee table. Someone pulled up to our house a few minutes later, and Denise quickly disappeared out the front door.

Dad emerged from the bedroom and plopped himself down on a folding chair, facing us. "You don't think she was telling the truth, do you?" he asked, slurring his words. "You don't know what went on here. She can't be trusted."

I remained quiet, unsure if he would turn on me as he had turned on Denise. My father had not touched me, yet I felt violated. He had protected his daughter while defiling someone else's.

Eddie sought refuge in the freezer and scooped himself a bowl of chocolate ice cream. Dad retreated back to the bedroom, and I cried while Eddie shoved ice cream down his throat. As I lay on the bed, I thought of the photo albums my dad and I had perused so many times during my childhood. The pages were filled with various women who had come in and out of my dad's life. I couldn't keep their names straight, nor did I much care to.

Eddie finished his ice cream. We lay in our respective places, holding hands, longing for sleep to take us away from the scene that had played out before us, yet afraid of the intoxicated man in the other room. The father I knew so well turned back into a stranger. I fell asleep consoled by dad's air pistol, which he had pointed out in case someone tried to break in. But I already felt in danger. Alcohol was its own beast. Dad could come out of the room much like the tigers on TV. He could throw me across the room just as he had done with Mom. The gun wasn't to protect me from Robert my father. It was to protect me from the alcohol zombie inside him whom he could not control.

16

OUR BODIES, OURSELVES
1996

THE RUSH OF THE WEEK had subsided, and my body and soul longed for something outside of itself, something higher than the limited view of everyday life—a place to think. I changed into comfortable clothes and stepped outside my front door. The air was crisp, refreshing. I walked along the busy university road until I reached my beloved Spring Street. Not far, just a couple houses. But houses that size took up a considerable space. Spring Street was empty that day and curved off into the distance. I walked past the all-American house with the United States flag, past the old VW camper van, past the trickling creek that led to a pond in front of the house across the street.

The road had a steep incline until its crest. I passed my yellow Victorian dream house with white gables. I climbed higher and higher. The road ended and the thin metal gate of Pogonip park welcomed me. As I stepped through, the world changed. The wild grass was spotted with purple flowers. The wind gently whistled through the tall blades. I was in the hills, at last.

The path was empty of people, and I heard my shoes as I walked on the soft dirt. The stones partly enmeshed in the dirt always gave me the illusion that I was in Ireland—a land that seemed full of mystery and romance, in the Anne Shirley sense of the word. Or maybe I was in her Prince Edward Island, off Nova Scotia, on the far-right coast of Canada. Up here in Pogonip, I was surrounded solely by hills and trees. Suddenly everything was put into perspective. God was by my side, and the solitude revived me.

I followed the path up to the highest point and sat, looking at the world below. Hills on my left, forest behind me, the ocean and town before me. I saw the roller coasters go round and round in the distance. And there it was—the town where I was so alone, yet so at home. I longed to leave but I longed to stay, and I knew I must choose. But the choice would come slowly. It would sneak up on me so quietly that I would not be aware of the change. I would think I was in Santa Cruz to stay, and one day I would find myself completely disconnected from it, not knowing that I cut the wires myself, oblivious to my own actions.

My good mood lasted until I got home. I walked into the kitchen and found Grandma making hamburgers. Grandma didn't like to cook, but throughout her life she had mastered simple American recipes— hamburgers, tacos, hot dogs, pizza, pasta, macaroni and cheese, grilled cheese sandwiches, and bean soup. Boston brown bread was a family favorite: molasses-rich bread, which, to my constant delight, came in a can. Grandma always chose the most trusted brands at the grocery store: Uncle Ben's, Martinelli's, Oroweat, Kellogg's. She used just enough spices in her cooking for a pinch of flavor, and just enough ingredients to make the meal. Food wasn't meant for experimentation. When I moved out and began cooking for myself, I adopted Grandma's asceticism.

"Are you home for dinner?" she asked.

"Yeah," I said.

"You could have told me ahead of time." She reached into the fridge for more ground beef.

"I have to call ahead?" I asked.

"Well, you're never here. How am I supposed to know?"

She had a point, but I didn't see it then.

Grandma rolled the ground beef between her palms until it formed a patty. Then she placed it, sizzling, on the pan.

I opened the cupboard and pulled out a plate, then opened the drawer for silverware, and placed them all on the table.

"By the way," Grandma continued. "You left grape juice on the counter this afternoon." She pulled the Welch's bottle out of the fridge and then grabbed a glass from the cupboard. "Let me show you the proper way to pour it. You have to tip it all the way, see? That way it doesn't dribble from the side."

"Uh huh," I said, as if I hadn't poured grape juice leak free 999 times out of 1,000. It was as if Grandma relished seeing me screw up. I didn't iron right. I didn't keep my nails clean enough. I didn't get a good enough grade on a math test.

After dinner, I called Mom to complain about Grandma and the grape juice. Mom had intimate knowledge of Grandma's "lessons." In fact, Grandma had stopped schooling all her children except Mom—the oldest but smallest, and the most childlike in demeanor. It's anyone's guess what came first, the chicken of Mom's struggle to navigate the world, or the egg of Grandma's infantilization of her, likely brought on my mom's cleft lip and palate.

After I had spilled my grape juice saga, Mom said Dad had called her about Eddie.

"He said he doesn't approve of Eddie because he lacks ambition. But it's not surprising he wouldn't like your boyfriend. That's pretty normal for fathers and daughters."

"Mom, there's something I have to tell you about the trip," I said. I recounted the night Denise came home with us and about Dad taking her into his bedroom. About how I didn't want to visit him anymore.

"No wonder he was upset about you and Eddie. There's nothing like projecting your own issues onto others. You have no obligation to visit him," Mom continued. "If you feel uncomfortable at your dad's when you spent the night, don't feel you need to spend the night. It's good that Eddie went with you."

"Thanks, Mom," I said in earnest.

Mom had missed both my birthdays since I'd moved out. She never called. I never seemed to cross her mind unless I was standing in front of her, and sometimes not even then. But when it came to Dad, she was the ideal therapist, trained by nearly twenty years of weekly Al-Anon meetings and their own complicated past. "I wish you and I could do things more often," I said. "Maybe Saturdays after book club?"

"Sure, that would be nice."

And it would have been nice, had it happened.

———————

A week later, Eddie and I kissed for the first time, in his cabin, from night until morning. That morning, as I lay holding him while he slept, running my hands through his soft curls, I felt the reason for my existence was finally revealed, much the way I had felt when Melanie was born. My completeness could no longer come from Melanie alone. She stayed for the occasional weekend, which we blissfully filled with cookie baking, walks to the park, and indoctrinations of my favorite childhood movies. But I needed more than a long-distance quasi offspring to love.

I returned to Grandma's later that afternoon with a contact rash on my chin from Eddie's goatee, which he had grown over the past couple months. His kisses branded me as a sexual being, officially ending my plan to save my first kiss for my wedding day. It felt like an initiation into womanhood, into love, into being loved. I had reached the physical ranks of my high school friends, had inched closer to the affection experienced by others under my roof. But I had also inched closer to losing what the church said was my ultimate gift.

Though Eddie wanted to touch me, to spend time with me, he still didn't want to make our relationship official. On the phone the night after our kiss, he said he wanted to leave and join the air force, somehow forgetting that his mental illness prevented him from doing so. Then he said he was afraid of relationships and wanted to become a priest, following his Catholic upbringing. If I had to lose Eddie to anything, the priesthood seemed the most noble. But I didn't want to lose him. His being, his body, felt attached to mine. If it strayed too long or too far, I feared that my own body and being would wither. I imagined myself collapsed on the floor like a rag doll.

The next day, determined to withstand his alienation, I drove to the linen room at Trinity Hills to get my backpack and the music I had left inside it. I opened my backpack to find a note from Eddie: "I love you. I love you. I love you. Guess who!" Eddie's declaration was different from Josh's, who had said he loved me like a sister, and different from

Brian's, who said he loved me like ice cream and his mother. That night, Eddie called and said he wanted to get married in four years, once he had become more stable.

I rode the wave of Eddie's mania, buoyed by his devotion, and was gutted each time he pulled away. I had no one against whom to measure his actions. Through the sheer act of showing up at my doorstep, of telling me I was beautiful, he was more present than either Dad or Gary.

Then Eddie started to blame me for our physical relationship. At first I balked at his mixed signals—his anger when I said no, and his subsequent anger when I said yes. In my diary, I quoted William Wordsworth from that semester's major British writers class:

> Strange fits of passion have I known:
> And I will dare to tell,
> But in the Lover's ear alone,
> What once to me befell.

Like Wordsworth's poem, I could explain our fits of passion to no one but Eddie. In each other's arms, we spoke a wordless language that had the power to enrapture or desecrate with one look, one touch, one silent promise. Just like that first night in the Garden of Eden, whenever my body pressed to Eddie's, my breath had no power. It ceased knowing its own cadence and instead matched the breath of my beloved.

Then I remembered a Bible passage from Romans: "In the same way, count yourselves dead to sin but alive to God in Christ Jesus. Therefore do not let sin reign in your mortal body so that you obey its evil desires." I remembered the monthlong sex talks held every February in youth group. My role as a single woman was to say no to Eddie, despite his anger. Enraging him in the present would make him respect me more in the future. It was a constant test from God, and I was failing.

Beyond even God, some voice inside me said my soul was corrupt, that I had the power to lure men into my web of sin, for my own selfish desires, and steer them off course. Eddie was proof positive that my powers were there, having lain dormant for years. I didn't know where the voice came from, but it would be mirrored back to me in the coming years when men would call me a vixen based only on conversation and a smile. I didn't take off my clothes in a striptease like the woman behind the door at Dad's house. In fact, I didn't do much at all. But these men were sure I possessed the ability to draw them to me against their will.

A week later Eddie and I sat on the floor in his cabin, listening to a cassette tape about a nun who couldn't say "Papa, I am your child." God wasn't just "Father," our spiritual authority up in the sky; he was also "Papa," our intimate father on earth.

"I can't say 'Papa' either," I told him.

Eddie was surprised. He took my hands and said we should pray in our heads and then say "Papa" out loud at the end of every thought. "Papa," Eddie said, his eyes closed tight, his mouth bent upward in a childlike smile. "Papa."

I searched my mind for a sincere thought to express to God. All that emerged was "I hate you." So instead of saying "Papa," I cried. My hate was for my dad's absence, for Gary's cruelty, and, if I were honest, for Eddie's ability to tear me down. Though I tried to dismiss the feeling as ridiculous, Eddie had always felt, in addition to a boyfriend, like a surrogate father, spiritually guiding me through his age-related wisdom. Just as with Dad, I never knew once Eddie left if I'd see him again. The dynamic was painful yet familiar, and, unlike with Dad, Eddie was with me more than not. He knew me more deeply than my father ever would. In this moment, I saw Eddie the child, attempting to heal the hole left by his own father.

Eddie's hands began to shake. I looked up, and he was crying too. There we sat, two wayward, abandoned souls, summoning the Papa whom the church said would never let us go.

Near the beginning of March, I was assigned to clean with my friend Michael, a seventeen-year-old from a drug-fueled home who had been given a cabin to rent on the premises. Eddie was a housekeeper now too, since the dining hall wasn't open much outside of the summer rush.

"Have you and Eddie kissed?" Michael asked me out of the blue as we tore the sheets off a bed.

I blushed. "Yes."

Michael tossed the sheets on the carpet. "That's really cool. I bet you'll get married. Eddie seems to change a lot, though."

"Yeah, he does," I answered, as I fluffed out the clean sheets.

Michael took a pause from making the bed and looked over at me. "If you get married, I know he'll be faithful to you, but his personality would be pretty versatile, in a negative way. His mood seems to change a lot."

I nodded. I attributed the mood changes to his rapid cycling—something I believed he could not control. In fact, he took pains to remind me of his condition whenever I wanted to hold him responsible.

A few days later, Eddie ignored me while we cleaned hotel rooms.

I peeked my head into one of the rooms, where he was wiping off the bathroom counter. "Do you know if we're supposed to clean room 208?"

Instead of answering, Eddie kept wiping in a deliberate circular motion, his eyes glued downward at the rag.

I returned to the room I was cleaning with Michael. "You should just forget about Eddie," he said. "What do you see in him?"

I didn't have an answer. As Michael and I talked about the music he liked to play on his guitar, about the grunge bands he had introduced me to on a mixtape, I sought to clear Eddie from my mind. The moment we dropped off our buckets in the linen room and signed out, I confronted him.

"Why do you like to ignore me at work?" I asked.

"I don't *like* to," he said with a smug smile.

When I left the linen room to head home, Eddie forced out a faux-casual "Bye!"

I felt used as I kept walking away, and like so many times before, I wondered if he would ever look at me lovingly again, or if I even wanted him to.

The next day, I went speed walking at Trinity Hills, secretly hoping to run into him. When I passed his cabin, I knocked on his door.

"I just can't work with you, because it's too weird," he said, once I'd closed the door behind me. "It's sort of like a husband and wife working together. The husband just needs his own territory, where he doesn't have to worry about how to emotionally interpret things with his wife right there."

Instead of acknowledging his not-so-subtle machismo, I swelled at his relating us to a husband and wife. He stayed over at my house that night. The next morning, as we stacked chairs after the church service, Eddie asked me to be his girlfriend.

His commitment didn't end the cycle of his push-pull, but rather he began a new one of breaking up with me and getting back together. I followed each decree, letting him steer the relationship this way and that, convinced he heard God more clearly than I did and followed his direction more closely. Eddie insisted that the purest couples kept nothing from each other, including their diaries. When he pulled away, I wrote freely, convinced he would never care to open my diary again. When he returned, I gushed at how he had changed. In his own diary, his handwriting had become more illegible, to the point that it devolved to scribbles haphazardly inked across each page. The scribbles matched the disorientation inside his brain.

In his diary, which he presented to me as if it were a sacred text, Eddie had written, "Father, please allow me to be strong against Shannon's seductions. Please don't let me give in to her temptations." I recoiled at the words and tried to quell their impact as they rang in my head. *Shannon's seductions. Her temptations.* Words I was sure I must not take seriously from a man with a mental illness, but, above all, words that felt true. I *had* wanted everything that happened, so I must have *willed* it to happen.

When we weren't together, I ached for Eddie until the aching passed, replaced with hope for a future path that didn't include him. One free of the roller coaster brought on by forces that felt outside Eddie's control, whipping me this way and that on a ride I couldn't seem to get off. But then I'd see him again at church or run into him at Trinity Hills, and my independence seemed trivial, selfish. Unbelieving of the transformation I knew was possible with God, which Eddie always said was just around the corner. I longed for a Trinity Hills bigwig to marry us in the wedding chapel, and for Eddie and me to live at the conference center. I wanted him to get the newly vacant custodial position and for me to befriend the mixed-race woman who worked at the soda fountain and wrote children's books, was married to the maintenance man at Trinity Hills' teen camp, and had two children. Her life was the epitome of my own dream.

––––––––––

At Cabrillo College, my major British writers class was made up of a white professor in cardigans and a smattering of white students, all of whom sat around four tables made into a square. As the professor expounded on Wordsworth and Coleridge, he and the students sipped coffee and hot chocolate in mugs brought from home. I had spent two semesters with my beloved lesbian instructor, Nancy, who had nurtured us with a belief in our ability to comprehend and analyze contemporary works. Now I was being taught by a white man whose world was made up of the old white men in heavy texts about white worlds that felt more foreign to me than my family's maypole dances and 4-H clubs and radios tuned to the Mormon Tabernacle Choir. While a smattering of the Romantic-era lines made sense in an abstract profundity, most never felt more than gobbledygook. I dropped the class with the belief that I had failed the ultimate test of English comprehension and that my deepest-held desire to major in English could never be realized.

My alienation wasn't limited to major British writers. In speech class, the white instructor placed a VHS into the VCR and turned on the box TV that sat atop the wheeled metal stand. She instructed us to take in an example of Black oration. The white students (and perhaps a couple of other races) listened to the words of the Black nationalist Louis Farrakhan, the leader of the Nation of Islam, who would become increasingly known for his anti-Semitism and increasingly shunned by the Black community. "You must recognize that your work is not more important than the *mission* of the resurrection of the dead," he shouted from a podium to an auditorium of followers, sporting a black suit and bow-tie, against a puke-brown curtain. "What you got is a job that the white man put you on." Students to my left and right began snickering.

Farrakhan continued, "What the hell is that but to keep the white man's world up?" The snickering turned to laughter. "You got a job; he gives you money to keep you going, in his world!" The students began hollering. I turned to look at the instructor, who seemed unfazed by her students' reactions. What had been her purpose to share the words of someone I knew most Black people rejected? Did she do it just for a laugh? Were there no tapes of Martin Luther King Jr., or of Malcolm X? "God wants to build a new world out of you and me. Somebody gotta take up the mission!" Farrakhan shouted.

As I ran from the classroom, I heard Farrakhan shout, "And many of us are runnin'. We're runnin' from the truth but we know the duty." I stood against the wall, anger bubbling up from deep inside. I wiped tears away and waited silently until the end of class, watching white student after white student pass by me from classes built just for them. When speech class ended, I returned for my backpack with my head focused on the floor. My instructor and I never acknowledged what happened, and I finished the class that semester with a C. Shortly after, with Mom and Grandma's blessing, I decided to take the following year off from Cabrillo. I didn't know what I was working toward, why I was putting in such effort with no clear direction. I wasn't sure where I wanted to go, but it no longer seemed to include Cabrillo.

One night in May, Eddie and I lay in my bed at Grandma's house. In the witching hour between wake and sleep, his hand found its way to what my friends and I called Mexico, the region south of our navels. (Our breasts were our Australias.) My ultimate gift was still intact the next morning, but we spent the next day depressed and drained, eating and sleeping until Eddie left for a walk. He came back around 10:00 PM and wouldn't look me in the eye.

"Can I have a hug?" I asked, trying to see if I was reading his body language correctly.

"No," he answered.

He grabbed his small red backpack and walked out Grandma's front door. I burst into tears and followed him to the porch in my brown bear slippers. To my relief, Eddie turned around and came back for me. We walked a few houses down to the two-story home on a large plot of land that overlooked the city. Next to the house was a grassy area with a tall oak tree in the center. The property was not fenced off, and Eddie and I quietly ambled close to the cliff's edge and gazed down at the city lights, and up at the stars that glistened over the water.

"I'm really hurt by what we did," he said, his eyes forward.

"Do you want to break up?" I asked, my voice small.

"Maybe. If I had a gun, I would probably kill myself."

Eddie walked off into the quiet night, and I ran back down the street and into Grandma's house, heading straight for Adam's back bedroom. He answered the door to my tears and waved me in. We sat on his bed and I cried as he put his arms around me. For the next hour, we spoke of Eddie and Stephanie and each of our futures, sharing more than we had in the past year.

The next morning, I woke from a dream that the world was encased in an ugly brown as I walked home from the metro. Once awake, I had meant to go to church but instead took the bus to Trinity Hills to give Eddie two letters assuring him that I was on his side. I knocked on his cabin door but he wasn't there. Then I remembered him speaking of suicide the night before. My stomach lurched as I imagined him ending his life. I called his uncle who lived in Santa Cruz. I let out my breath when he told me Eddie had spent the night there.

It wasn't too late to make it to church, so I took the bus to Santa Cruz Bible and saw Eddie seated in the worship room. The pastor spoke of the seven lies about what a woman should be; he preached that men needed to appreciate the women they love. Tears welled as I listened to the sermon and hoped the words had softened Eddie's heart. After the service, Eddie and I ran into each other in the back of the room.

"It's good to see you," we said at the same time. Eddie gave me a hug.

"I was worried about you," I said.

"I was worried about you too."

When I got home, I found a message from Eddie on the answering machine, asking me to meet him at church. That night I quoted Psalm 30 in my journal: "Pain lasts for a night, but joy cometh in the morning."

At every phase of our sexual relationship, Eddie punished me by pulling back. Purity culture had taught me that such a response was to be expected. I wouldn't realize until later that while part of Eddie's angst was genuine, another part of him used this punishment as a weapon—a way to maintain power over me.

The next day, Eddie and I sat across from each other at Taco Bell. Cars whooshed past us on Mission Street, a portion of Highway 1 than ran through town, past my elementary school, and up to San Francisco to the north and down south to Los Angeles. I longed to follow it in either direction—anywhere to finally start my new life, away from everything that felt so familiar. In a new setting, I was sure I'd be a new person: more confident, more eloquent, and more independent.

Eddie sat across the table from me, silent, pensive.

"You win," he said.

"What?" I asked.

"Will you marry me?"

Those four words were the culmination of everything a Christian woman was meant to want, aside from the two words that solidified her fate: "I do."

I smiled. "Maybe." I wasn't sure I wanted to sacrifice my Highway 1 escape, to start a new life north or south of where I now resided, however nebulous that escape might be. Longing for Eddie was different from making our relationship permanent. I wanted to be with him forever, but not as he was now.

Eddie took his straw wrapper from the table and fashioned it into a knot with a hole just big enough for my finger.

"Give me your hand," he said. He placed the wrapper on my ring finger, proud of his creation. "It would have to be right away or in four years. We either can't wait at all or need to get our lives together first. But we have to keep it a secret. We can't tell anyone we're engaged. It has to be between us and God."

Later that night we made theoretical wedding plans at the Crêpe Place, seated at a small round table on the back patio. When I went to bed, I got a stomachache that lasted throughout the night. I had read that the author Catherine Marshall, who wrote *A Man Called Peter* about her deceased minister husband, was sent to the infirmary right before Peter proposed. Maybe that was the cause of my stomachache too. "I'm sure it will pass on its own," Grandma said when I asked her for advice that night. Eddie came over in the morning and held me on my top bunk. As I lay in his arms, the stomachache went away. I was left with a peace about leaving my family for a future with him.

Eddie warned me that his Mexican family was from the South and might not approve of his marrying a Black girl. Later he told me that his grandma, who had met me once, liked me but worried about mixed kids, meaning kids that were part Black, not just Mexican, white, and Native American like Eddie. I had just recently heard from Amy that her fiancé, Kevin, wasn't sure if I should be in their Iowa wedding because his family might not approve. Amy said her father-in-law would yell "Run, n—r, run" as he watched football. There was never any doubt in Amy's mind whether I would be a bridesmaid, along with Jenna, Deborah, and Amy's college friend Dellie from Bahrain. After the ceremony, Amy took me aside: "One of Kevin's aunts said, 'What a colorful wedding.'" Amy rolled her eyes and we both laughed nervously. Dellie and I were flesh-and-blood minorities, real dimensional people whose existence challenged the stereotypes Kevin's family had acquired from only seeing people like us through a TV screen. I pictured myself back on the plane, above the backwardness of Iowa, headed to the Golden State.

Hearing about both Eddie's grandma and Kevin's family hurt. Their prejudices seemed outdated, out of line with the late 1990s. And yet their antiquated thinking reinforced that my feeling of racial otherness wasn't in my head; my being biracial, being Black, was too foreign for some people, even though we had lived in this country for centuries.

That summer, Crystal and I were back at Trinity Hills, staying in the front dorm room as RAs. Crystal now worked in the daycare, and I did housekeeping once again, not confident around children I didn't know, and waiting tables was too hectic for me.

Eddie was no longer in my safe haven. He'd been kicked out of Trinity Hills and wouldn't tell me why. Most likely from missing too much work. At the last minute, he got a job at the nearby Hope Creek Christian camp as a dishwasher. He decided the distance was divine intervention and said we shouldn't see each other all summer in order to be closer at the end. I took all his decrees as godly wisdom. And even without God, Anne Shirley and Gilbert Blythe had had a long-distance engagement. There was something romantic about being forced apart.

Two weeks after camp started, Eddie called the linen room and asked me to visit. I should have known his decree wouldn't last long. They never did. After work, I walked to the Safeway and took the bus through the winding hills to the camp fifteen minutes away. The camp wasn't far, but since I had never seen it, it felt like it could exist on another planet, with Eddie too far to reach. I could better withstand the summer if I had a clear picture.

Eddie may have said he wanted to see me, but his actions spoke otherwise. We sat outside against the wooden cross near the front of the camp, Eddie silent and munching on a loaf of sourdough bread. I asked him for a piece, and he said no. Then I shared a poem with him, and he said it was too sappy. His distance was haunting, like a recurring bad dream you forget about until you dream it again. I wondered if I was too late, if I had already lost him to this other world.

That night, I got settled on the worn leather couch in the lounge, which was more like an entryway. I prepared for a fitful night with summer workers eyeing me with curiosity as they came and went. Eddie joined me on the couch before retreating to his room, but sat on the opposite end. Once again, he said he was considering becoming a Jesuit priest.

"Women are too fickle," he said. "I applaud any guy who makes it through marriage."

I longed to break Eddie's trance, to remind him who I was and that he could trust me. My mom and Gary often fought, and after each outburst he would come back around and ask Mom for forgiveness. I hated the way he treated her, but acting out this dynamic in my own relationship felt like familiar ground.

"Can I have a hug?" I asked.

He gave me a half hug, then returned to the far end of the couch.

"Can I have a blanket?" I asked later as he walked away to his room.

"No," he said, and then returned a few minutes later with one in hand, plus an extra sweater.

The next morning, Eddie woke me up at seven thirty. "Can I have my sweater back?" he asked. I took it off and handed it to him. "See you in the fall," he said, and left.

I walked to the bus in a daze. Eddie always existed as some sort of apparition when I wasn't near him, and I filtered the world through his nebulous frame. The closer I got to the bus stop, the more the apparition faded, leaving me with an acute awareness of my surroundings. The morning air felt crisp in my lungs and fueled each breath as I took one step forward, and then another. I was convinced we should part ways. Eddie could stay there, at his new camp, and I could fully embrace my summer at mine.

Back at Trinity Hills, Crystal told Sarah about my visit with Eddie—the girl with the witchlike hair and crooked teeth whom Eddie and I had spent time with the previous year. Sarah found me while I was cleaning a cabin and handed me a pass-it-on—a laminated card with a Bible verse.

"He played the same mind games with me," she said, as she stood in the middle of the cabin. "I don't know if it overlapped with what he told you, but he told me he liked me but wanted to see what happened." I cried as she walked away down the narrow path. I didn't deserve her friendship. I had been so judgmental of her behind her back, and now that judgment faded. She understood Eddie's behaviors and mood swings better than anyone else I knew. Her words made me ready to leave him for good this time. I remembered a night in Eddie's cabin when he and I had been washing dishes. He had chastised me for not doing them the way he wanted. Then he held up an eggbeater and said with a deadpan expression, "Sometimes I think I'd beat my wife."

Instead of making a clean break, I wrote Eddie a letter saying I couldn't fully trust him. A few days later, he met me at a cabin where some of us had gathered for a Bible study class on relationships. The group discussed marriage and our definitions of ideal dating, including whether we should forgo dating altogether and go from friends to engagement.

After the class, Eddie took me aside.

"I was mad at the girl I work with," he said, about my visit to Hope Creek. "It's hard for me to work with women." Eddie's eyes lit up as he continued. "I wanted to teach her service. But then I started giving thanks to God for all of her qualities. I had to search for them, but they were there. When I started to serve her, she became the servant I was looking for. I left it up to God and then she started serving."

I folded my arms, unsure why his coworker would have to serve him. I was slowly coming to the conclusion that Eddie wasn't my spiritual leader. He was older, but that didn't mean he was wiser. At times God seemed to him a means to the end he wanted. A way to create a narrative where he was in charge. But my fear of abandonment spoke louder: the end result was that he appreciated women more than he had before. Maybe it didn't matter how he got there. To leave Eddie would mean that all the time we had spent together over the past two years had been in vain. I would have to admit that my instincts were wrong, and that I'd let someone touch me, defile me. No longer would I have a man who wanted to marry me. I'd lose the one person who had ever asked.

Eddie led me to a bench and we sat down. "You know that letter you wrote a couple days ago?" he asked.

"Yeah," I said.

"That really tore me up. I cried a lot, and prayed about it to God. Last Sunday I had a dream that I was in a maze of punching bags, like the ones that hang from the ceiling. All the bags were women. Then one fell and split open, and there were diamonds in it. The diamonds were you. God was telling me that you are the one for me. I want to marry you. And I want to try medication."

I turned and gave a cautious but hopeful smile. I hadn't expected my letter to cause him such emotion—not after his distancing at Hope Creek. I still didn't fully trust him, but I wanted to. I thought of God and the Israelites, how God didn't let his wrath against their rebellion harbor in his heart forever. Likewise, I worked to quell my own wrath and turn it to love, to be the diamonds he saw inside the punching bag. The harm of his dream was lost on me.

Eddie started making the trek to Trinity Hills often. Many nights we slept on the couch in the dorm lounge after talking for hours. In the mornings, he'd call his coworker from the pay phone and tell her what to do until he finally arrived, much to her annoyance on the other end.

Toward the end of camp, the summer staff were invited to an event at the house of a Trinity Hills executive. His house was huge, like a plantation home that had forgotten to add the slave quarters. As we sang in worship, I wiped tears away with my sleeve. I didn't belong there, in the opulence, and in the whiteness. One or the other caused little alarm, but when combined, I wanted to sink into the carpet, run out the front door, away from inherited wealth that I didn't yet have a name for but that I knew in my bones to be dangerous.

After worship, I saw Eddie standing in another part of the living room. We took a walk in the dark and I cried in earnest. I believed he was the only one I could talk to about feeling different. He was the only one who felt the same way. My crying turned to sobs, and he put his arm around me. As we walked, I told him why I was upset.

"I love you," he said, after I'd finished.

"Even though I'm different?" I asked.

"Yes. You're not an object to be placed in one ethnic category. You're just Shannon. But I know how you feel. I often feel that way too. There are so many stereotypes for white Christians, and we don't fit that. Sometimes I think I shouldn't use big words because I'm Mexican."

Eddie was the only person I knew like me—the only person I knew who walked through a white world with brown skin. Josh from high school, or Brian, might nod their heads and try to understand, but they hadn't lived it. They wouldn't have seen the way white people could look at you with fascination or surprise. The way they saw you as a safe link between their world and one they wanted to understand without getting their feet wet. The way they fluffed their feathers as they spoke of racism and equality, showing off their unbridled acceptance of your people, and their wisdom that they were sure surpassed that of their peers. Eddie moved through the world like me, unmoored and without the security that came from a family who reinforced your existence through their own. I took his hand and swung it back and forth as we looked up at the stars.

17

OF HUMAN BONDAGE
1996

WHEN SUMMER CAMP WAS OVER, I returned home. Uncle Adam, Stephanie, and I went out for ice cream at Marianne's, a local favorite, where Adam and I got our usual flavor, peppermint with actual peppermint pieces that crunched in our mouths. When we returned, Grandma took me aside and directed me to the gold velvet couch in the living room.

"I have some new house rules," she said, as she took a seat in her favorite hard-backed dark-brown wooden chair. "The past couple years have been stressful for me, and I need to make sure we have some structure. So, I don't want any friends over on school nights, and no friends spending the night on the weekend unless you give a couple days' notice. I think this will help you study, keep you focused on why you're here."

"Friends" meant Eddie. I had planned to enter this year with new focus, to return to Cabrillo even though for a while I had planned on taking the year off. Now, with rules, I felt my own resolve crumble. I'd have no way of proving myself to my grandma if I were just abiding by restrictions set in place for me as a result of perceived misbehavior. There was nothing to say except "OK."

I walked into the kitchen for a snack and found Stephanie already there, making her lunch for the next day. I opened the fridge and then slammed it shut.

"Grandma also wanted to give you a curfew," Stephanie said. "It could have been worse."

"I'm not a child," I said, folding my arms across my chest. This was my third year at Cabrillo. I was supposed to be off at a four-year college by now, but it still seemed as impossible as ever.

"If you don't like it, I'm sure your mom wouldn't mind taking you back in."

I bridled at Stephanie's comment. I was my mom's daughter; of course she wouldn't mind. She hadn't exiled me to Grandma's for misbehavior. She hadn't shipped me off to straighten me out. But I couldn't return to Mom's, because it wasn't Mom's, it was Gary's.

"It's not that easy," I said.

That fall I enrolled in one class: relationships. Eddie was supposed to join me but never did. The class lost its appeal and I stopped attending, and I failed with a no-credit mark. I kept working at Trinity Hills, and Eddie got a cooking job at Bethel Bible College, a nearby college in the Santa Cruz Mountains. I'd first heard about Bethel from Brian, who went there for a couple semesters. Bethel never seemed like the type of college I could attend—filled with rich kids from the surrounding area and expensive to fund. Now Eddie was in the same space as these spiritual women, who I knew must come from perfect homes with fathers who worked to provide for them, and mothers who cooked for them, and brushes that sat on their dressers to smooth out their straight, silky hair.

I still tamed my hair with chemical relaxer from a home kit sold in the small Black section of the drugstore, hidden in a far corner. I washed my hair every other day, putting it in a French braid on wash days, and wearing it loose the day after—the braid acting as a constrictor that provided frizz-reducing shape when I let it out. The natural hair care revolution was still years away, and most mixed girls like me washed our hair just like white girls, and brushed it dry just like white girls, not yet let in on the secret that for us, fewer wash days and brushing wet hair slathered with conditioner was the secret to beautiful curls. Fourteen years from now, Teri LaFlesh would publish the seminal hair care book *Curly Like Me: How to Grow Your Hair Healthy, Long, and Strong.* When laypeople first discovered the internet, mixed-race women bonded over one thing: hair. Those of us with white mothers lamented our lack of knowledge and the few options for our hair, none of which seemed to suffice. Once LaFlesh's book was published, we mixed-race women found a holy grail, something to guide us beyond our own meager understanding. LaFlesh received so many requests for guidance through Facebook messenger that she had to deactivate her account. Now, her hair care routine is second nature for mixed folks, and spiral curls are the it hairstyle, paraded by those who have them and envied by those who don't.

Back then, in 1996, wearing braids was one way to avoid using relaxer, to provide some long-lasting structure for frizzy hair. Grandma's influence had taught me the skill of talking to strangers; I got in the habit of asking Black women who did their hair as I passed them on the street. They likely took pity on me as they glanced at my unkempt hair. Many kindly answered: their sister, their aunt, their mother. One gave me her sister's phone number. I arrived at the house with hair extensions and left five hours later with braids that fell past my shoulders. Just like in high school, braids were my affirmation of my Black identity. They hung, radicalized, from my head, silently telling Mexican strangers that I might not speak Spanish, and telling white strangers that yes, their eyes don't deceive them. I am "other": I am of the Negro race.

"You know, you're my most beautiful grandchild," my grandma told me one evening during a commercial break of *ER.* The medical drama was the one thing that bonded all four of us together: me, Grandma, Adam, and Stephanie. We often ran to our two bathrooms during commercial breaks to brush our teeth or grab a container of floss.

Tonight, Grandma and I were alone while Adam and Stephanie raced against the clock. I blushed at her compliment. She didn't know how much I longed to hear her praise. Adria and Elsie were always considered the smart ones, the talented ones. Now I finally had them beat at something, and beyond saying "please and thank you," which Grandma had engraved as my best quality all those years ago. Being beautiful was a step up.

"You're the most beautiful because you're exotic," she continued.

Grandma beamed with pride but my face fell, at least on the inside. Her intended compliment set me in the African veldt, alongside giraffes and lions and zebras. It seemed to strip from me the Luders name, to reinforce the differences I saw between the pictures of my ancestors and the brown girl staring into their faces. I couldn't shake the feeling that I was adopted, even though I knew that wasn't true. But how else to explain the vast chasm between our lived experiences, as if I were set into a family and then forgotten.

When Eddie started working at Bethel, at first he assured me that though he was in the presence of godly women, even godlier than most at Trinity Hills, he wanted only me. Soon after, he said we should both date other people. While I pictured Eddie making new friends in the cafeteria, I was still scrubbing toilets with the same five people in rotation. One afternoon at Bethel, Eddie said I had power over him that no one else did, and he needed time away from me to respect me more. The bus was almost empty on my ride home. I sat near the back, by the window, and felt tears on my cheeks. At first they came without emotion, then fell in greater intensity until I broke down. I was only slightly aware of the few other passengers, and too distraught to care. By the time I got home, I realized Eddie always wanted me back once I had the strength to move on. Right now he had the upper hand, so he pushed me away. Eventually I'd have it again. I just had to wait.

My reasons for staying with Eddie were buried so deep, so layered, that I doubt I could have accessed them. If I had, I would have understood that some part of me—some large part in fact—felt unworthy of love, especially with a "normal guy." I didn't know what normal was, how to act around normal. My dad had an addiction to alcohol and abused my mom; my stepdad had indescribable rages that came at the drop of a hat. And even Uncle Adam—something was off there but I couldn't quite put my finger on it, now having completely forgotten about the visit from Child Protective Services and left only with my grandma's declaration that if anything had happened it had been my fault. Dysfunction seemed to follow me everywhere, even in the leaders I was assigned at Teen Missions. It felt like my cross to bear.

The next time Eddie came back around, he told me Bethel was hiring a library assistant. "It would be perfect for you." I imagined myself working during the day and taking classes at night with an employee discount.

On Halloween, one week after my birthday, I got my driver's license, I got the job at Bethel, and Eddie and I officially got engaged.

Over the next few months, everything continued in a predictable pattern, though I never seemed able to predict it. Eddie got close and pulled away. I alternated between feeling close to my family and feeling rejected by them. Each rejection from my family pulled me closer to Eddie. Each rejection from Eddie pulled me closer to my family. The back-and-forth of my allegiance was dizzying. Right when I felt secure in one camp, something would happen that—when taken together with the litany of hurts—would feel like the last straw of their alienation.

By April, I decided to go to Burnside Bible College in Portland, Oregon, the college that Eddie had shown me the pamphlet for that first night in his cabin. We planned on getting married and going together, but Eddie never filled out the paperwork.

On the phone, he said, "Maybe you should just go alone." Then, "You deserve the best. I don't want you to wait for me." Then, "I'll be so mad that you are living my dream." Then, "A friend of mine told me you were untrustworthy that summer. I should have listened to her. You're going to go off to Burnside and get another guy and sleep with him just to get back at me. It's what you do. You seduce men."

I pulled my robe a little tighter around my pink flannel pajamas.

"Meanwhile," he continued, "I've been waiting for you for two years."

If anything, I'd been waiting for Eddie for two years. Waiting for him to commit to me without reservation. Waiting for him to find his passion. Waiting for him to become the man I wanted him to be, not the man he was. If he could reach his full potential, he'd be able to hold down a job and hold his anger in check. He'd be able to release his hatred of women. I knew he wanted to change, but I wasn't sure he could. I thought of my dad and how, surely, he hadn't wanted to abuse my mom. But he couldn't change either.

In July, I wrote in my diary, "I don't want to be engaged. I don't think I love him. I think I am addicted to his manipulative talk. I want to get away. I want to run. I don't like his kisses. I don't think this relationship is right. I don't know how to leave." It dawned on me that I had moved from San Jose to escape my stepdad, and instead I found him again in Eddie. Eddie made fun of me—of the faces I made, of my hair, of my skinniness. He made fun of Black people, made fun of librarians, and called me and my family nerds. He sang a line from Prince's "Kiss"—"You don't have to be rich, to be my girl"—in a way that made fun of Prince's and my Blackness. In one of his usual mean streaks, he said he had only told me I was beautiful on faith, not conviction. I believed he didn't mean to hurt me, but he did just the same. The only thing my dad had made fun of me for was picking my nose, as he clandestinely snapped a photo. "Gotcha!" he had said, then laughed heartily.

One afternoon during my break at work, I went to the financial aid office on campus to ask about the FAFSA. Bethel didn't have night classes, so my dream of going to school there while working was long gone. But now Mom thought since I had a full-time job and was filing my own taxes, I wouldn't have to list Gary on the financial aid form and might be able to attend Bethel—or anywhere—as a full-time student.

The financial aid worker listened in her cubicle as I laid out my complicated family dynamic. Poor dad I never lived with. Well-off but poor-acting stepdad I didn't live with. Well-off grandma whom I did live with but was not my parent.

"I'm sorry," she said. "For these forms, it doesn't matter that you don't live with your parents. You have to put your mom and stepdad's information down until you turn twenty-four."

I took measured steps to walk, not run, from her cubicle. No matter how hard I worked, I could not escape the hold Gary had on me. His sole wish remained for me to get married, to transfer responsibility from him to a husband. Back in high school, when Mom had pointed to his income bracket on the FAFSA, it hadn't seemed real. Then he bought a plot of land in Oregon near his sister's house. Dirt that could have funded my education. Since he had paid for Nick's college, I thought maybe the issue was gender, but when Melanie grew up and enrolled, he paid for hers as well. I left the financial aid office and walked straight to the bathroom to sob in private. I kicked the handle to flush the unused toilet just to watch the water swirl away.

My full-time salary at Bethel couldn't afford me a room to rent, let alone an apartment. Later that month, I answered an ad for a cheap room in Hope Creek, the camp where Eddie had worked as a dishwasher. The listing, which I had found in the newspaper, was for a bed in a shared room with three other girls for two months. Though not permanent, it could afford me independence, at least for a little while. The girl who answered the phone was enthusiastic and asked to meet me in person.

The next day, I borrowed Grandma's car to check out the listing. As I stepped out of her black Mazda hatchback, I was met by a blonde girl and two brunettes. The blonde stepped forward as the one who had answered the phone. Immediately, her face fell.

"Hi, I'm Shannon," I said, smiling.

"Hi," the blonde answered, her mouth a straight line. "I guess I'll show you the room."

The three girls led me into a small, two-story country house and up the steps to the loft bedroom, just big enough for four beds and two dressers.

"This is it," the blonde said, with arms folded.

"Cool," I answered. "It looks nice. Is there an application I can fill out?"

"We'll call you if it seems like a good fit," she answered.

There was no question that I was not what she expected. I drove away painfully aware that I had sounded white on the phone. My inflection mimicked that of my mother, my grandmother, my aunt Deborah. It wasn't a choice but merely a reflection of my upbringing. The country home grew smaller in my rearview mirror, yet the image of the blonde girl's demeanor would never leave the glass, invisible but haunting like a ghost.

At the end of May, Jenna left her job as an au pair in France and returned to San Jose. On her first day back, she drove over the Santa Cruz Mountains to see me. Eddie and I borrowed Grandma's car, and I drove the three of us to Upper Crust Pizza on Mission Street. As I ate my giant slice of pepperoni pizza, I wondered if lightning could strike three times. Jenna and Eddie made eyes at each other across the table, just as she and Brian had last summer, and just as Brian and Amy had the winter before.

"So how did you like speaking French all the time?" Eddie asked. "Was it fun?"

"Oui," she said with a playful smile.

Jenna couldn't help but flirt. As we got older, her flirtations were often with boys who were already taken. I hadn't expected her to cross that line with Eddie, though. Along with Amy, we had been best friends for years. In high school, we took more walks than we could count through the hills in San Jose and up to our special spot that overlooked a quaint bucolic valley nestled against the mountains.

Moreover, though, I didn't expect for Eddie to return her flirtations.

"I'm sure you had all kinds of boyfriends over there," he said.

"Only one," she said, smiling. "I like American men better."

I looked over at Eddie. His cheeks were red and he looked down at his ham and pineapple pizza, then back up at Jenna. The two locked eyes.

"Yeah, American men are better," I said, attempting to break their spell.

"Excuse me," Eddie said. He got up from the table and walked toward the bathroom in the corner.

"Eddie is so sexy," Jenna said, once he was out of earshot.

Now it was my turn for a red face.

Jenna wasn't the only one who thought Eddie was sexy. Occasionally he worked as a model in bridal expos, through a job posting we found while walking along the back of the boardwalk. The casting assistant had taken in his dancing eyes, and the faint wisdom lines around them, his naturally tan skin, and his enticing smile. He had the body of a stereotypical, mythical Native American warrior.

That night after Upper Crust pizza, Eddie told me he had feelings for her. "She used to flirt with me last summer at Trinity Hills," he said. I remembered Eddie mentioning something before, but Jenna had a history of flirting, so it didn't stick. He had also hinted at liking her when she lived with me the previous year. Now I knew why he had always wanted to read her letters from France.

"Don't let me be alone with her," Eddie said that night. "I like her but I'm committed to you."

I spent the next two days sobbing uncontrollably while Eddie held me. He was the cause of my pain, but he was also the antidote. In my head I believed he loved me, but in my heart, I believed I manipulated him into loving me—that if I weren't in the picture, he and Jenna would be together. The dysfunctionality that bonded Eddie to me could also bond him to Jenna. She too had been raised by her grandmother and didn't know her dad. And she, even more than me, lacked a firm footing, with her grandma now deceased and her mom forever unable to parent her. Jenna looked more like what men I knew wanted: tall, slim but not stick thin like me, and, most important, she had the right skin and the right hair. Her race elevated her in my mind to someone who represented womanhood more than I ever could. To be white and from a dysfunctional family was one thing; to be Black and from a dysfunctional family was another.

The next month, Dad called, asking me to visit. Jenna said she and Eddie could join me, but I didn't want to watch them flirt. It would only add insult to the injury of Dad's erratic behavior, and I'd have nowhere to run.

By June, Eddie had unofficially moved in. He had no income and no place to go, so I had long since broken Grandma's rule about friends over on school nights. While her annoyance was palpable, she no doubt hoped Eddie's continued presence was just a phase.

Eddie told me he couldn't keep a job because he had been put on lithium when he was in the mental hospital a few years back. I imagined old brick or stone structures with doctors in white coats who injected substances that made eccentric patients go mad. I thought back to Eddie telling me that he used to stand on a street corner, unable to decide which way to go. I thought of Denise on the street corner with that glazed look in her eyes. How Dad did the right thing by taking her in and feeding her, even if he then did the wrong thing by putting his hands on her. I'd always felt close to madness, close to losing my voice forever, close to hiding in a closet and never coming out. Eddie felt like my madness personified. If I could tame him, maybe I could tame my own inescapable sadness and my inability to be happy with the cards I'd been dealt. If I could heal him, maybe I'd heal myself in the process. So in addition to my work at the library, I started working Saturdays at Trinity Hills to take care of us both.

With my Saturday job, Grandma seemed to appreciate how much dedication I was putting into work. One afternoon after I'd come home, she knocked on my door.

"I'm buying you a car," she said, beaming from the door.

She and Dennis drove me to a house in town where someone had advertised a car for $500. Instead, the man drew her attention to a $1,000 Saab, pointing to its sturdy doors and name-brand quality. After getting it checked out, Grandma handed the man a check. She and Dennis washed the car, got it smogged, and paid for the registration—all niceties I had come to not expect from anyone, especially since Gary wouldn't even pay for the hundred-dollar behind-the-wheel training my junior year. After Grandma purchased the Saab, she asked Gary to cover half, but instead he sent a check for the full amount. She felt like a good witch, able to put a spell on him that I couldn't. A week later I called Gary with a question. At the end of the call, he congratulated me on the car and said, "Bye, dear," the first time he had called me anything other than Shannon.

I still didn't trust Gary, but Grandma's kindness warmed over the parts of myself that had felt unloved and unseen. It healed my anger over getting a paperback for my birthday while Adam got a top-of-the-line mountain bike for his. Over Adam and Stephanie trying to outdo each other every Christmas, with increasingly bigger presents stacked increasingly higher around the tree. It wasn't the presents themselves, but the love the presents represented, and even the thought alone. Lately, I had felt only in the way—someone's offspring they had sprung off onto someone else, who also wanted to spring me off. But now I had a used gray sports car that hummed like an airplane as I made my way down the freeway. A car that had been bought for me specifically.

Then, my precarious position toppled again. "He can't stay here anymore," Grandma said on a Saturday morning. "I got up to use the bathroom in the middle of the night, and Eddie was taking a shower. I need my house back. And if you can't do that, then you need to leave." I wondered how my grandma could accept Stephanie but not Eddie—why Uncle Adam could have a live-in partner but not me.

Before long, Eddie was sleeping in my car, promising to pay me rent. And, soon after, I was sleeping there with him. We parked up on Spring Street, the steep street that led up to Pogonip park and my beloved bench overlooking the city. The incline proved too uncomfortable, so the next night we settled on West Cliff Drive, the winding road that followed the ocean. Grandma's gift of the car had no doubt been meant as a gift of freedom. Instead, I tethered myself even tighter to what she saw as my downfall. Her rejection of Eddie felt like a rejection of me—an extension that I felt showed parts of me that she didn't want to see: my fatherless-ness, my brownness, my working-classness. If he didn't belong on the quiet street of doctors and real estate agents and all manner of educated white folk, then neither did I.

One night, as the waves crashed peacefully in the otherwise still set-ting, we heard a car zoom past, screeching as it maneuvered each corner, and then all went eerily silent. Eddie and I emerged from the car and followed the winding walkway until we discovered the vehicle—a Jeep—overturned onto giant rocks near the waves. A group of people—likely from the expensive homes on the other side of the narrow street—were already gathered at the crash site. Eddie walked determinedly into the fray and located the survivors, checking to see if they were injured or otherwise shook up. He sat on the edge of the walkway with the young passengers and driver until the ambulance came. I sat next to him, proud that he cared so much about these strangers.

———————

In an attempt to give myself a bed again, I scoured the want ads for a place to live and found a room to rent in a home for just over half my monthly salary. I saw the place and promised to sign the contract but couldn't bring myself to pay for what I already had at Grandma's—a room to rent in someone else's family home, forever the appendage to someone else's life. Grandma, of course, hoped I'd choose her over Eddie all along and called the woman to explain my change of heart. But I couldn't quit Eddie. We continued to sleep on West Cliff Drive. Each morning, I'd awaken to my battery-powered alarm clock on the dash. The sun would peek in to the front seats, where Eddie and I reclined, facing the morning welcome of the comfortingly constant, gently crashing waves. I'd return to Grandma's to shower before making my way to work in the mountains. On my way home, I'd check my new PO box at Trinity Hills—a way to tie myself to the place I felt I could *be* myself, even if I couldn't afford to live there.

By August, the household was immersed in preparations for Stephanie and Adam's wedding and their upcoming move to Seattle so Adam could start work at Amazon. Grandma wanted me out by January and came around to the idea of Burnside Bible College, no doubt recognizing that an eleven-hour distance was the only way to get me away from Eddie. Stephanie had recently told me that financial aid would grant loans to anyone, regardless of income. Her words opened up the possibility of college in a way I never knew existed. Burnside wasn't yet accredited (though would be later), so the tuition was tantalizingly in my reach. While Grandma had come around, Mom still wasn't interested, over-whelmed by the responsibilities required to get through each day. In what I saw as a noble gesture, Grandma offered to clean Mom's house if she filled out the financial aid forms.

All my life I'd been put on hold while my mom got on with hers. Aunt Deborah once told me about Mom's political activism in the years before and after I was born—how she passed out fliers during Cesar Chavez's grape boycott in 1965, how she marched with farmworkers in 1966—but she did none of that now. She seemed unaffected by the world around her and didn't participate in civic events, especially ones geared toward people like me. It was as if I were a phase in her life, and the phase was over. I didn't know she stopped because the 1970s had felt unhinged and dangerous to her, with police brutality and Patty Hearst.

On a Saturday in September, Gary and my sister, Melanie, now seven, came over while Mom went to Stephanie's bridal shower. Gary plopped in front of the TV to watch *This Old House*, and Melanie and I escaped to the Capitola Mall. Aside from holidays, and sometimes not even then,

I hadn't seen Gary since I moved out after high school. Being in the same room with him was like turning the crank of a jack-in-the-box: I never knew when he'd pop out his shell and burst forth with a bang, causing shock waves that upset whoever was nearby. When Mom got back from the bridal shower, Gary decided to take her and Melanie to McDonald's. Melanie wanted me to go along, and I couldn't say no to her pleading eyes and her little hand that held mine. I wanted as much time with her as possible. When we got to McDonald's, Gary said the line was too long and that they would just go home. Melanie had an age-appropriate temper tantrum; she didn't want to say goodbye. Gary began yelling and pulled Melanie into the car. Mom then screamed at Gary. Anger bubbled up inside me and had nowhere to go except out my eyes. I wiped away tears as I made my way back to my own car.

The next day, my mind kept flashing back the look on Melanie's face pressed against the car window as they drove away.

It brought to mind the time I left for Wednesday youth group as Melanie stood crying in the doorway. My heart had broken as Amy and I pulled away in her car. I had feared leaving her with Mom asleep in the back room before her night shift at the care home, and with Gary, who had a habit of falling asleep sitting up on the couch or busy in the backyard working in his garden. Three-year-old Melanie was too young to care for herself. She could have gotten into anything, or hurt herself, or wandered into the street. Later that night I called from a pay phone and was relieved to hear Mom on the other end.

Now Melanie and I had been separated again, and my heart ached for both her and my mother. But for all the difficulties I had in Grandma's house, it separated me from my family's dysfunction—with Gary at the root—in a way I couldn't return to.

The night before Stephanie and Adam's wedding, I sat alone in my room, made impersonal by my packed boxes going nowhere and Grandma's insistence that it be neatly arranged for the aunts, uncles, and cousins coming to stay the night. Grandma thought I'd stay in my car at West Cliff, but a wedding overrode my desire to escape, even if it left me unsettled in a way I couldn't understand. Adam snuck into my room on his way out the door for the dress rehearsal. He sat next to me on the bed and wrapped his arms around me in a silent promise that he would always be the man I could look up to. The next day, he and Stephanie married in a friend's backyard on a beautiful day much like that of my mom's wedding day. And just like with hers, the weather seemed to taunt me, creating such beauty on the day I would lose someone I loved.

———————————

A few days after the wedding, Stephanie and Adam left for Washington, Grandma and Dennis went on vacation, and I quit my job. Eddie had dislocated his shoulder, and even though it was a common problem from an old injury, I wanted to take care of him. It felt more fulfilling than working full time for a paycheck I couldn't even live off of outside of Grandma's house.

During one of Eddie's routine breakups, I decided he was no longer allowed to read my journal. He said we had to start learning how to say no to each other, so I said no to him.

Just as he had feelings for Jenna, I had developed feelings for another guy at church. Eddie encouraged me to go to one of the guy's monthly game nights, while Eddie himself wanted to go on a date with Jenna. (Jenna said no; she was still on-again, off-again with Brian.)

I drove out to the guy's house and heard laughter on the other side of the door. The laughter felt so unencumbered, emanating from young people I was sure had mothers and fathers who guided them and provided for their futures. Laughter from young people who didn't sleep in cars on West Cliff Drive and wake up to alarm clocks on the dashboard. From people who didn't sleep on the beach under pieces of cardboard as Eddie and I once had at his insistence. Who hadn't woken up under those pieces of cardboard to hear a wealthy woman run up and down the steps of her fancy home or rental as she breathed in the morning air. The guy's friends likely knew what was in front of them. They pursued the dreams their parents had laid out for them—or didn't—but the dreams were there. Recently, I had found a box of old family photos in my closet, photos of my grandfather and my great-grandmother. I searched their features for a connection to my own and found none. Perhaps melanin erased any kind of resemblance. I wondered if my grandfather would have approved of me, had he lived. (He would have.)

And I wondered if the chasm between me and my living family felt as great to them as it did to me. It sure seemed so. What the door represented felt like an abyss, too deep to cross. I turned around, got in my car, and drove home.

In late November, I sat on my floor, looking through my box of photos from high school. The lives of my friends and me had felt so complicated, yet now I yearned for that simplicity. In high school I had imagined my first boyfriend, my first kiss, my first child. I hadn't expected that God would give me a broken man and that I would become broken as well.

"Yoo-hoo," Grandma said from my doorway. "I just talked to a counselor at Burnside for the past hour." Then she started to cry. "My heart is changed about you going away to a Bible college. I realize now that Christianity isn't all bad."

I smiled tentatively.

"And I convinced your mom to sign the loan papers," Grandma continued.

And just like that, a path lay before me for attending Burnside in spring session.

That night, I drove through the Santa Cruz Mountains to Mom's house in San Jose. I knocked on the door, and when Mom and Melanie answered, I stepped inside for the first time in three years.

Everything was as I had remembered it. They had replaced the worn-out sofa with a fuzzy red antique, but the girl in the picture whose eyes followed me across the room still hung above it. The fireplace warmed the living room. Melanie took my hand, and as we all walked to the bedroom, the heat wafted away.

"Where's Gary?" I asked, afraid of the answer.

"He's in the backyard."

Mom and I sat on Melanie's white trundle bed with delicate flower designs on the metal posts. I picked Melanie up and put her on my lap, and she twisted around and wrapped her arms around me.

"Here's the paperwork for the parents' loan," I said. It was a federal loan Mom would be responsible for; it would accompany the ones I had taken out myself. Without it, I wouldn't have the money to attend. I handed her the small stack of papers.

"OK, I guess I'm really doing this," she said. "Gary wouldn't want me to."

"Mom, I'm worried if you don't sign the papers, I'll become barefoot and pregnant in the kitchen with an unstable guy."

Mom knew intimately what such a life held. She hadn't been barefoot, but she and Dad had always been near destitute, with Dad accusing Mom of being a seductress just like Eddie did with me, though I hadn't shared with her that aspect of our relationship.

"OK," Mom said, with more determination. "I'm just not going to tell Gary."

I exhaled, my body relaxing more than it had in a long time.

A few days previously, I had paged through a recent journal. In the back, amid a bunch of empty pages, I had found an unfinished letter to Eddie:

> You know what I think? You and I, we are like those birds. It's time
> for us to fly south, but we never had parents to show us the way.

Finally, I did.

Mom flipped through the papers and signed on the dotted line. I had crossed the threshold of Gary the dragon and exited with a ticket to my new life.

18

GOOD-BYE TO ALL THAT
1998

I FLEW TO PORTLAND for spring semester with an old, rust-yellow leather suitcase that Grandma had used in the 1970s. Its loud color was long out of fashion, but I carried it proudly, a piece of family history.

I arrived on campus once again engaged to Eddie and wearing a promise ring with an emerald stone. One foot was firmly in my future, and the other chained to my past: I had jumped states but still remained tied to Eddie. His promises of getting help for his mental illness, which he still argued was the reason for his manipulation, made me believe our struggles were about to end. Deeper down, I felt too broken for anyone else, and still too addicted to our roller coaster. I wasn't ready to get off the ride, but I had taken the first step.

The Burnside campus sat on twenty-five acres in the heart of northwest Portland. Cherry trees dotted the commons and would bloom to a glorious pink that spring. I saw students with backpacks walking to administrative buildings, to the cafeteria, to the dorms, and soon to classes. I breathed in the homogeneity that I'd longed for all these years—a community enclave where young people lived and learned and dined together.

The student body reminded me more of my Teen Missions team than of my high school youth group. Like with Teen Missions, many of the students had been homeschooled in small towns. On any given day,

"My Heart Will Go On," *Titanic*'s theme song, emanated through open dorm rooms, though there was a campus-wide debate about whether it was appropriate to see Kate Winslet's breast. We were forbidden from seeing R-rated movies, female students weren't allowed to wear spaghetti straps or hems above a certain length, and the dorms had the curfew I had longed for in high school.

Burnside offered few majors and wasn't yet accredited, just like most Bible colleges. I had selected women's ministries in order to be a good wife and mother and to teach women about God through writing, though I wasn't yet sure how. All my life I had wanted to major in English, but Bible colleges didn't offer it, so I chose something as close as I could find.

My first week of school, I logged on to one of the three Macintosh computers in my dorm hall's common room after my shift at the campus library. I was pleased to see an email from Grandma. Reading through it, my face fell. Through the impersonality of a computer font, she said I was not to come back to her house, even for spring break. It was the second house I had lost, and I'd lost it twice. Before I left for Burnside, Grandma had said I'd be back soon. Now it all felt like a ploy to get rid of me. I faced my future at Burnside with a resolve to grow, but I also felt completely untethered once again.

In March, my grandma sent me a letter in which she addressed her decision.

> I wanted so much for your enrollment at Multnomah to give you the opportunity to explore a side of yourself that I felt was being neglected because of your immersion in your relationship with Eddie. I wanted for you to give yourself space between Eddie and yourself. I am delighted that you will not be down for spring break, much as I would love to see you. I wanted all along for you to give yourself at least until summer to find other places for your emotional energy and for intellectual exploration.

Her words healed the part of me that was ready to accept them, and angered the part of me that didn't want to move on.

That weekend, as the RA and I sipped Orange Juliuses in the mall's food court, she told me of her white friend with a Black son.

"How does it feel to be mixed race?" she asked.

I took a long slurp and then answered. "I'm proud of my identity, but I don't think couples should have mixed kids and then separate. The kids need both parents to feel complete. To get both sides of their culture."

It was a belief that would change in the future and was firmly tied to my own experience. I felt Dad's judgment for my not being more Black, for coming across as a white person with Black features. And yet, his judgment felt hypocritical because he was the one responsible for shaping me—or not. Television shows and the occasional visit weren't enough to teach me Black culture.

Later that night I entered the cafeteria to grab a snack and sat with a group of students I recognized from classes. One asked where another was from.

"I'm from Grants Pass," she said.

"That town has the highest KKK population in the country," someone replied.

I looked down at the table, my ears burning.

"I'm not proud of that," the girl said.

As I walked back to the dorms, I began to cry. I pictured the Klansmen in their white robes around burning crosses. My mom liked to tell me that when I was little, I saw a picture of Klansmen and started to cry. She said my dad had responded, "Don't worry, I won't let that boo get you." Now Dad felt not only miles away but in another dimension. I was at the highest echelon of Christian life but couldn't escape my difference, my inability to feel settled anywhere. I thought of the one other Black female student, a seminary student who worked full time. Though I didn't know her well, we were connected beyond any affinity I could make with my dormmates.

In mid-February, I took the Greyhound to Seattle for the long weekend. Uncle Eugene's company in the Bay Area had been bought by Microsoft, and he'd been acquired too. Uncle Adam had followed them north for his job at Amazon. Both families bought houses outside the city. Aunt Deborah and Uncle Eugene had a log house that sat off a winding two-lane highway, then ten minutes up a winding road, then up two unpaved roads. Their four-acre property was surrounded by dense trees. The sun felt eons away, and the air was crisper and colder than in Portland. Their house was technically in an unincorporated part of the county, a short drive from their borrowed zip code of Carnation, a farm town of just over two thousand residents in a secluded valley. The valley was as picturesque as a postcard, and the Murphys' living room with its fireplace was the epitome of cozy conviviality.

Over cups of hot chocolate, Aunt Deborah assured me I was welcome anytime, even during the summer break. I couldn't imagine being even farther away from Eddie. But if I had to be, Carnation wasn't a bad option. I had secretly imagined becoming part of my aunt and uncle's household for as long as I could remember. I imagined what my life would be like with two "parents," and one of them an at-home parent at that. But I couldn't get too comfortable. The rug had been pulled out from under me too many times before.

A few days after my trip north, Jenna called me.

"Eddie and I kissed," she said quietly. I continued to listen as the room spun. "Brian brought his new girlfriend to Graceland," she said of the college offshoot of Santa Cruz Bible. "Eddie and I sat in his truck in the parking lot."

Eddie's grandma had passed the truck down to him just days before I left for Burnside. I had driven Eddie around for three years, and now here he was escorting Jenna around and kissing her in the front seat.

"How long did you kiss?" I asked. I felt out of body, almost like I had willed this to happen by my fear of this exact scenario.

"I dunno," Jenna replied. "I guess just two minutes or something."

"Two minutes! That's a long time." My mind immediately went to everything that could be done in two minutes. Nuking a plate of dinner, impatiently waiting for the ding. Getting through commercials that felt like they lasted forever. Waiting for a light to turn green at a busy intersection. Thinking of me and pulling away.

"Will you still be my friend?" Jenna pleaded. "You're my only friend. I don't want to be alone."

With that, I hung up the phone. Jenna had visited me the week before I had left for Burnside and told me to let go of Eddie. "You deserve someone better," she had said. When Eddie and I started getting close again, and she emailed him to ask him not to call me so much. Now it all felt like a ploy to get Eddie for herself. Though it's easier to look out for your friends.

In the common room, I clicked on a new email from Jenna. She said she was sorry and hadn't been a good friend. I returned to my dorm room, anger coursing through me with no outlet. I kicked the drawer of the dresser and threw my desk chair on the ground. It wasn't the first time my anger had flown out of my body. Back in September, Eddie and I stood on the beach and were taking in the glittering stars above the water when he told me he wanted to date Jenna. I felt tricked, like a plaything, like someone with whom he had merely bided time. Before I knew it, my hand flew across his face. My demureness kept it from being a strong swing, however, and my slap landed limply, with the crashing wave simulating the force I wished I had mustered.

Soon after kissing Eddie, Jenna went off to the military, training to be a nurse. I didn't have to worry about her kissing Eddie again. I judged her for kissing men in relationships, but I hadn't expected that she would cross that line with my fiancé. It made it easy to blame her almost entirely for seducing him. Just as I still blamed myself. As if we gave him permission to act out his naturally lustful desires when, without us, he would have remained pure. Eddie said Jenna didn't want a relationship. The audacity of his request that she be his girlfriend while engaged to me didn't register to me, only that she had kissed him with no intention of getting together. "Now I know you love me because you stood up for me," he said on the phone. "You defended me for being violated." He equated kissing Jenna to looking at porn on the internet, dirty and satanic. I clung to him even more tightly, sure we had passed the most difficult spiritual test.

———————————

One evening Tracy, an acquaintance, and I stood in the dairy aisle of Fred Meyer, the local grocery-department store. My friend Matt, who had driven us, was off in the electronics department. Matt had been subtly flirting with me for the past month, holding his gaze past the friend limit during conversations in the cafeteria. He had the look of an all-American boy, with short, slightly tousled light brown hair. Unlike many at Burnside, he came from a broken home, with a single mom who scraped by. He drove a clunky VW van, a smaller version of Grandma's old Volkswagen camper. Matt felt within reach, the possibility of him upsetting the balance of my devotion to Eddie.

In Fred Meyer, Tracy opened the door to get milk.

"It's a bummer I won't be home when my parents call," Tracy said. "But they'll understand because they know about Matt."

Earlier, Matt too had expressed concern about her missing the call because of this outing, which I had requested. I wondered what it would be like for my mom to call at a set time, and to do so sitting side by side with some theoretical father of mine. I also wondered what it would be like to have a guy worried about me missing it.

"Oh," I said. I stared at the next display over, trying to act nonchalant. "Are you guys dating or something?"

"I don't know," she answered. "I don't really know what's going on." Tracy shrugged as if she were tossing the idea off her uninterested shoulders. But I knew she was just dying for clarity. I thought back to my other outings with Matt and her, and realized I always sat in the back of the car, while she was always in the front.

This short conversation in the dairy aisle felt like a last straw in my feelings of belonging—it spoke to my absence of schedule-keeping parents who wanted to talk to me, and the absence a caring guy who saw that I had caring parents, the lack of being chosen by a man and loved by family. Guys had overlooked me at youth group, at Teen Missions, at Trinity Hills, and at Bethel. Even Amy had said that Northwestern College in Iowa wouldn't have been right for me. We had flipped through her yearbook and I had noticed white face after extremely white face, most of whom, she said, had come from farm towns nearby. They were even more sheltered than the students at Burnside. But Bible college was supposed to be God's chosen path for me—the place where my life would match the novels of Christian heroines who find their God-given mate in their new surroundings.

My thoughts were taken back to Southern California, to the long drive to Disneyland, to Brian and Amy in the front seat, and to me, in the back of the van, the extra, invisible guest. The pain of it all ran down my cheeks in Fred Meyer, before I could quickly wipe the tears away. I thought of myself as a little girl, watching my mom flirt with a man who would come to rule my life, a man who would separate me from my mother's protection, who would place me on the outside of the circle.

I thought of the house in Santa Cruz that I called home but wasn't. I remembered everyone standing in the backyard while being introduced to a distant relative at Thanksgiving. I saw the new cousin's eyes scan the extended family around him, separated into clusters of immediate families—mothers, fathers, children. I saw his eyes come to me, the darker one without a darker parent to explain it. He looked puzzled, perplexed, as if he were seeing a goose among chickens. "She is not part of the circle," his eyes said. I smiled, pretended that I did not know my difference. Pretended that I was indeed a chicken among chickens.

I thought of the community group of a church I attended before Santa Cruz Bible. On a Saturday in the wealthy host's house, a guy whom I thought was attractive pursued another girl after the meeting, asking about her high-up missionary father. "Do you need a ride home?" he had asked her. But she didn't need one. Her father had provided her with a car. The guy did not ask me to be a front seat girl. My father had been in prison, had lived in a shelter, had always been beaten down by life. Did that make him any more lacking in love? Did that make me any less of a catch? Did that mean I was destined to be a backseat girl?

As I drifted off that night, I thought about my dad molesting Denise, and the tears came again, this time with no need to wipe them away. When I fell asleep, I dreamed that Eddie came to Burnside and tried to propose at his friend's suggestion. In my dream, instead of feeling excited, I felt fear.

The next day, I had renewed confidence about my worth. After all, during our trip to Fred Meyer the day before, Matt had said he wished he had a crate in the middle of the front seats so I wouldn't feel so isolated in the back. Maybe Tracy was making a mistake in thinking she was more important to Matt. Either way, in the friendliness of daytime, I knew I was worthy of being a front-seat girl. I just didn't know if worthiness would ever translate into actuality. I was twenty-one now and older than most of my dormmates. A carton of milk that was soon to expire.

At the beginning of the semester, Eddie had encouraged me to talk to someone about his mental illness. Little did he know, this request would result in regular sessions with Dean Margaret, who slowly fostered in me a sense of independence and a view of Eddie that I could trust. Through her, I found books in the library about codependency, furiously underlining sentences and paragraphs that spoke to my experience. Eddie and I had gone to codependency classes back at Santa Cruz Bible, but they were led by laypeople. We followed workbooks on how to curb our own issues in order stay together. Now, through these library books, I learned success wasn't measured by weathering the storm. Like Portia Nelson wrote in "Autobiography in Five Short Chapters," instead of falling into the hole on the sidewalk each time I walked up to it, I could alter my course and go around.

In the cafeteria in March, a friend said she was driving to California for spring break and asked if I wanted a ride to see my family.

"I can't even stay at their house!" I exclaimed, then immediately regretted it. I had learned not to talk about my dad, and now I had to learn not to talk about Grandma.

Tony, a Mexican American friend who knew a bit about my family life, picked up on my discomfort. "So tell me about your extended family," he said.

I proceeded to lay out my story.

"Were you depressed when you came here?" Tony asked.

"Yes," I said.

"Are you still depressed?"

"Yes."

I answered because I felt like I had to, but as I did so, it became clear that he wanted to know about my life merely because it was an interesting story. In that moment, I understood that I had a habit of being so open because I thought people could save me: from my dad, from my stepdad, from my Santa Cruz house, from Eddie. Being saved was a core tenet of the church. It was in the sermons we heard, in the songs we sang. Jesus was our savior, not just from the evils of the world, but from inside ourselves. Self-sufficiency had no jurisdiction.

Eddie's phone calls vacillated between multiple times a day to almost none at all. If he sensed I wasn't swayed by his emotions, the calls grew more frequent; when he knew my heart was once again fragile, he grew near silent. Just as I had recently seen in an episode of *Dr. Quinn, Medicine Woman*, where she and the community tried to help someone detox off drugs, I felt like I was being purged of Eddie at Burnside, even while I wanted to hold on to this old world. I didn't yet believe *he* was bad, but that my unhealthy addiction to him was, the way I needed the confirmation of his love each day to function. I convinced myself that if I could just hold on less tightly, loosen my addiction to Eddie, our relationship would be healthy.

Over time, Eddie remained in the background of my mind for longer stretches. I became absorbed with classes and new friends. While I started getting stronger, feeling his power lessen, and coming back into my body, increasingly unencumbered, I also still felt I was the main source of our problems. I was grateful when he said he needed to love me despite my actions. It was a mindset that had always been reinforced by my family and by Christianity. We were to come to Christ broken in order to be healed of our selfish natures.

As I majored in women's ministry, college became almost intensive therapy, with classes like Social Factors of the Family and Spheres of Relationships. The classes placed a mental emphasis on my own family and how I could begin to heal those wounds. I wanted to communicate with my dad while doing so safely, to keep him part of my life without the threat of drunkenness or guns or strange women in hospital gowns. I started writing Dad letters, aiming for one a month.

Between the classes and my visits with Dean Margaret, and the codependency books I found in the library, I began mending my relationships with both my dad and my grandma. Grandma and I began to exchange heartfelt emails. I opened up to her about the difficulty of being measured against my cousins, and she began to understand how she had compared me to them unfairly. And, in March, I got my first letter from Dad since I was a kid:

> *I felt (feel) I may not be around maybe (10) years . . . I have another settlement forthcoming, and when it does, it will be earmarked specifically for you. . . . When I start working again I'll be able to send you money on a monthly basis. Keep your eyes*

on the prize and know that you will persevere. Again, I remind
you how proud I am of you. . . . Hit the books and always keep
yourself out of harm's way both on and off campus.
    With much love,
    Your Father,
    Robert C.

The letters weren't much different from when I was younger, but
now that I was twenty-one they took on more meaning. I saw the desire
between the lines of text that I knew would not materialize. I knew I
would not receive checks each month. But I was also aware that he longed
to send them. The letters also included each new place of employment:
administrator of a satellite office of the Sacramento County office on
aging; paralegal to eight hundred clients of the Women's Civic Improvement Center. Without context, his job titles felt like ethereal worlds that
existed in some other dimension. I had no idea what he did each day, or
whom he helped, or how he helped them. But the letters felt meaningful
anyway—something tangible I could hold in my hand.

———————

Matt and I grew closer as the semester went on. He had in fact been
interested in Tracy. After a couple months, she ended it. He shared
his heartache over their breakup, and I shared mine over staying with
Eddie. One night we stood in line for an intimate concert by the biggest Christian artist of the time—Michael W. Smith—along with a few
other students from Burnside. Matt and I were extra quiet during the
long wait on the city sidewalk. We hadn't seen each other in person
in a few days.

A couple weeks earlier, Matt and I had played a duet in the practice
room, he on the piano and me on the violin. We planned to prepare it
for class, but after practice, Matt had decided we shouldn't risk bonding
over music. He saw the obvious attraction between us, he said, but he
wanted to steer me away from Eddie, not toward himself. It was a refrain
I'd heard many times before, so many in fact that they all began to bleed
together. I didn't know where Eddie ended and Matt began—if God had

made me unworthy of Matt because Eddie had made me damaged goods in God's eyes. All I wanted was for someone to hold me. Instead, I stood precariously on my own feet.

Matt kept his promise of friendship and called most evenings, genuinely interested in the latest Eddie saga. He knew how those sagas went because of his mother's past husbands. Now we stood in line, shy about all we had expressed on the phone.

After the concert, Matt took me out to eat, let me pick the place (Taco Bell), and paid for my food. Afterward he took me on a drive around Portland. Without a car, my Portland experience was mostly limited to campus and Fred Meyer. Now I saw different parts of downtown, lit up against the night sky.

"You still have the card on your visor," I said, pointing to the handmade birthday card I'd given him on which I listed attributes for each letter of his name.

"I kept it up there even while I was dating Tracy," he said. "It meant a lot to me."

Once we found ourselves at the Portland State campus, Matt taught me how to drive his van in the parking lot. He guided me from between the two front seats as I drove us home, just as Brian had guided Amy on the way back from Disneyland. As we talked, I learned Matt believed in tithing, in balancing his checkbook, and in being honest about his tips as a waiter. Completely opposite of Eddie, he thought it was wrong to ask a girl for money and thought the man should be the breadwinner.

I pictured a future with Matt that resembled the one between Aunt Deborah and Uncle Eugene—he the worker, she the homemaker, both literally making beautiful music together. It was an image I always held up as the epitome of a happy family. Parents helping their children with homework at the kitchen table. Fostering in them all manner of journeys into the worlds of their imaginations. All the Murphys lacked, in my opinion, was a devotion to God. The missing ingredient I would bring to my own domesticity.

Back at campus, Matt called me. "I had so much fun with you tonight, but I don't want to give you the wrong idea going into summer."

"OK," I said, sucking in my breath. "Does that mean that you're afraid I'll take your friendliness as being more than a friend?"

"No," he said. "Your perceptions weren't wrong. A relationship *is* forming between us. You have all the things I want in a woman."

"You have all the things I want in a man too," I said.

Matt continued. "You totally understand me, and you're a great listener. But I feel like God is telling me that it isn't the right timing. Our plans may not be his plans. I was wrong to have had that date with you tonight. It *was* a date. I was wrong to have led you on. We can't spend time together anymore."

I took a deep breath. "Would this be temporary or permanent?"

"I don't know," Matt said. "I just have to obey God in this area and see where he leads."

I watched boys and girls pair up all around me at Burnside, and my feelings of unworthiness compounded on themselves. I wouldn't have the gentle guide, the provider, the partner I could count on. Eventually I told my roommate Michelle everything as we walked around campus. Michelle said that Matt had tried to "save" another student, just like he'd tried to save me, perhaps stuck in his own cycle of wanting to save his mom from bad husbands. His words of promising to come to my rescue if I were in danger now made me feel like a project instead of someone worthy enough to be saved in their own right.

And Eddie began to feel more dangerous.

One day toward the end of the semester, I opened my email to find a message from Eddie so threatening that I quickly closed it, but not first without forwarding it to Matt. Someone needed proof of Eddie's ominousness, and I did not have the space to hold it. All that has remained in my memory was knowledge that Eddie saw me unfit to live in this world. I wanted to follow Matt's advice of breaking things off completely with Eddie, but I didn't know if I was strong enough. I didn't know whether to think him dangerous or harmless. Whether I should show him mercy and begin a friendship or cut off all communication with him immediately.

On the phone, Eddie said he was coming to visit. I didn't agree to the visit but I didn't refuse; I highly doubted he would actually come. The Greyhound required money and forethought, and I knew firsthand his troubles with both.

Eddie continued to call a lot. He wanted me back, wanted another chance, but I told him I didn't have another chance to give him. Then he began to beg and plead. Out of my mouth came "No. No. No." Eddie always said his actions were connected to his mental illness. Now, when I learned how to peel back those layers, I saw he was also just a jerk.

His mental illness hadn't caused him to disagree when I said fathers who wouldn't let their white daughters marry Black men were racist. It hadn't caused him to say he thought I was beautiful on faith but not on conviction. And for the part of me that still loved him, I knew letting go was the most loving thing I could do. He couldn't break the cycle, but I could.

A couple days later, my stomach was in knots at the library and I didn't know why. Some vague forewarning about something in my future. After work, I walked into the cafeteria. My eyes automatically zoomed in to the back of a head a knew too well. Eddie's head. He nervously ran his hand through his fluffy hair, with his curls bouncing back each time.

My gaze shifted and I spotted friends at the next table. I calmly walked over to my friend Alexandra and put my hand on her shoulder.

"Eddie's here," I said.

Tony, my friend who had asked if I was depressed, gave me a concerned look. "Where is he?" he asked. "I'll beat him up for you."

I couldn't tell if he was serious, or even if he knew who Eddie was, but the protective offer made me cry.

"Do you want to leave?" Alexandra asked. "Do you want me to come with you?"

"Yes."

At that moment, Eddie turned around and spotted me. Once I saw him seeing me, my gaze didn't lift from the floor. He held too much power, like a wolf in lamb's clothes. I turned and ran. Alexandra met me out in the commons and then we escaped to a room to pray. I knew I had to talk to him. To confront the wolf.

When we finished praying and returned the cafeteria, we ran right into him.

"Hi," Eddie said, smiling.

"Hi." I couldn't help but smile back, a reflex I didn't know how to stop. Or maybe because I wanted to deflect the intensity of the moment, like speaking to an animal in soft tones to prevent it from attacking.

"You look good," he said. He held out his hand. "My name is Eddie. What's yours?"

The trick, which had worked on me once before, now made me sick. Nothing could erase the torment of the past three years.

"I don't want to play that game."

Without my even asking, Tony walked up and offered to walk Alexandra and me back to the dorms. "I like hanging around you anyway," he said.

My dorm section was going out for ice cream, giving me the perfect excuse to leave campus. Surrounded by other girls, some who knew my boyfriend saga and others who didn't, I felt a swath of protection—and even a smidge of joy. I was beginning to feel as strong as I had back in my senior year of high school, surrounded by friends who at the time were such pure connections that it felt like nothing would ever go wrong. Most of these girls didn't have boyfriends and looked to each other for comfort and connection. Bonding over servings of ice cream melted away the heaviness of my loss of innocence.

Later that night, Alexandra and I worked out in the gym, a practice we had taken up off and on throughout the semester. Working out always brought me back to my father, to lifting dumbbells and doing push-ups before bed. Whenever I worked my arms, I felt the Manuel blood course through me. Blood of warriors and of slaves who had lived through centuries of oppression. But when I stepped off the stair climber, I felt the air drain from my body and slowly collapsed to the floor in exhaustion. I waved off Alexandra's concern and let her finish her workout. As my shock began to disappear, tears took its place.

So far I had made it through the evening unscathed. Eddie hadn't found me at the gym, and he wasn't waiting for me at the dorms when we returned. I wanted my ability to walk freely to continue, to not be locked inside because of the monster looming outside. Plus, I had books to return and the library was closing in fifteen minutes.

My path to the library was straight, and the stars kept me company, though my head turned this way and that as I peered into blind spots. Once safely inside, I stood at the checkout counter and erased underlinings from *No Longer the Hero: The Personal Pilgrimage of an Adult Child* by Nancy LeSourd.

Then Eddie walked in. I continued erasing as he walked up to me.

"Hi," he said.

"Hi," I said with restraint.

"Are you OK?"

"Yes."

As we spoke, I didn't look up. A dorm friend appeared then, as if from nowhere, staring absentmindedly at the card catalog while keeping an ear attuned to the scene nearby. "Can I talk to you?" Eddie asked.

"Sure," I said, carefully avoiding his eyes, knowing I needed to get the conversation over with so we could both move on. Andrea continued to eye us from the card catalog.

Eddie got down on one knee and handed me a sterling silver ring from his own finger—I had long since put away the emerald ring he gave me before Burnside. "Will you marry me?"

The audacity of his question bolstered my resolve even more. I looked him squarely in the eyes and said, "No." I said no with the power of the books in the bin behind me, cheering me on for breaking the pattern of Shannon the Adult Child. Shannon who clung to broken things because they were familiar. Shannon who was more comfortable with chaos than calm.

Eddie stood up and left, and my friend and I walked out together arm in arm.

"Shannon, do you know what you just did?!" my friend said. We squealed under our breaths into the night sky.

Later that night, a student who worked as a security guard called me. "Do you know someone named Eddie?" he asked.

"Yes," I said. I hadn't escaped Eddie. At least not yet.

"A student said they saw someone acting strange in the coffeehouse," he said. "Kind of out of control. Rambling to no one about someone named Shannon. So I went over there and walked him back to the guesthouse, and he asked if I knew you. Is everything all right?"

He asked with such concern that my tears fell again. "We were together for three years and it was an abusive relationship." It was the first time I had uttered those words out loud. Maybe even silently too.

"You don't have to tell me," he said.

"No." My voice cracked as I struggled to continue. "I want to tell you so you know."

"Do you want us to keep an eye on him for you? And make sure he stays away from you?"

"Yes, please," I said.

"If you want, I can tell the head security officer your situation."

"Thank you."

Shortly after, a friend from the dorms, on duty in her security guard uniform, knocked on my door.

"Jimmy told us all about your situation," she said. "Do you want security to kick Eddie off campus?"

"I'm not sure," I said. "I don't know if that will make things better or worse." Eddie might get into my building, even though it was locked for the night. Or he might tell everyone we did everything but actual sex back in Santa Cruz. He might prove to everyone that I didn't deserve to be here. I needed to remove him from my life in the least dramatic way possible. But so far, my efforts hadn't worked.

Eddie called later that night from the guesthouse.

"Can you meet me for lunch tomorrow?" he asked.

"OK," I said. As I hung up the phone, I immediately regretted my answer. I decided I would take my roommate and another friend along with me. But about five minutes later, we got another call. I answered the phone. No one was on the other end. Then it rang again, and my roommate answered. "No one was there," she said as she hung up, her eyes wide with alarm. "There was just heavy breathing and laughing." We told our resident assistant and director and unplugged the phone.

The next morning, a security guard escorted me to class. I didn't feel nervous, but my mouth was drier than it had ever been. On the way back to the dorms, another security guard escorted Matt, my roommate, and me to Dean Margaret's office, where I left a letter asking if she could make Eddie leave. Then the guard walked us back to the dorms.

That afternoon, Dean Margaret called and said she and an admissions counselor talked to Eddie before escorting him off campus with the promise to never return. Later that day in her office, the dean lifted her shoulders and sighed in relief as she dropped them back down. "I watched Eddie move through all his stages," she said. "Elation, anger, tears. He kept trying to steer the conversation back to you, but I kept it focused on him."

I nodded.

"I told him it's his choice, whether to be happy," she continued. "And you've made that choice for yourself now."

It wouldn't be until 2024 that I'd realize his mental illness had little to do with his abuse. My sister told me that when she was six, Eddie said she must be jealous that he was with me and not with her. And in a phone call with Crystal from Trinity Hills, who did in fact remain a good friend just like I had blurted out when I first met her, I asked her about Eddie. "He always made me uncomfortable," she said on the phone. With prodding, she said cautiously, "He was a predator." My eyes welled instantly and I felt the color drain from my body. What I thought had been a relationship never was. Eddie had preyed on the youth and innocence of Sarah and me at Trinity Hills. He used classic religious abuse tactics to control me.

In the coming days, weeks, months, there were no phone calls. No pages. No emails. I had walked around the hole in the sidewalk to the other side.

19

THE SUN ALSO RISES
1998

At the end of the semester, I flew to Columbus, Nebraska, to take a summer biology class with Amy at her local community college. It was my second time in the Midwest after having been bridesmaid for Amy's "colorful" wedding in Iowa.

Amy's town of twenty thousand people was as flat as the land around it. The one small incline on a two-lane road was referred to as "the Hill." Amy, pregnant with her second daughter, lived with her husband and their toddler in a white, two-story apartment complex. Through their red door was a sparsely furnished two-bedroom and the domesticity I longed for. I shared a room with Amy's daughter, her blonde hair, blue eyes, and unencumbered laughter a comforting reminder of the years I had spent raising my sister. On free afternoons, I took Amy's daughter on walks around the cookie-cutter neighborhood. Here, even more than in San Jose, I looked like the babysitter—a role that felt as comfortable as an old shoe. Which, incidentally, is what I wore.

A week or two into my stay, I took a job as a janitor in a needle factory down the main road. The factory employed much of the town, who worked long shifts to keep the factory going night and day, 365 days a year. In one room, employees sported all-white coverall suits as they stood in front of conveyors. I removed the giant filters near the ceiling with an extra-long pole and replaced them with fresh white ones, then watched them turn black in the few seconds before I left the room for my next duty.

For the Fourth of July, I joined Amy and her family at a parade in Platte Center—a village of about 350 people. We sat on the edge of the sidewalk with our feet in the street. Next to us was the one Black family I saw in attendance. The parade was the smallest I had ever seen, with tractor trailers carrying cattle as a main attraction. Partway through the parade, a man in a flannel shirt, jeans, and cowboy boots rode through on a horse. He carried a giant flag, the design of which looked familiar but I couldn't quite place. "Rebel without a cause!" a man shouted from the sidelines. The man on the horse looked over at the Black family and me. "I've got a cause all right." The Black family and I looked at each other, then to the man on the horse, then down to the ground. There was no mistaking the significance of his piercing stare, of the way his mouth curled up at the corners. The flag's message became clear.

Later that night, Amy and I sat at her large computer monitor and connected to the internet. The familiar dial-up singsong static came through the speakers. On the AOL search engine, we typed in keywords to research for our biology papers. When Amy left to grab a snack, I typed "Confederate flag." Something told me that was what the man on horseback carried so proudly. Images popped up identical to the one I'd seen that day. On the computer screen, the blue X against the bloodred background screamed, "You do not belong here."

––––––––––

That summer, I was surprised to receive a forwarded letter from someone back at Burnside. One night before spring semester had ended, I had walked to a practice room only to find that I couldn't get the code to work. I saw a security guard doing rounds down a walkway nearby, and I flagged him down for help. Barry was just a couple inches taller than me, with straight brown hair that had premature flecks of gray, which he kept short in a 1960s, military-style flattop. He jiggled the knob to let me in.

"Is that a violin?" he asked.

"Yeah," I said.

"How long have you been playing?"

"On and off since fifth grade," I said.

He seemed suddenly aware that he had opened his mouth and asked questions, as if he weren't used to tainting the quiet night with language. "Well, have a good practice."

I ran into Barry a couple more times that semester and learned that he was nine years older than me, in his final year of seminary school, and would stay on the next year as a full-time graveyard security guard. After finals, I meandered through the campus bookstore and came across a display for graduation cards. I wondered whom I could give one to and landed on Barry. Before flying out to Nebraska, I slipped the card into his slot in the mailroom.

After a week or two, I received a letter from Barry, forwarded to Amy's from the mailroom. In near perfect handwriting in friendly blue ink, he spoke of the peaceful night sky during his graveyard shift. "Wow, he sounds just like you," Amy said as she looked over my shoulder. Our nightly viewing of M*A*S*H took on new significance; I saw Barry through the character Radar, the somewhat homely company clerk who embodies the straight man TV trope. He's the sole cool head in the army hospital unit. Barry and I continued to write over the summer; his letters followed me from Amy's home to the Murphys' until school started up again.

While at the Murphys', I learned from the car radio that Tiger Woods was in Redmond, near Carnation, for the PGA tournament. Buses and charters passed by each day as I drove to and from my temp jobs in the city. I had an overwhelming obsession to get a ticket for the tournament, even though I knew nothing about golf, and even though I knew it wouldn't happen. Each time I saw a charter bus pass, I pictured Tiger Woods spotting me on the tournament sidelines and falling for me at first sight. He was the first mixed-race man to make a big impression on the country, and thus the first celebrity that actually matched—or near matched—my racial makeup. This was before his infidelity scandals. He was a sports golden boy.

When fall semester started, my mind was a frenzy with how to make a living and support myself in the coming spring. My financial aid was running out for Burnside, and I didn't know how much longer I could hold on to my student status there. Mom had been making the parents' loan payments that had to begin right away but said she couldn't much longer. I didn't ask why but knew Gary still oversaw their money. Since the summer, I'd been thinking about pursuing an associate's degree in medical transcription, which Cabrillo offered back in Santa Cruz. I considered that, or taking the courses in Portland, though I wasn't sure how to pay for an apartment while going to school. I laid out my struggles for Dad. In September, I received a new letter:

> *Hello Shannon,*
> *Sorry not to have written sooner. Health problems have been occupying a portion of my life-style at a greater frequency.*
>
> *I'm having pulmonary difficulties that affect the breathing process. Some of the medications that have been prescribed have side effects such as fatigue and tremors.*
>
> *As you well know, I'm no stranger to tremors so I try to communicate by letter at stable times. . . . Your methods of pursuing higher education may, at times, seem to be random. There are powerful forces at play that are guiding you into a place higher than basic academics. Within that sphere you will develop into a person richer in the knowledge of life. I need to discuss this with you in depth. Let your intuitions guide you BUT reflect upon them periodically. Look hard at the forks in the road upon which you're traveling. At times you will note a need for directional changes. Think it thru!*
>
> *At the moment my mind is arush with the intensity of the raging elements being unleashed by nature in the current hurricanes and tornadoes. I will rest and recuperate at this time. I just spend a week in the hospital and I'm exhausted.*
>
> *Take care Baby Girl, your father loves you.*
>
> *Hope to hear from you and hopefully see you before the next century.*
> *Love*
> *Robert C.*

Dad's words were characteristically vague, but getting his letters felt like proof that I'd found a way to communicate safely. Through his familiar cursive, increasingly stilted from arthritis, he was able to express sentiments that had remained unspoken when we saw each other face to face—namely, his belief in my future. While he talked poetically, I wished he had more concrete advice. My books on codependency and adult children of alcoholics had taught me to identify that sweet spot between aching for what a parent cannot give and understanding the value of what they can. In a return letter, I wrote that though our relationship had been rocky, the older I got, the more I recognized the importance of having one. I still valued hearing from him.

Barry and I started spending time together as soon as fall semester started. We went to coffee shops, to movies, to hiking trails, to church. We discovered a shared love of literature, and poetry, and cats. We pored over the giant Writer's Market book, almost the size of a phone book, to find places to submit our written work. Barry seemed less conservative than some of the guys at Burnside. Charles Bukowski was his favorite author. He liked jazz and Dire Straits and didn't listen to Christian music. He wanted to go to a graduate seminary to become a drug and alcohol counselor. There was just one thing that held me back, that called to me from the recesses of my mind that my faith had taught me to ignore: I didn't find him attractive. His eyes were beady behind thick, circular glasses. He chewed his nails past the free edge. When not in uniform, he looked like he'd stepped out of the 1960s: collared shirt tucked into tight Wrangler jeans with a thick black belt; freshly shined, black military-style boots or oxfords. I didn't want to rip his clothes off. But he was the opposite of my father and Eddie, who were charming but ultimately destructive when you got too close.

"Maybe I'm not attracted to healthy men," I told Dean Margaret.

"Just give it time," she said.

Over the next month, as I told Barry about my past, his interest didn't waver. He learned about my codependent relationship with Eddie, about my dad's alcoholism, and even about Denise. He learned about Gary's rages. But nothing made him run.

At the end of October, Barry said he wanted to invite me over the next Saturday to talk about spending more time together. When Saturday arrived, he picked me up in his white Mazda Protegé and took me to the apartment he shared with a roommate. He led me to his immaculate room, which he said he cleaned just for me. Instead of a mattress on the floor, like at Eddie's cabin, there was a real bed, a desk, and a dresser—a grown-up's room. He warmed up water for peppermint tea and turned the radio to a jazz station. Barry motioned for me to sit on the bed while he took the comfy chair just across the small room. He told me of his interest, then laid out four points indicating why we should wait six months before officially dating.

"One," he said, lifting a finger for each point. "My last girlfriend and I broke up eight years ago, so I haven't dated in a long time. Two, I'm a staff member and you're a student, and there are probably rules about that. Three, I want to get myself more established to be able to provide for someone. Four, I was looking for someone for a long time and thought I would find them at Burnside, but it was harder than I thought. Now, just in the past year, I've been focusing more on writing and being single, and it's hard to switch gears all of a sudden."

I found his four points cute, and while his desire for six months had the faint aura of Eddie's instability, Barry had proven himself different in every way. He picked me up when he said he was going to. He opened the car door for me. He paid for almost every meal. He asked if I was too hot or too cold. He valued my opinions.

The next day after church, Barry took me to Powell's City of Books, a new and used bookstore that takes up an entire city block. We meandered through the ten rooms, silently taking in row after row of high shelves and the unique smells of our favorite pastime. I wanted to grab everything. Every world that existed between the covers of each book. I found the small multicultural section, which had three books about being biracial. I pulled out the one I hadn't read yet, a small, yellow book of essays called *Half and Half*. I turned it over and flipped through the pages, debating whether to buy it with the bit of money I had in the bank. Sensing my hesitation, Barry suggested we split the cost and read it together. His interest in my race didn't come from warped curiosity. He saw both sides of me in a way that other men hadn't. He was interested merely because my races made up who I was. And now he wanted to read about my identity with me.

That month, we read essays from the book when we met on the weekends. After we finished one essay, I got up the courage to ask him a question.

"Do you think your parents would mind if you dated a Black girl?"

It was a question that haunted me whenever I was interested in anyone, and it had proven a valid one. Eddie's grandma liked me after my visit to Hollister, but she worried about us having mixed children. She hadn't considered Eddie mixed: Mexican and white didn't count. It was the introduction of Blackness that made the concoction dangerous. Parents' fear of mixed children never seemed fair. I was already mixed. Was I not supposed to have come into this world?

"I don't think they would mind," Barry answered. "I've never seen them be prejudiced against anyone. And if they did have a problem, I'd tell them I'm a grown man and can make my own decisions."

I smiled and took a deep breath. "Good."

Barry continued. "One of my cousins is marrying a girl from Jamaica, and my uncle is warning him that the family will do anything they can to break them up, but if they do get married, they'll support him."

"Hmm," I said. That sounded the opposite of being supportive. Supportive out of duty, if they must, if their initial lack of support didn't get the result they wanted. I thought about the Jamaican girl among Barry's family in eastern Washington, just outside Spokane. I hadn't been there, but I knew it was white, just like a lot of the Pacific Northwest. My heart went out to her.

"They're also really young and come from really different cultures," Barry continued. "Not like us. We're basically from the same culture."

I nodded. "Yeah, that's true." I still only knew Black culture from books and TV, and short visits with Dad to Black neighborhoods. I knew it in a way outside myself, as a thing to purposefully study in the words of Maya Angelou, in the music of Bell Biv Devoe.

"Maybe I'll ask my parents what they think when I go home for Thanksgiving," Barry said, breaking my thoughts. I was flattered that he wanted to ask, but afraid of the answer. Barry looked at me. "Your nose kind of shows your Black ethnicity," he said. Then quickly continued, "Not that I think you have a bad nose or anything. I hope that doesn't sound offensive."

"It doesn't," I said. "I like my nose."

He said, "I like it too."

When Thanksgiving weekend came, schoolmates asked me the standard, innocuous question meant for small talk, but which for me always cut deeper into my feelings of abandonment than just about anything else: "Are you going home for break?" Ever since I'd left Mom and Gary's, the question had no simple answer. "Home" had changed twice since I'd moved out. I chose the path of least resistance, answering honestly but without making the asker uncomfortable: "I'm going up to my aunt and uncle's."

Thanksgiving in Carnation was identical to Thanksgiving at Grandma's, just with different dinnerware. Our dinner menu had been passed down to us from my grandfather's mother, with every food item made from scratch. In the living room, Deborah accompanied me on the piano while I played Suzuki songs. Later, at Deborah's suggestion, Uncle Eugene played Christmas duets with me on his violin. I was scared of Eugene, the way I was scared of all men in the family except Uncle Adam. Men were a foreign species to me—a species that yelled and drank and wielded power. But Eugene had never been anything but quiet, and our musical melodies diminished the danger sign that hung over his head. I left Carnation with my first pair of wool socks from Deborah and twenty dollars from Stephanie. A week later, Deborah sent me a batch of homemade chocolate chip cookies in a festive tin. It was a simple act that held more meaning than I could express, a motherly act that made me feel less of an orphan and more of a daughter off at college, fawned over by her mother. At the end of the semester, I earned my highest GPA thus far: 3.27.

In spring, my dormmate and I moved into an apartment near campus with two other girls. We ignored the bright green shag carpeting and the small bedrooms and reveled in the $400-a-month rent, split four ways. Since Deborah and Eugene had offered to send me $300 a month and take over Mom's loan payment, I could attend spring semester. I felt enveloped into the family fold from their generosity. At the same time, it was hard to get too comfortable. My money woes had ceased for the semester, but I couldn't get them extended for another year. I pled lightly with Burnside's financial aid department but was met with resistance. By the time they had a solution, I'd already made plans to return to Grandma's house in August, the prodigal daughter now free of Eddie, to attend Cabrillo's one-year program for medical transcription. That summer I worked full time in the Burnside library and took a medical terminology course at Portland Community College. Learning how Latin prefixes, roots, and suffixes came together to form a medical meaning felt like being ushered into the inner circle of language. It was a stronger connection to learning than I had felt in my semesters at Burnside.

While there was plenty of introspection to be had at Burnside, questioning was strictly forbidden. Burnside required all its students to sign statements of belief at the beginning of each school year. If you didn't sign, you didn't get to attend. One student had been kicked out for being gay the year before I came to campus and had only been reinstated after conversion therapy. We were taught that if a person were truly listening to God, they would choose Burnside; there was no other right choice. Which meant every other college—even every other Bible college—was inadequate in the school's mind. I couldn't reconcile this belief with my own views.

Bible college was supposed to be one of the pinnacles of Christian life, but it came to seem like lots of arbitrary rules, and interpretations of a text that I was ever so slightly beginning to question. How could anyone be sure that the words of the Bible had come from God and not from man? And if they were from God, how could we be sure we were interpreting them correctly? Barry never seemed to waver, not even when we checked out a church whose pastor outed an adulterous couple before the congregation and spent the entire sermon publicly berating them instead of guiding them in private. Adultery was wrong, but it felt just as wrong to revel in their humiliation.

In May, Barry's and my six-month hold on becoming official was almost up. One afternoon we walked downtown after a visit to Powell's to buy a copy of Queen—a book by Alex Haley I had pulled from Mom's bookshelf in high school, about an enslaved woman and enslaver's son who fall in love and have a mixed-race baby. Barry and I stood at the corner waiting to cross the street when a Black man Barry's age walked up to the light.

The man turned to Barry. "Is that your girlfriend?"

"Yes," Barry answered.

"All right," the man said, and nodded his head. He patted Barry on the shoulder. "You take good care of that Black woman."

I blushed as the light turned green and Barry and I crossed from friends to partners.

Burnside "Bridal" College felt different with my new partnership. The school's nickname among students was a tongue-in-cheek nod to the high number of marriages it produced, specifically between future pastors and pastors' wives. I was no longer jealous of my classmates' wedding announcements and of newly engaged female classmates retelling their fiancé's proposals as we listened with reverent attention. But I was honestly surprised when I saw one couple after their honeymoon. They were driving the same beat-up car and wearing the same clothes as they had before the wedding. Realistically this made sense, but I imagined marriage as so life altering that nothing could be the same as before the "I do." And I imagined my slight physical distaste—at best, physical indifference—for Barry would dissipate once he put the ring on my finger. Marriage would change everything.

Over spring break, Barry took me to meet his family in Chattaroy, a small town outside Spokane. We left just before noon and listened to Natalie Merchant and Tori Amos on the way. Barry's lack of interest in Christian music released me from guilt over two of my secular favorites. In some Christian circles, the cover of Amos's latest album—in which a pig appeared to be suckling at her breast—proved that she worshipped the devil, and that the listener might worship the devil, by accident, if they listened.

We drove up to his parents' modest home in a somewhat remote rural part of town. His mom answered the door; she was my height, thin like me but strong, with a hint of a sallowness in her face and bright eyes.

"Hi!" she said, drawing me in for a hug. "You're so pretty. Your mom must be pretty." And with those words, I knew I'd won her favor, and she mine.

The inside of the house was furnished neatly with unremarkable, mismatched, mostly oak furniture. Barry's father got up from the kitchen table, leaned on his cane, and reached out his hand. He was tall, much taller than Barry. His wide smile matched his wife's, and I saw no hint of prejudice in his eyes. Later that day I played my violin for Barry's mom at her request. As the weekend continued, I met his fortysomething-year-old sisters and his grandparents, all of whom welcomed me warmly. Their closeness reminded me of my own extended family. I could see myself becoming part of this one.

The next day, Barry took me across the state line to Idaho, just a hop and a skip from Spokane. Idaho was even whiter and more remote. I wasn't used to fully Black spaces, but having at least some pops of color made me feel safe.

"I'm always a little afraid of going to a new place," I told Barry. With all our reading of *Half and Half* and *Queen*, the admission felt safe. "I never know how people will treat me."

Barry turned to me and said if I was ever in danger because of my race, he'd point to the sky and say, "Look at the helicopters." That would be my cue to run as fast as I could to a public place, and that he would stay and fight if he needed to. Barry wasn't a fighter, and I couldn't picture him swinging his fists against a racist assailant, but I felt protected just the same.

"The helicopter reference is because of the president," Barry said. "Whenever he flies, another helicopter flies right behind him. And if someone starts shooting at him, his helicopter is supposed to fly straight up, while the helicopter behind him takes all the shots. Not that I think anyone is going to shoot at us, but it's good to have a plan."

Back in Spokane, we walked halfway across a bridge and stood looking at the water below. Barry and I were official now, but he still hadn't made a move. If I didn't make one first, it might never happen. So in an uncharacteristic act of forwardness, I kissed Barry's cheek.

"I don't think anyone is looking," he said, and kissed me on the lips. The kiss was awkward, and it took me by surprise, even though I had given him an opening. The next day, on a rather silent walk near his parents' house, Barry spoke up: "Well, I don't have much to say, but I do feel I need to kiss you one more time." The second kiss wasn't awkward at all.

As the summer progressed, we talked of weddings and marriage. Barry made a mock budget. I knew a proposal would come soon, but not before he'd met my parents. He had guidelines he felt he should follow. In June, I returned home from my shift at the library and found a letter from Dad.

Dear Shannon,
My health situation still has the professionals shaking their heads
in wonderment. Bottom line—lungs and heart appeared to have
mysterically healed. I no longer need oxygen. In contrast to the
six (6) heart medications I'd been taking . . .
      You mentioned a friend as someone you would like me to
meet. Be aware, if you are not already so, that your choice of a
companion ~~represents~~ *reflects a mirror image of self and a reflec-*
tion of your upbringing, of which I have played a major part.
Now, decisions are to be made by you depending, in part, of your
earlier parental and social experiences. I, as a man and Father will
see far deeply into what you've become by the choices you make.
I will not judge or influence, it's too late for that! I look forward
to meeting someone chosen by you.
      Your Father,
      Robert C.

I hadn't expected Dad to revel in my new relationship, but I found
his tepidness frustrating. His letter reminded me of our past visits and
phone calls, the way he tended to insert himself not into my actual life
but into the one that existed in his head—he as a major player in my
upbringing, and he as the one I needed to please. Instead of heartfelt or
even-tempered congratulations, his letter was a warning wrapped in the
impersonal, philosophical language he loved so much.

Later that summer on visit to my grandma's house in Santa Cruz
and my mom's house in San Jose, Mom drove Barry and me three hours
to see Dad in Sacramento. Mom liked Barry immediately. She liked his
calm demeanor and quiet personality. It wouldn't be long before I realized that they were two peas in a pod—both gentle souls who recoiled at
arguments and preferred a steady life over grandiose ideals.

Barry and I didn't have a car with us, but even so, I was glad we
needed my mom to drive us to Dad's. She'd be there for protection.
Emotional protection, but that was all that I needed. Dad's and my
letter-writing relationship filled a void, but it was a connection that
felt safe because it existed in the confines of pen and paper. This visit
would be the first time I'd seen him in four years, since that fateful day
with Denise.

Barry stepped out of the car and I realized he was dressed all wrong. Penny loafers and a tucked-in shirt, a crew cut and pleated pants. I glanced at the backseat, but there was no casual attire to save the day. No "Guide to the Black Part of Town" or "Meeting the Black Father for Dummies." There was nothing but a piece of paper with Barry's perfect rows of handwritten directions.

Barry looked down the street, eyeing the rows of chain-link fences and windows with black steel bars.

"Don't worry," I said, smiling at my honky-tonk husband-to-be. "No one is going to shoot you. Not today, anyway." Not that I'd ever heard gunshots in my dad's many neighborhoods.

Mom waited in the car while Barry and I opened the metal gate and walked along the concrete, and then up the steps of a converted house with well-worn shingles to Dad's second-floor apartment.

Barry knocked on the front door, and I heard him suck in his breath. The door swung open. Dad looked Barry up and down through the screen and his face fell ever so slightly.

"Well, well," he said, and I knew he was thinking he could take him.

Inside, the light was slightly dim. Barry and I sat on the couch, and my dad took the chair facing us.

When Barry asked for my hand, my dad said yes, but he seemed less than thrilled. Barry was a socially awkward white conservative, though liberal enough to not seem racist. It must have seemed obvious that he and I didn't hold hands or look longingly into each other's eyes. But maybe Dad was glad to have been asked. Or maybe he knew it didn't matter what he said.

The three of us met Mom at her car, and Dad followed us in his to the nearby park. We sat at a table—four adults made relatively silent by the awkwardness of the situation—and breathed in the quiet, sunny day. I had Barry take a picture of my dad and me as we sat side by side. I wanted it to replace the one good picture of the two of us since childhood—a photo Amy had snapped during our trip to see Dad my senior year. In that photo, Dad and I sat next to each other on an Amtrak bench. He rarely smiled in photos, but in that one he smiled proudly. Last year I'd sent the photo to a boy I'd met online, along with others. We'd promised to send a handful to each other, but I'd never received his and never got mine back. Losing that photo was the biggest regret of my life. I wouldn't get it back again until my forties, when Amy happened to find the negative in a box of photos after moving to a new house.

This day at the park, I saw an opportunity to re-create the warmness of that missing picture. Only, when I got the prints, I saw two individuals sitting rather far apart. My dad sat with one leg crossed over the other and his arms crossed loosely in front of him. My legs came together at the knees, and my feet turned inward—a pose that matched my insecurity next to the man who now seemed so distant from me. So much had changed in the past four years; I wondered if we'd ever get that smidgen of closeness back. Two hours after we had arrived in Sacramento, Mom drove Barry and me back to her house. It was the last time I saw Dad until he was dying.

——————

Toward the end of the summer, I leaned into the balcony ledge of the Pittock Mansion—a converted museum that at the time held historical artifacts from Lithuania. My eyes blinked against the sun, unnatural now to a once-native Californian who cried at Portland drenched in gray. The Columbia River, forty-five minutes east, was a steadily flowing stand-in for my coast-born need for water. The familiar brown hills enveloped me; the flames of the nearby wildfire danced around in my mind, red hot against the untamed wilderness, while peacocks flaunted their beauty on the manicured lawn just below.

Barry looked over at me and smiled, his gaze falling to his feet before he could receive my return on his investment. My own smile hung naked, somehow ashamed.

Barry leaned over and rubbed my back, eyes safely looking east. I looked west and wondered how a back rub could feel territorial like a leash and collar. I glanced at the birds as they flew out of sight. My eyes followed their course until they were nothing but black specks, gone completely when I blinked my eyes.

The museum, the landscape—it all felt scripted somehow. The sky was never that blue for nothing. People didn't get permission to cross the rope inside the museum and ascend to the balcony for nothing. My boyfriend could not have been quite that uneasy for nothing. Maybe this would be the day my heart would start to flutter after two years of being completely still.

Barry pointed to a frame on the one high outer wall of the balcony. I ambled over to investigate. Inside the frame was a poem about a girl. I read, half-interested, until I discovered the girl was me.

Just as I turned to face Barry, he got down on one knee and took a ring from his shirt pocket.

"Will you marry me?"

I thought of Tiger Woods, and of the make-believe mixed man named Brian Scott that I had been sure I'd meet. But Barry was the one who stood before me with a ring in his hand, so he had to be the one God had chosen for me. To say no to Barry would be to say no to God.

"Yes," I said.

I observed my lips moving from some anonymous location in the blue sky. I was the heroine in a romantic comedy, and this was the ending of a two-hour chase to get to this very moment. He would slip the ring on my finger, the camera would slowly zoom out to encompass the museum, the gorge, the hills, and the credits would begin to roll, sealing our happy fate.

Barry did slip the ring on my finger. Or at least he tried. He got to my knuckle and froze, unable to force the ring past the little section of resistance. The ring wasn't too small, but his fear of hurting me was too big. This is not how the romantic comedy is supposed to end, I thought, as I did the work of putting the ring on myself. I slipped the ring—a rose gold band with the small diamond in the tall setting—easily past my knuckle and glanced at my fiancé with a hint of disdain for his timidity, for his unromantic faded shirt, for his now grown-out hair on top that blew in the wind much like that of the googly-eyed Steve Buscemi in *Con Air*. Then I kissed him, ashamed of my antipathy.

20

ANNE OF WINDY POPLARS
1999

THAT FALL, I RETURNED TO GRANDMA'S TO start my year-long medical transcription program at Cabrillo and the completion of my associate's degree. Barry and I wrote letters, just like Anne Shirley and Gilbert Blythe during their long-distance engagement in *Anne of Windy Poplars*—still my favorite book series—and we talked on the phone on Sundays. I didn't fully realize that our nine-month-long separation was what moved me ahead so confidently. Letter writing felt safer than actually living with a man.

Two weeks after I arrived, I sat with Mom and Melanie at Grandma's kitchen table. Melanie was almost ten, and she and Mom would often spend nights here now that there was an extra room. Grandma's probably felt safer to her than her own house. Mom had slept in Melanie's bed for a couple years after I had moved out after high school. Later she would tell me it was her small act of defiance against Gary for treating me poorly when I lived there. It was nice to know that she had been paying attention, but her sleeping with Melanie did nothing to mend my time there.

That evening, I looked out the window to see Eddie standing in the road, waving. My heart dropped. As if on autopilot, I went through the dining room and into the hallway, and opened the front door. Eddie wore a white Lacoste shirt with its signature green alligator on the breast. He handed me a congratulations card—somehow he had learned of my engagement—along with flowers he had picked from someone's yard.

"Hi," he said, as I took the card and flowers. "It's good to see you. Can I have a hug?"

Despite my better judgment, I leaned in for a half hug.

Eddie began to cry. "I'm so sorry," he said. "So sorry. Can you forgive me?"

I pulled away and said, "Yes, I forgive you." I closed the door and returned to the kitchen, throwing the card and flowers away before sitting back down. Mom leaned over and rubbed my shoulder as I sat, stunned. Eddie no longer had power over me, but witnessing him on my doorstep was like seeing the ghost of someone who had died.

Five minutes later, the doorbell rang. Eddie was once again on my porch, this time holding small plums he had picked from the neighbor's tree. Same old Eddie, I thought, giving me gifts he didn't buy. Out of curiosity, I asked him questions about his life. He was still landscaping for his uncle, which he had done off and on (more off than on) when we were together; still taking classes at Cabrillo (and, I assumed, still dropping those classes without finishing); still doing housekeeping at Trinity Hills. His pupils looked dilated and somewhat sparkling, and I knew from experience that meant he was manic.

The next day at the kitchen table, I was afraid Eddie would walk by the window. The day after that, I wasn't afraid, and he did walk by. There was no reason to pass my house except to see me. It didn't lead anywhere he knew. I got up from the table and took my dinner to the bedroom, safe out of sight. I ate at my desk and thought about what I'd say if I saw him again: "I don't want you ever coming to this house again. All that we had is in the past now, and I have no desire to be friends with you." Maybe he stopped coming, or maybe he came by one day and Grandma scared him off. Either way, after that day, I never saw him again. The year and a half since we had been together felt like three and a half years of sobriety. I wouldn't have traded it for anything.

That school year, my ability to flourish in school was tested by my eighteen-unit course load. Armed with the success of my previous school year at Burnside, I dug into classes with more fervor, and more determination, than ever. I followed a strict schedule of classes, studying, and sleep. Most of the classes were too easy, but I knew they were building toward a future less than a year away when I could finally make my own living. And I'd get to do it beside Barry.

Most evenings I took in two rerun episodes of *Friends*, which I watched in wonder for the first time, even though it had debuted four years earlier. Though I was still a Christian, the show opened my eyes to secular life. Over the next few months, I took walks down to Blockbuster to rent straight-to-video romantic comedies starring various *Friends* cast members, expanding my worldview beyond the rom-coms we watched in the Burnside common room where the characters fell in love—and the movie often ended—before sex: *Ever After, While You Were Sleeping, Runaway Bride, Sleepless in Seattle*.

One Sunday, I took Grandma to the Black Baptist church downtown. The classic structure with the staired entrance and the classic cross at the top of the A-frame roof had called to me for years. Sometimes I saw parishioners stand outside after the service in jovial conversation. Eddie and I felt alien at the church we went to with Dad, where the pastor had spoken about the valley of the dry bones, but I longed once again to immerse myself in Blackness, with Christianity as the familiar tie that binds. Santa Cruz Bible had not called to me since I'd been back, but maybe this church would.

The church held about thirty people, all of whom welcomed Grandma and me. Even though she didn't believe, Grandma joined me in clapping along to the worship songs—unfamiliar to me but close enough to those I knew that I was able to pick them up quickly. A young woman about my age sat at the piano, her fingers gliding over the keys with ease as she moved her body to the music. After the sermon, Grandma and I left with hearts full and smiles wide. It didn't become my church—I couldn't shake the feeling that the white half of me, and my white culture, would set me forever apart in a different dimension that neither Black nor white inhabits. If I joined, it would have felt performative, adopting a culture that was mine only in melanin and not in practice. But Grandma and I were accepted, and that was enough that day.

Toward the end of October, just after my birthday, I received a letter from Dad:

Hello Daughter,
You spelled out your future in some areas, but I'm curious about
your plans for life's many facets. Plan to acquire a B.A. or B.S.?
And if so, in what disciplines? You stated a goal of practicing
medical transcription. To what length? Today's realities all but
demand that one establish a career that will be sustaining, regard-
less of one's status as married or single. You're doing good with
your life but I'm not the least bit surprised. That's just Shannon,
of whom I've always been extremely proud.
 Much Love,
 Your Father,
 Robert C.

Despite my continued disinterest in a career, Barry and I discussed my future. I'd never fully let go of the desire to attend an accredited four-year college. To my surprise, Barry was highly supportive of this goal, and that support hadn't wavered. We planned to put him through school for counseling first, and then focus on my plan to major in English. "You can have a creative writing emphasis," Barry said. "I'm sure one of us is bound to become a published author."

Barry's mom sent me a birthday present—something my own mom had never done. Inside the box was a homemade card, a necklace made of Black Hills gold, and two bottles of body wash. "Shannon," she wrote in the card, "we love you and promise our love and support." It was the type of motherly gift I had always wanted. My own mother failed to call. Many years later, when my sister was grown and had a family of her own, she and I made a pact to remind our mom of each other's birthdays. Until then, no matter how many calls I received, no birthday would feel complete without it being acknowledged by the one who birthed me.

Even before he proposed, Barry said he wanted to put me up in an apartment at the beginning of summer, and then join me there after we got married. I began buying items in Santa Cruz in anticipation of my new home: dish towels, silverware, salt and pepper shakers. I imagined a future home as fulfilling as the apartment I had shared with Mom in San Jose, which was filled with coloring and puzzles. A home where I could get undressed in any room of the house. Where I would be able to fall asleep under the fuzzy brown comforter Barry and I had bought for our future before we even became engaged. I imagined the death of "Shannon Manuel" and the birth of "Shannon Carver." The death of a bastard mulatto and the birth of a mixed-race wife and mother. No longer would a feeling of rejection descend on me whenever I entered a family member's home, because I'd have my own home to return to. Holidays would be sweeter. The future would be brighter. My life would be more secure.

A friend asked me how important passion was in a relationship. I said, not very. Barry and I didn't have passion, but an all-the-time good feeling. Passion fades, I said. Companionship was most important. But even as I spoke these words, I questioned them. Sometimes I wondered if what I saw in Barry was a father figure, not a spouse. A best friend, not a lover. Barry sent me a letter, and on the stationery he drew a stick figure dipping a stick figure with hair, as one does in ballroom dancing. "I can't wait to kiss you like this," Barry wrote. I looked at the stick figure in fear. Later, I sent him a clipping from an article about a condition called vaginismus. It was a term I'd never heard before, but it gave a name to a condition I thought plagued me, in which the pelvic muscles tighten up, preventing intercourse. Back when I was with Eddie, we never consummated our relationship. In part because we were Christians, but also because the time or two we tried, it didn't work. Vaginismus can be a physical reaction to a mental state, and I was sure I could beat it. I was sure God wouldn't have picked Barry for me if I couldn't have sex, and I knew Barry was who God had picked for me because he was the one who proposed. Not a Taco Bell proposal with a straw wrapper, and not a desperate proposal while stalking me, but a thought-out, eyes-wide-open, fairy-tale request for my hand.

Barry came to visit over Christmas break, and I visited him right after the New Year, and then I headed to Carnation. Aunt Deborah was making my wedding dress from a Renaissance costume pattern and fabric I had found with Grandma, with money Mom gave me for the wedding. Mom's contribution was extra special because it was from her, not from Gary, from a bonus she had received from work.

My cousin Elsie was home from Oberlin College for the holidays, and she brought home her friend Kisi, originally from Ghana, who had an internship nearby at Microsoft. Kisi was the first African I'd spoken to in such an intimate setting, and I longed for us to be friends, away from the confines of my white family. As she sat playing a game with my uncle and cousins, fitting so well into their family unit, I felt tears well in my eyes. I'd always felt that part of my alienation was due to my race, but here was someone even more Black than me, and she fit in fine. But she had something I didn't: a nuclear family. She was able to give of herself freely because she came from a stable home. Her cup was full. But an empty cup is nothing but an empty cup. I wanted desperately for my cup to be full, instead of feeling on the outside of any given situation. I wanted to stop the lie that told me I was being excluded. Sometimes it was true, but more often it wasn't. Sometimes I excluded myself without trying and then got upset that I was excluded. It was a habit I performed subconsciously; exclusion was somehow more comfortable.

When Kisi left, Deborah told me about their conversation.

"Why is Shannon so light?" Kisi had asked her the first night.

"Well, she has a Black dad and a white mom," Deborah explained.

"We call those half breeds," Kisi said.

"Well, we don't," Deborah said emphatically.

I was glad Deborah stood up for me, but knowledge of their exchange quelled any hopes I had of Kisi and me becoming friends, and reinforced my belief that I didn't fit in anywhere.

In December, Grandma flew to Washington to meet Uncle Adam and Stephanie's new baby, born the day after Christmas. In January, Grandma sat me down at the kitchen table with news. "I've decided to sell the house and move to Washington," she said.

"Wow," I said. It was inadequate, but it was the only response I could muster for losing the first and longest home I'd ever known.

"These people down the street were having an open house," Grandma continued. "Dennis's son asked me what I would do if someone offered me good money for this house. I said I didn't know. So I talked to the real estate agent, and she came over and gave me a bigger estimate than

I had imagined, and then she called back yesterday and went up even higher. So, I'm pretty set on selling."

"What about the business?" I asked.

"I'd sell that too," she said. "It's a prime time to move. Everyone wants to move to our neighborhood. And houses in the Seattle area are a lot less right now."

I understood why she wanted to go. She worked so hard at her business, and all her life she had taken care of other people. Not even just her own kids, but also me as well as some second cousins before I was born. If I hadn't been about to start my new life, I would have been devastated at losing my old one. The tree I used to climb in the backyard, the street I used to fly down on my bike, the stop-start, stop-start of each car as it braked at the stop sign on our corner, and the way I jolted awake when someone ran the stop sign in the middle of the night.

By the middle of February, I realized the house would sell fast. I arranged with all my teachers to finish classes two months early. Doing so meant I had to spend more hours in the computer lab working on my typing speed. I hunched over in my chair, hitting the keys with fervor in an attempt to be able to cross this chore off my list. But as the week went by, my wrists revolted, and I developed tendinitis. At first I thought it would pass quickly, like a stomachache or a cold. Just a few days off the computer would do. But days turned into weeks, and the house sold. I moved to Portland one class short of my associate's degree and with no ability to perform the job I'd trained for.

Work that didn't involve computers was hard to come by. I settled on a job as a janitor for Burnside, reverting to a state of employment I thought I'd put behind me. I worked with a small team, cleaning alongside them as intimately as I had with my cohort at Trinity Hills. One day, one of my coworkers asked me how my walk with God was—a common question in evangelical circles.

"Great!" I said. "I think of God right away when I wake up each morning."

She answered with a smile, "Now the trick is to think about him all day long!"

That moment felt like a last straw. I became fed up with the arbitrary methods of proving one's dedication in a way I never had before. If I had been honest, ever since my conversion ten years earlier, my relationship with God had centered around being attuned to following his path for my life, of waiting patiently for my future, which had now come to fruition—almost. There was no more giving my desire for a husband over to God, because God had now given me one. And there was no wondering if I'd meet my future spouse at a Sunday morning service, because my future spouse came with me. With such an uncertain future in my teen years, believing that there was someone in charge of the minute details of my life felt reassuring. God had been in charge of making sure I ended up with a home, and now I had one. What would I need from him now?

While the conversation with my coworker was a seminal moment, the beginnings of my disbelief didn't begin that afternoon. A few months earlier in Santa Cruz, as the Planned Parenthood building peeked out between trees while I sat at a bus stop, I suddenly came to believe that a woman had the right to choose what to do with her own body, finally seeing the choice through her eyes instead of the church's. And during a class in my last semester at Burnside, a husband-and-wife missionary team from a Native American reservation spoke about their experience.

"How do you keep your kids away from the untrustworthy, alcoholic men?" someone had asked.

I found myself disgusted with the equally stereotyped answer. "We let them come on the porch but we keep our limits." Why not let the men inside? And why assume they were all untrustworthy alcoholics just because they lived on a reservation?

But I wasn't done with God yet, just the people who believed in him.

———————

That summer, Dad and I exchanged letters in which I shared about my upcoming marriage and pushed back when he showed concern. In July, he sent a letter devoid of its usual joviality and with harsher words than he had ever written before.

Dear Shannon,
I have no desire to oppose your marriage. Your choice is yours
alone. In a letter you said that I probably misunderstand Barry

and don't know his true personality. His personality or he as a person has never been an issue to me. I don't know him and I'm sure I never will. My concerns and interests focus entirely upon you and your welfare and future.

Throughout the period of your entry into academia, the goal, the path has been upon completion of your education and its resultant affordance of a better and independent life. With a degree and your being who you are, the world would then be your oyster. You would thus have assured your lifetime of independence.

The shift of focus mentioned is illustrated glaringly by your entire goal is that of getting married. Your recent writings have been exclusively that.

No mention of credits, courses, summer and part time employment, which affords you the freedom to "pay your bills" while you pursue your career.

Your choices are fraught with evidence that you are walking away from beliefs that I hold dearly. It is a firm separation in many respects.

An analogy would be your boarding Amtrak and venturing off to China, into a world completely alien to me.

I should hope I've outlined my thoughts and position as precisely as can be done by pen. If you stepped into the world of China or boarded a rocket to Mars, you will always be my little girl and my adult daughter. I love you with all the fibre of my being, and will always love Shannon D., God's gift to me and to the world!

Have a good life,
Your Father,
Robert C.

Dad's letter left me confused. Myriad roles suddenly presented themselves. Conflicting roles, it seemed. According to the church, I must be chaste for the five weeks left before my wedding, and then I must be sexually active and open to my partner. If I tried to hold back physically, Barry felt rejected, but I was not supposed to give in. Barry was upset at my having physical boundaries, my dad was upset that I was focused on marriage, and a friend rebuked me for being too sexually free before marriage, sure that her own sexual freedom before marriage—with her now husband—has caused their present friction. How could a woman and wife expect to have so many roles? Sexual woman, pure woman, submissive woman, independent woman.

Barry and I talked about school and what I should focus on now that I was getting married. Without a clear career path now that medical transcription was off the table, we came to the conclusion that my role was now wife and worker, not student. My love for Barry in part rested on his belief in the importance of my higher education, but now his beliefs shifted, and so I shifted mine alongside him. It was Dad's responsibility to pay for my college, we told ourselves. If he wanted me to go, he could pay for it. In the meantime, we talked about my taking one class at a time at Portland State.

What right did I have to attend school anyway? My mom got her bachelor's, and even her master's, but she had a father to take care of her, albeit one who had passed on. Being with Barry had improved my life beyond the confines of what it had been. I had a home. I had a man who loved me, who kept a steady job and wanted to provide for me. I had a man who was going to make me a wife and mother, and give me his last name.

One afternoon I stood at a stoplight with a Black man, his white wife, and their mixed-race daughter on a pink bicycle. I pretended, as we stood there, that they were my parents and that the girl on the bicycle was my sister. It was a nice fantasy, to feel part of an interracial family. I was excited as the wedding grew closer, but I also grieved the life I would never have. I wondered what my life would be if I had gone to a Black college, if I had found a mixed-race man. Barry wanted to learn about my identity, but he didn't know it in his bones. Not the way a mixed man would. Would my children identify as mixed? Would they resent me? Would they think I wasn't worthy? Black men never felt like an option to me, in large part because I never saw them. With my dad as my sole Black figure, picturing kissing a Black man felt like kissing my father. Perhaps my desires would have been different had I not known Dad at all.

Shortly after Barry's and my talk about school, a library job I'd been counting on fell through. Barry suggested we postpone the wedding until I was financially stable, but through the help of a friend, he found ways we could cut back. Though we kept going ahead with the wedding, my sense of security diminished. My role of wife and future mother became dependent on my ability to provide—and provide without the possibility of an education.

Barry and I got married in the A-frame rec room on the Burnside campus. My old roommate Michelle and another friend acted as my wedding planners. I didn't realize until after the wedding that their drive came not so much from a sense of closeness to me but because I held the golden ticket: a wedding. Once I was married, I barely saw them again.

The morning before the wedding, I told a white hair stylist to do what she thought best. I had debated which race stylist to see and came to the conclusion that neither would know how to do my hair. (Natural hair was not in vogue for Black women at the time.) The end result affirmed my fears. The stylist ironed the back of my hair into a bow and combed out the part that remained free. As the afternoon went on, my hair expanded until it formed the dreaded triangle it liked so well.

Everyone I loved came to the wedding—everyone but Dad. Amy, Jenna, Heather, and my sister Melanie were my bridesmaids, everyone but Melanie wearing the dresses from Amy's wedding in Iowa. My cousin Adria was my photographer. A friend made the cake. We served finger food—carrots, celery, crackers—and sparkling cider. Adam walked me down the aisle—the best substitute for Dad. There was no alcohol and no dancing: both were prohibited on campus and for students to partake in elsewhere. I asked the pastor not to talk about salvation to keep from upsetting my family, but he did so anyway. After Barry and I exchanged our vows, we jumped the broom, a tradition I had learned about in *Queen*.

In my apartment before the ceremony, with all my friends, I felt stirrings for Brian, who made the trip from Santa Cruz. Amy had moved on, but he and Jenna keep up their flirting. "I can't have Brian," I thought. "So that feeling shouldn't keep me from marrying Barry." Later, I would realize it shouldn't have to be between Brian and Barry, that the feeling itself had importance. That I should marry *someone* who gives me that feeling—it didn't have to be Brian.

"Is it hard to be away from Barry?" Grandma had asked me in Santa Cruz when he sent a delivery of flowers for Valentine's Day.

"Not really," I had answered.

Grandma would later point to that conversation as a missed opportunity, an observation that she later would say she should have acted on. Likewise, Uncle Adam said he should have spoken up when the pastor asked the wedding guests to speak now or forever hold their peace. But no one but me could have kept me from marrying Barry.

21

THE SCARLET LETTER
2000

BARRY AND I CAME BACK from our honeymoon in Victoria, BC, as married virgins. The day before Halloween, I finally got a diagnosis: a thick hymen. Surgery was scheduled for the end of the year. Even with my condition, Barry's actions on our wedding night were more methodical and less passionate than what I'd imagined. Leading up to my surgery, I followed a home treatment without much success. If I failed, what would become of my marriage? I knew Barry would stay with me even if he was relegated to a sexless marriage. He'd do so because it was noble and selfless. But I didn't want him to. I thought of Eddie, and how I had stayed with him despite his untreated mental illness that I had thought caused his abuses. I had gained a sense of pride from my sacrifice while silently filled with resentment. Barry would resent me too. Not because he was a bad person, but because this wasn't what he had signed up for. I didn't want to be the good deed that tested his piety.

I walked through life as if I had a scarlet *V* on my chest, as if everyone could tell I was a married virgin. I had gone through with my marriage in part because I didn't want to fail in front of my family, and now I'd failed anyway—only in a manner I couldn't discuss. I thought I was a woman, but I was still a child. My one solace was that it wasn't in my head.

But there was something else. If I didn't have pain, I could imagine Barry was suave and knew just what to do. I could imagine that I looked at him with the passion a wife is supposed to feel for her husband. But the block in our sex life magnified my indifference, and almost repulsion, to the man I married, through no fault of his own.

In December, I was wheeled into the surgery room with my stuffed dog Dominic in my arms. The next weekend, Barry drove us to the beach expecting a mini honeymoon, but while I could now use tampons, I still couldn't have sex. The scarlet *V* grew larger, more permanent. Marker instead of crayon. A capital *V* instead of a lowercase one. Movies that culminated in sex taunted me. Songs mocked my inability to live out the lyrics. And amid it all was my continued lack of passion for my husband.

A couple weeks after the surgery, Barry and I lay in bed, under the plush brown comforter we had bought before he proposed. Our apartment had slowly come together over the past few months. I cleaned regularly and vigorously, making our home as spotless as possible. Barry reached over and took his wire-rimmed glasses from the nightstand and lifted them to his face.

"Are you attracted to me?" Barry asked.

It was a direct question, with an answer I had been trying to hide since the wedding.

I suck in my breath. "No. I'm sorry."

I thought this would end the charade of our marriage, but Barry surprised me by saying he didn't believe in divorce. "I wouldn't do it again if we had a choice, but we made the choice, so we have to live with it."

After I said "I do," I realized I was not cursed. It wasn't a messed-up childhood that made me feel perpetually tepid toward Barry. I simply married someone I wasn't attracted to, which wasn't doing him any favors. After all, beauty is subjective, and I was keeping him from someone who would love him with abandon.

Our relationship moved forward as best it could. We still held out hope for the consummation of our relationship, but Barry understandably touched me less. I thought about his first visit to Santa Cruz and how he had rubbed my back at the boardwalk as we stood in line for the Giant Dipper. The public display was uncharacteristic, and I wondered if it was in response to the men around us. If he was marking territory. Now, he no longer desired to do so. When Valentine's Day came, I found a rather pitiful bouquet of flowers, their stems untrimmed, the tie still on. I was losing the partner I was bound to for life.

After we got married, I worked part time in temp jobs while searching for something permanent. Barry had set parameters: it must pay a certain amount, it must be full time, and it must provide me with my own health insurance. Barry didn't understand my struggle until he went to a career fair and saw the background necessary for finding a good job. Finally in November I got hired at a transportation company in the accounts payable department. At CNF, which stood for nothing, I sorted and delivered mail and kept records, sometimes scanning, sometimes printing, and sometimes taking a coworker to the empty, old bank building where we stored physical records on several large floors illuminated by hanging lights and accessed by an elevator with a hand crank.

My coworkers seemed somehow satisfied driving to a cement building on a cement freeway with identical cars moving slowly in the same direction. They seemed happy enough to rise before dawn, take their seats before the sun had fully taken its place in the sky, and do the same tasks today that they did yesterday. It's not that I didn't enjoy my job. There was something satisfying about taking a bucket of mail, tearing open each large manilla envelope, and allocating the various pieces of paper into the appropriate cardboard mail slot. I started with disorder, and I made order. I listened to music on my Discman while I made copies. I said hello to my coworkers as I passed them their respective bundles of freshly opened invoices. But the fluorescent lights beat down on me with indifference, and I couldn't remember the last time I'd felt the sun on my skin.

During the best half hour of every day, I scarfed down my lunch while I befriended the Bennet sisters, Bigger Thomas, and Rodion Raskolnikov. "Are you going to read *all* the classics?" a coworker asked. I shrugged my shoulders, tickled that she thought there was a finite list. "Why aren't you in college?" she asked. I silently wondered the same thing.

On an afternoon in March, I left my desk and ran to the bathroom. I opened a stall and cried, much like I had when the financial aid counselor at Bethel told me I had to list my parents on the FAFSA until I was twenty-four. Here I was, now twenty-four, and I was no closer to getting a formal education. Barry and I had talked on and off for months about what role education could play in my life and what my future job could be, always vacillating in our decision. That day in the stall, I couldn't stop crying and left work early. Then I called Grandma for advice.

"You're not alone in trying to find a good balance between work and family," she said, her comforting voice soothing me through the phone. "All the women in our family have this struggle."

I asked, "So what do you think I should do?"

After a slight pause, Grandma answered. "If you could do anything you wanted, without having to worry about training or capability, what would you do?"

"I'd want to be a writer," I said, without hesitation.

"I'm not surprised," she said, and her voice cracked in that special way it did whenever she was moved.

"You know," she continued, "Gary told me once, very passionately, 'Shannon should be a writer. She writes *so well.*'"

"Really?" I asked. It was the first compliment I'd received from Gary, ever.

"Really," Grandma said.

In January, I received another letter from Dad. It was his first letter since last July, before I got married.

> *Hello Shannon,*
> *Thought I'd attempt writing if the tremors will allow. Health problems have been the focus for the last 5–6 months. The pulmonary problems are limiting my life style at the present, compounding the situation has been the onset of crippling arthritis, which causes serious pain in the hands, knees and shoulders. For quite some time I had difficulty holding a toothbrush or opening a medicine container.*
>
> *During a consultation with the primary care physician the issue of long term health issues was introduced. Question was . . . if in the unlikely event I reached a level where personal care or residence in a nursing home was in order, would I be prepared for it. I think NOT! Having worked in those places I know my independent personality would not set well. Without family or a strong support system the quality of life under those circumstances is bleak.*

As usual, my health is improving and I'm becoming stabilized. With that in mind I have closed the books on California and the interim period of my existence. I am 100% focused upon returning to Kansas City as soon as humanly possible. Jay's mother and 5 grandkids are in Wichita Kansas, my ex-wife Lillian (Damon's mother) and my 6 grandkids live in St. Louis. They each have for years sought to have me return to the area. Also, I'll be much closer to Jay and his family and kids.

This move will provide a Richer, more Rewarding life style. As you must know, a Father always looks forward to a daughter's marriage and the possibility of grandkids being added to the mix. That happened in your case completely devoid of my involvement.

It's unlikely I'll ever see you again because it's unlikely you will come here or to the Midwest once I've moved there. Good luck and God Speed.

Your Father
Robert C.

Dad's letter felt so red hot that I blocked its contents as I wrestled with my own struggles. I didn't know it, but his plans were a fabrication. His exes had no desire to see him. He hadn't seen Damon since he was a baby, and he'd seen Jay once as an adult. Perhaps he needed that fantasy to face his own mortality—happy progeny running around him in the warm afternoon sun.

Two months later, I got a call. Dad had terminal lung cancer.

22

DREAMS FROM MY FATHER
2001

I WOKE UP TO A LOUD KNOCK on Dad's front door. I got off the floor where I had slept on a mishmash of piled-up blankets. Dad was asleep on the couch, but it would have been a stretch to say that either of us slept at all. Dad had lost all sense of time, of night and day, in that liminal space that those on the threshold of death inhabit.

When I arrived the night before, I had exited the cab to find a pale, thin woman with an almost full beard coming to greet me.

"Your dad's inside," she said. Her speech slurred like that of an elderly white woman who had misplaced her dentures; even though the stranger standing before me couldn't have been more than thirty, her front teeth were completely gone. My father was no stranger to strange women, so I followed her lead as I had countless others. I walked up the rickety wooden steps to the second-floor unit of the dilapidated house. It sagged under the weight of dreams that would never be reached and a life that would end before it could make peace with the world it was leaving behind.

When I stepped inside the doorway, I still somehow expected to be met by my father's magnetic energy and six-foot-tall frame, but he was nowhere to be found. Peering into the dim light, I saw a dark figure prostrate on the couch with an oxygen tube in his nose, and suddenly

I felt as if the entire world could come crashing down. My father was huddled up like a baby; his glassy eyes beckoned me forward.

"Dad?" I said questioningly, as if he were merely pulling one of his pranks.

"There's my baby girl," he said.

That night I lay covered in blankets on the living room floor while Dad slept fitfully on the small couch. My eyes followed helicopter searchlights as they blazed into dark corners, the intrusion reminding me how far I was from home. During our visit, Dad would tell me he was proud of this apartment because his last had mice running across the floor and stray bullets blasting through the windows.

Throughout that night, Dad's oxygen tank followed him to the bathroom and back in a series of false attempts at urination, and I jumped in a frenzy each time to make sure he got there before christening the carpet. When he wasn't trying to urinate, his teeth ground together like a skeleton in a lab. Hardly a word had escaped my dad's mouth since I entered the apartment. It was easier for him to maintain a somewhat full lung capacity by pointing. My own vocabulary seemed inadequate to make sense of what I had walked into. Watching a parent lose sense of their faculties is beyond words, beyond the language we are taught for life's other events.

Beard Lady, otherwise known as Janet, was his part-time caretaker. She had mentioned something about a doctor's appointment last night before she disappeared into the darkness. Between her toothless explanation and the harrowing night, the details were completely lost on me. I scrambled to the door that morning and found a man standing on the porch, with a service van parked down below.

"Hi, I'm here to pick up Robert?"

I waved him in and scrambled back to the living room. I knew I was supposed to be some sort of authority in that moment, but I was sure he could tell I was a phony. I was convinced that something in my face revealed that I hadn't seen this house before yesterday.

The man entered with another man behind him, and they placed Dad in a wheelchair and carried him down the steps. Dad was in the same clothes as last night. There was no time to change, not that I'd know how anyway. How does a daughter of average height change a six-foot-tall man? I did a quick search for his wallet and then stumbled out the door.

In the oncology unit of the hospital, the receptionist asked for Dad's insurance. I pulled his wallet out of my purse and emptied his cards on the counter. I picked one that said State of California Benefits Identification Card and handed it to the receptionist.

"That's not the right one," she said. Then I handed her the Medicare card with my dad's signature at the bottom. "That's not it either." I spread the cards out in front of her and she picked up the purple one labeled UNIVERSITY OF CALIFORNIA, DAVIS MEDICAL CENTER. She asked me to verify information. "Address?" she asked. My face flushed as I said I didn't know. "Phone number?" I didn't know that either. This was 2001, before smartphones, before Google Maps, when addresses and phone numbers were tucked away in address books. She looked at me sideways and told me to take a seat.

Dad glanced over at me from his wheelchair. He was slightly hunched over and his hands rested on his legs. One socked foot sat peacefully on the footrest while the other one escaped to the hospital floor.

"When I look at your eyes, I can see myself staring back at me," he said.

I couldn't tell if this is his way of staring into a proverbial mirror to bask in his own reflection, or if he really could see the daughter sitting before him—the daughter who hadn't sat before him for two years, and only then for two hours so her fiancé, now husband, could ask for his blessing.

A nurse entered the waiting room with a clipboard in hand. "Robert Manuel?"

She weighed my father on our way to the exam room. We lifted him out of his wheelchair and helped him hobble onto the scale. His slacks dropped straight down to the floor, his cancer pantsing him right there in the hospital. The scale read ninety-four pounds.

My naive plan had been to spend the weekend with my father and then return home with the satisfaction that I had done my part, had been the dutiful daughter who overcame her disappointment in her estranged father to say goodbye. But from the moment I'd entered his apartment the night before, I knew I had to stay put. The doctor gave him one week to live. I didn't know what I was doing, but I knew I couldn't leave. Aside from visits from Janet, there was no one he could count on but me. Damon lived in the Midwest and hadn't seen his father since he was one year old. Jay lived across the country in Florida and had only seen him once or twice. The twins and their sister had been adopted out as babies. I was the only one who'd had a relationship with my dad, limited as it was. I called my brothers in case they wanted to come say goodbye.

I was surprised I hadn't killed Dad yet. He took five different medications at different intervals. Some he took on a regular basis, and others only as needed. Some required food, and others didn't. Some were pills, and others were inhalers. No matter how much I stayed on top of his medication, he was never well. It was the kind of sickness that suffocated the caretaker while it literally suffocated the sufferer. My dad's lungs were slowly deteriorating. A year from now I would watch my mother-in-law die of lung cancer in a nice hospital bed as her children sang Christian melodies and strummed guitars in a circle around her. This sixty-year-old marathon runner would have a perpetual smile on her face, even into death. My father had been dealt an entirely different set of cards. His oxygen tank seemed to tease him, providing just enough air to keep him alive but not enough to relieve him of perpetual anxiety.

I pondered this as I sat on the porch steps with the caseworker. She was about my age and there to offer support to my father and me as we navigated the ironic isolation of hospice care. When she first arrived, I invited her into the dim living room. She had plopped herself down on the couch and I couldn't find the courage to tell her she just sat on my dad's urine from the previous night. Her pants let her know about five minutes in.

"Did Robert pee here?" she asked.

"Yes," I said. "I'm sorry."

She shrugged and said in her line of work, it was par for the course. When she was through with her prearranged question set, I asked her to the porch. I wanted to get this twentysomething out of my dad's field of vision, because I was in desperate need of care.

"It's so hard," I said. I uttered the words with just the right amount of stoicism. A veil to test the waters and see if it was safe to swim.

"Yes," she said. "I can imagine."

"I hadn't seen my dad in two years."

"Really?" she asked. But it wasn't so much a question. More of a half-hearted reply—as if she was as aware as I that this didn't fall into proper caseworker–family member relations. So instead, I spoke without a word and hoped she could see that I was drowning in an abysmal ocean, with her as my only hope for a life vest. *I'm a fraud of a daughter because my dad was a fraud of a father. I feel nothing. Can you tell me that's OK?*

"I think I need to stay longer," I told Barry over the phone. I wrapped and unwrapped the cord around my fingers, and then tried to clean the dirty parts with the tip of my fingernail. I wondered what would happen to the phone when Dad was gone. It would probably end up in a dump somewhere. My fingernail still cleaned off the dirt. Old habits die hard.

For a while Dad was declining quickly, but now it seemed his body had forgotten he was dying. His appetite returned, and he no longer complained about the oxygen tank. But no matter how well he was doing, I knew I couldn't leave him. Death wouldn't be on pause for long.

Barry had a different opinion. "I think you need to come back. You don't want to lose your job. They can replace you just like that."

I felt accusation in Barry's voice, as if I were doing the wrong thing by taking care of someone. As if I were selfish for getting two hours of sleep a night to watch over a parent with one eye open. But Barry was forever afraid of making waves, and a year from now, he would see his mother right after she was diagnosed with lung cancer but would send me to the funeral to avoid missing more work. My bills weren't on hold just because I was.

Weddings in movies always came at the end, a culmination of twists and turns that led to their own happy ending. Sometimes, right before the credits, the plot would jump forward in time, allowing the viewer to glimpse into the couple's future. A plus sign on a pregnancy test, a swelled belly, a blissful walk in the park with children in tow—whatever that glimpse was, it included none of the mediocrity that preceded it.

I was an underpaid paper pusher for a transportation company and I didn't even know what that meant. What did they transport? Where did they go? Saturdays were spent recovering from the week. Sundays were spent preparing for the next. On payday weekends I scoured the mall, desperate for deliverance, as if new cotton against my skin was the key to my own jump forward in time, just before the credits closed my story, since the wedding itself didn't do a good enough job.

I promised Barry I'd try to figure out how to leave in a few days, and I hung up the phone.

That night, I couldn't keep my eyes open, even though I said I'd watch Dad through the night. I didn't want Janet the Beard Lady to win—for her to have this superpower that gave my dad exactly what he needed, while I succumbed to the influence of sleep. This thirty-one-year-old lived on coffee and cigarettes. Literally. She smoked her cigarettes and drank her coffee while sitting in her doubled-up pairs of sweatpants, staring at my dad with the fervor of a religious zealot. This goateed woman was so in love with my seventy-one-year-old father that she volunteered to watch the rise and fall of his chest for hours on end in his darkened bedroom so I could sleep, never breaking her gaze or even relaxing her shoulders as she rubbed her hands over his face. If I were him, I'd drift into eternal slumber just to get away from her. So much easier than all the documentation involved in a restraining order. And yet, I needed her, and she knew it.

I tried to drift off to sleep on the living room floor. The couch was tainted now, with urine that seeped into the fabric of Dad's thrift store find. So instead I placed blankets under me and blankets over me. I smelled each to ascertain its worthiness, discarding those that matched the stench of the couch. Through my closed eyelids, I saw long periods of darkness followed by quick periods of light as helicopters searched overhead. This otherwise urban street, with its hand-watered grass lawns and barred windows, was filled with the chatter and laughter of neighbors making memories. Sometimes the chatter turned to raised voices at raised pitches. I lay prostrate on high alert as I waited for the voices to die down again.

I wondered which of the voices belonged to the woman who had entered Dad's house the day before. Her tall frame stood a few inches above mine, and her dark skin made mine look pale by comparison. "This is Loretta," Dad had announced. I knew instinctively that she was Dad's latest flame. Their eyes matched each other, sparkle for sparkle, and she leaned over to hug Dad on the couch. She pecked his lips and kept standing, while speaking in jovial tones. Then she was out the door in five minutes.

Loretta loved a memory of my father. The man who stood before her just two weeks ago, not the one who now shrunk into the couch. She likely cooked for him, possibly cleaned for him. But she had no shoulder to lean on for cancer. And I didn't blame her. And then I thought, maybe this is divine retribution. After all, Dad never could stay with one woman for long. I was glad to have Dad for myself—to be the woman that stayed till the end. If I could only get Janet to follow Loretta out the door. And yet, I kept wanting people to walk in.

Dad told me I shouldn't have married a white man—that Black folk need to stick together. It seemed contradictory, since he had lived with my mom. I felt like I had no identity, or at least not the identity I wanted. I had felt completely untethered since I had gotten married—a time when I should have felt the most tethered. I made a list of who I was: "employee, wife, daughter, sister, writer, future mother (hopefully)." But I was not at the right job, I married the wrong man, I felt like I had no mother, I lived too far from my sister, I couldn't get the training to be a writer, and kids seemed far off.

––––––––––––––

My first day in Sacramento, I called my mom, desperate for saving.

"I'm glad you're there to take care of your dad," she said. "I always worried about who would be there in the end."

I knew it wasn't fair, but I couldn't understand her nonchalance. She was the one who lived with him for five years, bore his child, and made some sort of promise to be by his side. My mom always corrected me when I said she and my dad were never married. "We basically had a civil union," she'd say. But it seemed this civil union allowed her to walk out, to move on with her life, and to leave behind her dabbles in Blackness to marry a straitlaced white man. Parents could get divorced, or separate, but children didn't have that luxury. It's not that I didn't want to be there for my dad, or thought my parents should have stayed together, but if there was a time I needed my mother, this was it. Not an unknown girlfriend, not an obsessed caretaker, but a woman who knew my father better than almost anyone—even better than me. Mom must have sensed my desperation. She jumped in the car on my third day to spend the long weekend with me, leaving my stepdad and half sister behind to rescue her cast-off daughter. At least for a while.

When Mom drove up, I rushed out the door and skipped down the uneven wooden steps to greet her. My parents and I hadn't been in the same space for two years, not since she drove Barry and me to Sacramento so Barry could ask Dad for his blessing.

Mom walked through the kitchen and into the living room where Dad sat in his wheelchair. I almost expected the rapture to begin that very moment, only because it was such an odd sight to have both of them in the same room. The odds seemed so much better that one of them would mysteriously disappear into the kingdom of heaven. At the same time, my heart leapt in my chest. My mother loved me, my father loved me, and in this very moment they were loving me together. I tried to forget the diary I had found on Mom's bookshelves that described her fear of my dad. I tried to forget her reluctant tales of being thrown across the room, being accused of adultery, and acquiring sexually transmitted diseases from his philandering. Part of me wanted to leap to my mother's rescue, even though Dad couldn't get out of his wheelchair if he tried. I wanted to protect her even though it was Dad who needed protection now.

Mom walked up to Dad's wheelchair and reached down to give him a hug.

"I'm glad you're here," Dad whispered, which was the loudest he could get his voice now.

They smiled a knowing smile, of memories past, of before I even came into being. Their smiles transported them to their apartment in San Francisco. To the now-funny story of watching their car amble down the road, stolen before their very eyes. To the joy of winning their grant proposal for a new Head Start location for preschoolers in low-income families. To making a daughter together who was now standing before them, ready to offer support.

———————

Mom went and picked my brother Damon up at the airport. Only, she didn't know what he looked like and finally had the airline worker call for him to meet her at a gate. Damon walked up, dark skinned, heavyset, and almost a full foot taller than my short, tiny white mom.

Mom opened the door of Dad's house, and she and the brother I had only talked to in scant letters and phone calls walked through the door. Damon and I reached out our hands timidly and then went in for a hug. He and my mom told Dad and me the story of their confusion at the airport, laughing at their inability to find each other. They were no doubt relieved to have a story—something to talk about to break the awkwardness that loomed between us all. Damon walked over to our father and marveled aloud at the strong Manuel blood that bonded us. Dad smiled genuinely but feebly from his wheelchair.

Later that day, Damon drove me in Mom's car to the laundromat while my mom stayed behind to watch over Dad. It was the first time I'd left my dad's house since I had arrived five days before, and the first time in two days I'd have clean clothes. The sun shone bright blue out the tall windows as the dryer cycled my few items of clothing. My brother sat across from me at the small table. I had a brother, I thought in wonderment. A Black brother. It was the first time a blood brother had been more than a voice over the telephone or large cursive handwriting over pages of legal-sized paper. It was the first time I could reach out and touch a lateral male relation on a family tree, instead of staring at blurry photos sent by mail.

I didn't know what to do with a brother. My stepbrother Nick moved in for a year when I was thirteen, but Nick was a live-in brother, and just one year younger. Damon was a forty-five-year-old stranger with a handful of kids I couldn't keep straight, save for the daughter he named Shannon: a namesake who wasn't named after me.

My brother and I sat in relative silence. There was so much to say but there was no way to get there. Instead, we smiled big smiles, both of us revealing our Manuel grins that stretched from ear to ear. Though Damon had traveled hundreds of miles to sit across from me in a laundromat, there was something remote about our visit. How do we traverse the twenty-year age gap between us? How do we cross the twenty-four years that stretch before our first meeting? How do we, related as we are, share hopes and insecurities without knowing our sibling beyond the very base details of age, location, and occupation? Our one partnership, sharing the frail, dying father in the frail, crumbling house, was something so far beyond words that the only confident speech came from the dryer, as it signaled the new life of my clothes.

———————

Dad got outfitted with a hospital bed after his visit to the oncologist. I had moved my well-worn blankets to the foot of his bed so I could help him walk to the bathroom or to hold his hand during a nightmare. That night I slept enveloped in a new sleeping bag. While Damon stayed with Dad, Mom and I had scoured Target for something to replace Dad's worn blankets—not for him, but for me. The clean aisles of untouched linen had called to me like a long-lost paradise. Everything was untainted, nothing was dying, and my only responsibility was selecting an item of personal comfort. I drifted to sleep in a cocoon of warmth and protection, where two hours stretched forth as if it were a lifetime.

A couple days after arriving, Damon flew home early. I had wanted him to be a normal big brother, to step in and help his little sister with their father. But it had been too much to ask of someone who was watching a veritable stranger die. Mom left shortly thereafter, returning to her home of the living. It was back to just me and my father.

———————

A week or so into my stay, Dad called to me from his bedroom. It wasn't words I heard, but a deep, insistent groan. As I stepped in, a pungent odor permeated the room, and I instinctively plugged my nose.

Dad was tangled in his blankets. One arm lay limply outstretched, past the end of the bed, as if reaching for another house, another body, another life.

"Let me get you cleaned up."

Dad didn't take up much of the bed. He had always been a string bean, but now he was more of a twig. I wondered whether to get him to the bathroom or get the bathroom to him. I settled on a combination. Folding away his layers of thin blankets, I helped him turn on his side so I could reach his bottom with the toilet paper I'd confiscated from the holder in the bathroom. Luckily hospital beds are made for situations like this, so I didn't have trouble reaching his behind from where I squatted at a safe distance. Only, I didn't know what to do with the toilet paper after the first wipe. I settled on tossing it on the carpet, then getting the next wad ready and doing the same.

I couldn't get Dad sufficiently clean. The poop had escaped while Dad wrestled with the blankets, and it left its mark on both him and his sheets. I helped him get out of bed and led him to the bathroom. Dad took feeble steps, summoning his resolve to lift each leg and place it a few inches closer to his destination. His oxygen tank followed us. We were never alone.

When we got in front of the shower, I untied his hospital gown and balled it up in the corner. Dad still had hair in delicate places, and it covered what I preferred not to see.

We took a few steps to the bathtub. I placed his hand on the towel rack on the outside of the sliding door, then lifted his leg over the top of the basin and placed it inside. In the midst of our delicate balancing act, I wrapped my arm around my dad's body and lifted the rest of him into the tub. Dad was surprisingly light but floppy. His arms and legs didn't know what to do with themselves, and it was difficult to help him turn in order to sit down on his shower chair. Once he was seated, I ran the water and turned on the shower hose when it got to a lukewarm temperature. Dad sat like a shell of flesh and bone with no life inside. He was breathing, but his mind was somewhere I couldn't reach. Perhaps he was already gone, and all that was left was a heart that wouldn't stop beating. The heart made his lungs fill with the little air he could muster. It kept his eyes open and aware of his failing body.

When my sister was little, I used to fill a plastic cup with water and pour it over her body in the tub, so I grabbed a cup from the kitchen to do the same. It was just another day of me bathing other people's children. I thought, when my husband Barry got to be Dad's age, I would probably bathe him with a plastic cup too.

I stripped down to my bra, shirt, and panties and hopped in the tub, taking advantage of this opportunity to bathe myself and keep an eye on my dad at the same time. Dad shivered a bit in the shower despite the warm temperature. I cleaned him as quickly as I could, and then grabbed a fresh hospital gown from on top of his dresser and a fresh change of clothes for me.

I couldn't put Dad back into a soiled bed, so I walked him to his wheelchair in the living room. I stripped the bed and checked each blanket for Dad's accident. Luckily it had only reached one, so I threw both it and the sheets in the trash can outside, along with the soiled hospital gown. I said a quick prayer that the number of clean sheets left in the closet would outlive my father.

The next day, the landlord came over from another unit and threatened to evict us. My dad never filled out his Section 8 form and had been paying lower rent without documentation. I assured him he'd have the apartment back in a matter of days.

I was sure Dad was a con man, and this Section 8 business verified that in my mind. I thought back to his false birthday on my birth certificate, to the fake first name I saw on one of his bills. I thought about all the times he said wealth was just around the corner. And, in the future, I thought about his saying he was the mastermind and the getaway car for a bank robbery, when in truth he had stolen TVs off the backs of trucks. Maybe "con man" had entered my mind because "compulsive liar" hadn't yet reached the mainstream lexicon. Either way, it would be decades before I'd realize many of his fibs were born of a need to keep his head above water—to craft the identity that suited him. As my mom would later say, in his defense, "I think of a con man as being more successful. Your dad didn't get away with a whole lot."

The next day, hours passed without Dad eating. While he sat breathing, his new full-time job, I scrambled some eggs and buttered a fresh piece of toast. It was what I always wanted when I didn't feel well. Dad wouldn't reach for the fork. He wouldn't pick up the piece of toast. So I scooped up a bit of egg onto the fork and gently placed it between his open lips. He was a starling who couldn't quite leave the nest to enter the heavens.

"Thank you," he said. "Thank you."

That night, I dreamt that Dad started calling my name. I heard his voice behind a tree, but when I got to it, he wasn't there. Then the voice was behind another tree, and then another. I sprinted from tree to tree but his voice moved on too quickly. I'd never catch up.

"Shannon." My eyes fluttered open and I realized Dad really was calling my name.

I jumped up like a cadet in military school. Dad wasn't my sergeant—the cancer was. "What's wrong?"

"Something's wrong with the oxygen. I can't breathe."

Dad's breath came in and out more strongly. His chest rose and fell, then rose again, like a frog. I checked the oxygen tank but it all looked fine. I pulled it slightly away from his face and placed my hand in front. The pressure hit the palm of my hand.

"It's OK, Dad. I think it's working."

In the morning, the hospice worker checked the tank after receiving my call to the hospital. "It's working fine," she said. "His lungs just can't get enough air."

———————

Someone knocked on the door and I crossed through the kitchen to answer it. A middle-aged man stood at the threshold. He had strawberry blond hair, shining blue eyes, and a wide smile. He was wearing a lightweight, dark green sweater and a red, patterned prayer shawl over his shoulders.

"Hi, I'm Chaplain O'Malley," he said with a smile. "Kevin O'Malley. Is Robert here?"

I led the chaplain into the living room and he took a seat on the couch next to my father.

"Hey, man," my dad said softly. "Good to see you."

Chaplain O'Malley stretched out his hands and held my father's with a gentle squeeze.

"This man right here is one of the most giving souls I've ever met," he said.

I nodded, but not in understanding. That wasn't the Dad I knew.

"I'm sure he's told you all about his paralegal work?"

I stared blankly. I knew Dad used to work for the NAACP, but that was ages ago. I couldn't remember what job titles he'd sent me in recent letters.

The chaplain didn't seem to notice my hesitation and continued. "He helped over a hundred people apply for food stamps and low-income housing. Many people have full meals now and a place to sleep because of him. You must be so proud."

"Yes," I said. But what I really wanted to do was punch Chaplain Kevin O'Malley in the gut. I wanted to reveal to him that my dad beat my mom. That he drove drunk with me in the car. I wanted to tell

him about all the times he said he'd see me and didn't. My dad may
be a hero to strangers, but he stopped being a hero to me a long time
ago. Now he was just the guy I couldn't find an appropriate card for
on Father's Day.

But I didn't say any of this. Chaplain O'Malley saw the man my dad
projected to the world. He saw my brown-skinned father, his tales of
growing up poor in St. Louis, of enlisting in the army just in time for
the Korean War. He saw the man who was incarcerated and taught himself the law in prison, who went on to win a grant proposal for a Head
Start, who met Black Panther Huey Newton. It was a nice story, and
not wrong. But all I saw when I pictured my father was an empty chair
in my house that was never filled. He was too busy saving the world to
save his daughter.

"Did you know I interviewed your dad for TV? A segment for the
news about men in hospice. He was so eloquent. He couldn't stop talking about you."

I pushed down a slight rise in my chest—a slight longing for comfort.

I would see this segment sixteen years after my father died.

———————————

There was so much I wanted to forget about this experience. I existed in
a perpetual daze with scraps of sleep in between unbearable wakefulness.
My dad sat for hours in his wheelchair, his head drooping to his chest.
Every so often I scrutinized him from the couch to ascertain whether his
chest was still rising and falling. Sometimes it was hard to tell.

Watching someone die is a painfully slow process. I hoped to be in
the room when he died because I'd rather watch my dad pass than walk
into a room with a dead body. I thought about how my dad always said
we needed to have a deep talk, but we never did, and now we never
would. In middle age, a new peacefulness has come with this revelation.
If my dad had passed before I had the opportunity to see him again, I
would have berated myself for missing what I would have imagined to
be that elusive big talk. But in flying out, in taking care of him, I wasn't
left with what-ifs.

As I watched my dad mentally prepare for his own death, I felt something shift inside me—something that had begun to shift long before I arrived: Dad didn't need to be saved by God. He didn't need a Jesus to secure a place in heaven. The afterlife was unfathomable. My youth pastor didn't have special knowledge, or my college pastor, or Teen Missions or Trinity Hills or Burnside Bible College. No one knew what lay beyond life. In discarding my belief in heaven, I was faced with the reality that my dad would just die and go back to the earth. That that was just the natural order of things. And in this apartment, away from everything I knew, and with grave responsibilities I never imagined I'd have, I didn't need a spiritual father, because I had a corporeal father right there.

I pictured my dad's body slowly becoming one with the ground—ashes to ashes, dust to dust. I knew Dad was born from the chaotic universe. Not from the grand design of a creator, but from cells and other biological transformations that I didn't quite understand and never fully would. God didn't work in mysterious ways; nature did. Nature brought him and nature would now take him away. Just as it would one day take me away. He would become the tree root and I the tree, the physical evidence that he had existed. There was no heaven above, no hell below. No angels and harps and wings. I knew, for me, there was also no reincarnation, no ancestors who spoke from beyond the grave.

And yet, there was something. Some connection between this world and whatever lay beyond. I would first feel it three years from then when I heard Dad's song, "I Just Called to Say I Love You," play over the speakers as I checked out at the grocery store and realized it was his birthday—the first and last time I ever heard that song in a store. I'd feel it a couple more times when Dad came to me in my dreams. Once in his wheelchair in Grandma's entryway, beaming, his eyes welling up with pride for his daughter. Once in a doorway as family members gather in a room of someone's home, the night before Aunt Margaret—Joseph and Charlie's mom—dies of lupus in real life, in her home, surrounded by loved ones. "I'll take care of her," he seems to say. And in another dream, we meet by chance in a park. As we hug goodbye, he says, "I'll see you again soon."

All I knew while caring for him, however, watching his chest rise and fall with slow, faint breaths, was that the faith I'd carried since I was fourteen was gone, and a surprising serenity had taken its place.

———————

Nine days in, I hadn't slept more than an hour at a time. My dad's lips became cracked and gooey from the morphine. At one point, he said, "You're so pretty." I took a mental image of the moment to hold on to after he died. Later he said, "You're kinda ugly." He didn't remember who I was, but it stung just the same. In his more lucid states, my dad told me he was leaving everything in his apartment to me. He said it with pride, but it was nothing I wanted.

Dad started peeing in a urinal bottle instead of the toilet, grunting through his UTI as he tried to get trickles into the jug. On day ten, he couldn't hold the bottle. "Just do it for me," he said. I expected him to laugh and then do it himself, but he was serious. In that moment, I became my father's mother, even more so than in wiping his bottom. I raised his penis between my fingers and delicately placed it in the jug. He grunted and peed in a start-stop fashion.

"You're a good girl," he said when he was done. "I'm so proud of my daughter."

Dad had professed his pride in letters, on cards, but never in person. I smiled despite myself. I clung to his words with all my being.

———————

On the eleventh day, my mom came back to help me pack up Dad's things. We decided it was time to send him to the nursing home, despite Janet's objections. Janet decried Mom's and my decisions for Dad's funeral arrangements: the cemetery wasn't nice enough; the funeral home wasn't good enough; Mom and I were too stoic. I could tell she thought she loved him more.

I didn't know what was wrong with me; I couldn't inspire feeling beyond excitement that I'd finally be able to sleep. Part of me waited for the time Dad's head would never raise again, when he'd never let me down again, and I'd be able to remember the good things without worrying that more letdowns were just around the corner. I felt like a monster for being OK with his passing.

The notary came to the apartment so Mom could help me fill out power of attorney paperwork. The notary checked my dad's driver's license against his birth certificate and noticed a nine-year discrepancy in ages. "Oh, the DMV got it wrong," Dad said. My father was seventy-one, not sixty-two, a fibber even in the most ordinary ways. The notary nodded, unsure, but continued the process.

The next day, the medics placed Dad in his frail wheelchair.

"Where am I going?" It was the fifth time he had asked in the past hour, and each time I answered, my words fell flat.

"I have to go home and back to work," I told him. "The people at the nursing home will take care of you."

The medics carried him down the wooden steps with the peeling paint. I picked up his box of possessions—his picture of me as a little girl, his wallet that he would never use again—and I closed the front door behind me.

One of the medics opened the back door of the ambulance, and he and the others helped my father out of his wheelchair and onto a stretcher. They lifted the stretcher off the ground and glided him in.

It was a hearse for the living.

The ambulance came to a stop on the freeway. I sat on the hard bench next to the stretcher and held my father's hand with one of my own and my worn-out purse with the other. Rows of gridlocked cars stretched forth before us through the rear windows. The medic checked the oxygen pump and looked at his watch in resignation.

"Ambulances should have conveyors," I said. "That way they can rise above the traffic and get to their destination easier." Sirens did that job when needed, but an hour of sleep at a time had rendered my plan brilliant in my mind.

My father looked at me and smiled. "That's my little girl," he said. With a labored whisper, "So smart, this one."

I squeezed my father's hand and steeled my heart against the now continuous forward motion of the ambulance.

Dad's eyes brought themselves to mine, and his pupils became those of a child, the startled irises staring back at me as if I had the power to stop time.

"When can I go home again?"

His alcoholism had led him to lie almost by default, and now lying was the kindest thing I could do.

"Soon," I said.

Mom and I visited Dad at the nursing home, and when the caregiver saw my white mother, she looked confused. The nursing home was depressing beyond belief. Dad shared a room with other men, with each cot lined up next to the other and a small curtain in between. Everywhere we looked and listened, elderly patrons stared vacantly, cried out in pain, mumbled incoherently, or slept peacefully as near-living skeletons.

At the end of the day, we drove to my stepbrother Nick's mother's house, just a few miles away in the same town. I ate my first full meal in days.

"I don't feel much of anything," I confessed to her.

"It's perfectly normal," she said. "There's no 'right' reaction to death, and you and your dad had a complicated relationship."

It was the first time I had let that out, and the validation felt incredible.

The next morning, Mom and I returned to Dad's neighborhood. We stopped at the bank to drop off the paperwork for financial power of attorney. Then we went to the funeral home to make arrangements for when we would return. At 11:00 AM, we met Dad for the last time, before my flight at 2:00. There was so much to say to Dad and no way to say it. I wondered if I was leaving at the right time, or if I would miss his death by just one day in my haste. Words of no consequence were our last. Maybe it was "I love you." Maybe it was "See you later." Whatever they were, they were lost to me in the flurry of the day, mainly because there was no good way to say goodbye to a father forever. We were both too poetic to platitudes, both now too agnostic for prayer.

At the airport, I fell asleep before the plane took off. I woke up after it touched down.

On a Monday, two weeks after I flew back to Portland, my mom called to tell me that Dad had died. He'd had a heart attack after falling out of bed while reaching for his urinal bottle. I felt a pit in my stomach at his dying with so little dignity, especially because handing him the bottle had been my job. Mom and I flew back to Sacramento to pack up his things and give a small memorial. My half brother Jay, whom I had never met, flew out from Florida. The service was led by Chaplain O'Malley in a small room in a Black-owned funeral home. About ten people were attendance, including Mom, Jay, my dad's elderly sister, and some members of the community. Janet, dad's bearded caretaker, sat in the back and cried.

I had never felt so outside myself as I got up to speak. I stood in front of the metal stand, the same kind I used for violin performances. As I talked, I stared at the funeral program.

"Dad was very encouraging to me. He never put me down and he was always proud. Everyone always knew me because he would brag about me, even if I didn't know them. Dad spent his whole life being stuck in the same ruts, mostly due to his alcoholism. He accomplished a lot, but we never got close enough for me to really understand what those accomplishments were. But he was my dad, and I will miss him."

When I think about it now in middle age, I wonder if his frequent listing of personal accolades, if his promises of money and houses and pets and security, wasn't so much to make promises as to try to make himself worthy in my eyes, while I always questioned if I was worthy in his. Maybe we didn't know how fundamental and pure our love was, unconnected to any status or performance of self.

Back at Dad's, Jay, Mom, and I sorted Dad's things. Mom stood in the bedroom doorway, holding on to the side while she leaned her body forward in jovial yet reserved conversation, understanding the complexity of events that brought us here. As strangers to the city with limited time and resources, we took papers and photos, signed Dad's car over to Janet, and left much of the rest of the apartment in disarray. In Dad's unredacted psychological evaluation, we learned we had another sister, born between Jay and the three girls given up for adoption. At about age forty, I would find her through DNA, and we would text each other a warm emoji every now and then from our opposite sides of the country.

A year after my dad died, I would get a phone call from the funeral home that my father's ashes made it to the national cemetery for war veterans. Dad had received a free plot for his service in the Korean War. Only, unbeknownst to me, it took a year to verify him as a veteran. Mom and I laughed when I told her. Even after death, his identity still felt elusive. He had moved almost every year since my birth.

Mom and I took a trip to the cemetery in the months after Dad arrived there. We wound through Route 152, past the eighty-five-square-mile San Luis Reservoir, and entered the long road that fed into the memorial. The sun warmed our legs as we delicately traipsed between the urn plots to find Dad. Rolling brown hills cradled the cemetery on one side, and, so far off the beaten path, the only noise was the slight rustling of the grass.

"I bet your dad is finally warm," Mom said, smiling. "He was always perpetually cold."

I laughed. In my gut, I knew Dad would approve of this place. And for the rest of my life, I would know where to find him.

Epilogue

I KNOW WHY
THE CAGED BIRD SINGS

I LEFT CNF AFTER ONE YEAR and worked in the county library system as a page. I hoped to advance to a clerk until I learned the job called for a degree. I decided once again that I wanted to go back to college and finally major in English. Barry decried the expense, even though we paid for him to get a counseling degree that he didn't really want.

I still couldn't have sex, and Barry decided he didn't want children even if we could. He had told me he wanted them before we got married because he figured eventually he would, but now he realized he never would. We had both married thinking our minds would change about significant issues: his regarding children, and mine regarding attraction. As I became more acquainted with his desire for order and calm, I realized not having children was a good decision for him, but it left me feeling trapped. If I were to not have children, I imagined doing so with someone a little more spontaneous—someone who gently challenged my inhibitions. Instead, because Barry didn't want a divorce, we both felt completely stuck—he with a wife he couldn't sleep with, and me with no prospect of children and a job I couldn't advance in because I didn't have a degree.

Barry preferred holding things in to fighting. I reverted to my child-hood self when he seemed upset, at one point ensconcing myself in the closet because I felt I failed him when I insisted on doing both our laundry and then didn't get it done on time.

In the spring of 2003, two years after my father died, Barry and I drove home from a visit with his family. In the stillness of the open road, Barry broke the silence.

"I've been thinking," he said. "What do you think about getting divorced?"

It was the question I had been waiting for for almost two years. In preparation for my single life, I applied for a library job at the University of Nebraska, near Amy, and flew out when I was one of two candidates being considered. I didn't get the job and then wondered what to do with my future, since I couldn't make a living as a library page.

"Didn't you want to go to school?" Amy asked.

Her question made me realize that I finally had permission to do so. I moved into Deborah and Eugene's basement and got a summer job as a uniform attendant at the Space Needle while I waited for the fall semester to start at Southern Oregon University in Ashland, the closest in-state school to my beloved California, which I had never ceased to miss.

After Barry and I signed our final divorce papers, which happened to coincide with our three-year anniversary, I signed my new name: Shannon Luders-Manuel—continuing to honor my father while also feeling part of the family that raised me. Barry and I left the building and went out to dinner and a movie. Our relationship had been built on friendship, and it ended in the same way.

That fall, Uncle Adam and Stephanie dropped me off on their way to Santa Cruz with their two kids. Now twenty-six, I hadn't needed to list Gary on my financial aid forms, and I received enough in grants and federal loans to attend, plus I took a work-study job at the campus library. I poured myself into school and graduated with honors three years later.

———————

I stopped attending church the moment I left Barry, with no reservations. Some church friends thought I must have done something that I felt was unforgivable, and that I was banishing myself from the church out of shame. It was inconceivable to them that I just stopped believing in something that was so real for so many years of my life. I couldn't explain it to them either, except that the transition was as black-and-white as realizing Santa Claus wasn't real. The only thing that tugged at me, and still does, were the formative years I spent with the Crossroads youth group, immersed in an all-consuming extended family. Many of the most active high school members married each other, and many still attended the same church. My recurring dreams about Crossroads reflected my reality of being on the outside. I dream I'm back in youth group and ready for the next adventure. "Can I still be part of the group even though I'm not Christian?" I ask. In some dreams I vow to pretend I still believe. But I haven't lost everyone. I've held on to friends like Amy, who doesn't question my changed beliefs, and Crystal, from Trinity Hills, who changed along with me.

Southern Oregon University is a tiny, white, liberal enclave nestled in between mountains, with the highest KKK population in the country in the expanse outside its protective walls. A Black classmate invited me to join the Black Student Union, but I turned it down. The organization felt foreign, filled with a race of people I had still barely encountered. When the same Black classmate invited me to dance in an African style for the international festival, I turned that down for the same reason. But in one way, I began to connect to my Blackness. I found a Puerto Rican hairstylist who instinctively understood my hair. I did the big chop, cutting away inches of limp, overprocessed hair damaged from years of relaxer, and sported a new style of perfect curlicues.

My first professor of color, a Mexican American woman who rose up from poverty in Southern California, said I had to go to grad school. My linguistics professor, a white man near retirement, wrote in his letter of recommendation that I was probably the best student the department had seen in ten years. After graduating with honors, I enrolled in the University of Massachusetts, Amherst, for a master's in English. There I was welcomed into an unofficial cohort of about six Black academics (one mixed-race), in literature, MFA, and history programs, all of us experiencing the racism unique to the East Coast. Years later, three are still close friends. Their acceptance was an invaluable gateway to finding a Black community that has flourished in my life since.

As I entered my thirties, my mom and I talked more on the phone, sometimes chatting up to an hour. We talked about our lives, our ailments, and our pasts. In one phone call, when we were discussing my paternal grandpa's "penchant for young girls," she said, "When you were three, child protective services came to the house about your uncle Adam. Your dad called them because you told him about things Adam had done."

My ears were red hot. I thought it was the first time I had heard about the CPS visit, forgetting that it had come back to me when I returned to Grandma's house. Now I remembered things from my past. Running after a paper airplane that Adam put in his underwear, back and forth, back and forth. The smell that came from the paper. Him standing naked in front of his bedroom window while I played outside. I knew there was more that I may never remember.

"You told me in high school," Amy said when I told her about the paper airplane. I had no memory of remembering.

The caseworker knew my mom and had volunteered to be the one to come. Because of my dad's drinking, because they were in the middle of their custody battle, and because my dad was a compulsive liar, the case was closed. But my mom had a feeling—so deep down that she wouldn't let herself believe it—that my dad may have been right, and she had kept Uncle Adam from babysitting me. We lived in the same house for four more years.

The only thing that had stayed with me, since I was seventeen, were Grandma's words: "If anything happened, it was your fault for being a flirt." I had always believed her, but I also thought I had been older than three. Learning of my young age was the first giant step in letting go of her accusation.

With my clear memories, and with her long-repressed hunch, my mom came to believe me and confronted Uncle Adam about the past. For me, large facets of my life suddenly came into clear focus, and I never again repressed the memories. Uncle Adam apologized and, after reading a published essay about the abuse, encouraged me to write more.

Learning that my dad had been the one to call CPS drew me to him more than ever before. He had tried to protect me. He was the only one who had.

After graduation I cast about, ultimately returning to California. In 2014, I dated a man from Colombia. It was my first serious relationship since Barry and I had divorced in 2003, and since my diagnosis of vulvar vestibulitis in 2009 and my subsequent surgery to fix the pain I had experienced all those years. My boyfriend started our relationship with talks of marriage and children, but then he pulled away. At first I pled with him that anxiety is normal, but as it became clear that our relationship was ending, I fell into an almost catatonic despair, crying frequently at home and performing my work as a tutor devoid of expression.

During those rough days, I held my sister's new blonde-haired, blue-eyed daughter, Maya, who reminded me of her as a baby, and I worked on a growing memoir about my dad that I had started just before grad school. I applied to be a featured writer at Mixed Remixed, a mixed-race festival in Los Angeles. As part of my research, I dug out my folder of letters Dad had written to me over the years and reread each one for the first time in years. The folder that contained all his paperwork was always both enticing and like a hot potato, replacing the quietness of his death with his eloquent yet emotionally charged words.

Most of Dad's letters from toward the end of his life decried my focus on marriage instead of on my financial and intellectual future. One section stuck out to me, and he seemed to be speaking these words now, even though he had written them years earlier:

> There are powerful forces at play that are guiding you to a place higher than basic academics. Within that sphere you will develop into a person richer in the knowledge of life. . . . Look hard at the forks in the road upon which you're traveling. At times you will note a need for directional changes.

Dad seemed to be calling me out, just like he had back then, only with the added years, I better understood his words. I was once again trying to fit myself into a common mold. My thoughts had been filled with plans to marry my boyfriend, and I had applied to a fast-track credential program at San Jose State—Mom's alma mater—to teach high school English. But my acceptance letter filled me with dread, much as my wedding day had.

I submitted my materials to Mixed Remixed in the wee hours of the very last day of open submissions. A few weeks later, I received an email that I had been chosen. At work, the older, Black female tutor, who acted as somewhat of a mentor, suggested I practice my material on our colleagues during our lunch break. As I stood at the front of the classroom and read from my pages, I watched the faces of my peers transform. I always felt like an average tutor, effective but shy. Their close attention gave me confidence. They were silent when I finished, with eyes wide and jaws dropped. At that moment, I knew I needed to make writing my true focus, working only to support that passion. I declined my acceptance to the teaching program with relief.

From the moment I walked into the Mixed Remixed event space, celebration filled the air. A woman with big curly hair like mine checked me in. Participants of all ages gathered to hear stories, watch films, and view art exhibits. I read from my pages while Amandla Stenberg, newly famous as Rue from *The Hunger Games*, sat in the audience. I knew a duo named Key and Peele would be winning the Storyteller's Prize later that night but didn't know who they were until I saw their faces go by on the side of a bus as I parked my car. I ducked out early to meet up with a Black friend from UMass who had moved to Los Angeles County. "I'm moving to L.A.," I told her definitively, and transferred to my job's SoCal location.

I found a studio apartment in Hollywood. The neighborhood in general, and in particular my little corner, was a race haven: My apartment complex was made up of all manner of folk, as were the cashiers and customers at the stores on Hollywood Boulevard. On a walk down the street to run errands, I'd pass families speaking various languages as they looked up at the Roosevelt Hotel and down at the stars on the Walk of Fame.

My extended family was becoming more diverse as well, adding Mexican, Korean, and Taiwanese members. In a few years, I'd sit next to my cousin Elsie's half-Mexican daughter, who struggled as I had with looking different. She would look at my arm next to hers at the table and announce with a smile, "We're the same color." I needed that too.

In 2017, two mixed-race friends and I drove south from Los Angeles to Imperial, California, for an end-of-year festival in the desert to release paper lanterns into the sky. My friends both looked like versions of me.

Though I had known them for two years, our mirrorlike qualities still felt joyously surreal.

In Imperial, the three of us sat on a blanket and decorated our lanterns along with hundreds of other participants. Out in the desert, the sky was immense. Nothing was visible before us except the occasional gently sloped mounds of sand. My two lanterns were in honor of my father and of my grandmother, who had died earlier that year. On Grandma's lantern, I drew her VW camper. On Dad's, I drew a black cat with a crown on its head in honor of the "Black Prince." When the emcee on the stage far ahead of us directed everyone to release their lanterns, we heated them with the electric torches that stood on tall sticks pressed firmly into the ground. The three of us looked up in wonder as we released our creations. I watched my tributes to my grandma and my dad soar above me, merging with hundreds of others to create a glowing mosaic in the black sky.

Hello Shannon,

It was great seeing you and we will do it again soon.

I saw you as you were skipping down the street with D'orrie, going to the car.

I thought, "there goe's my Baby and I'm going to miss her Berry, Berry much." I hope your record played O.K. on your stereo.

Tell Funshine Bear hello for me and tell him to eat all his meals. I will call you sometime. I love you.

Your Daddy
Robert C.

ACKNOWLEDGMENTS

THEY SAY IT TAKES A VILLAGE TO RAISE A CHILD, and this book is my child. It couldn't have come into this world without my community.

First and foremost, thank you, Mom, for answering so many questions about a past that must have been challenging to revisit. This book likely wouldn't exist without your exceptional memory. Thanks to both you and my sister for believing in this project and supporting me along the way.

Thank you to my best friend, Ingrid Boswell, for being my biggest cheerleader ever since college, for believing in my desire to be an author even when all I had was a bad first draft.

Thank you to my editor, Michelle Williams, for taking on this project and pushing me to dig deeper than I thought possible, and to Alicia Sparrow, for finding it worthy. To Jonathan Hahn for the beautiful cover design. And to my agent, Farley Chase, for connecting with this story so strongly and being the best champion.

Thank you to the Leporine Conspiracy—Alia Volz, Jacqueline Doyle, Sasha Vasilyuk, Caryn Cardello, Rose Andersen, and Matthew Clark Davidson: the harshest and helpfullest critiquers. Thank you for tearing my work apart in the best way. To Christina Hoag for giving peer feedback on my proposal. To the SBs for your camaraderie in writing and in life. Also a big thank-you to other writers who have been with me on this journey: Lauren DePino, Melissa Blake, Ruksana Hussain, TaRessa Stovall, Chanté Griffin, Mike Young, Erin Khar, Karie Fugett, Simone Gorrindo,

Janice Littlejohn, A.K. Whitney, JoBeth McDaniel, Eboni Rafus-Brenning, Nicole M. Young-Martin, Jamie Beth Cohen, Allison K. Williams, Laura Carney, Sharon Van Epps, Ana McNaughton, and Nabil Ayers. If I've forgotten any of you, you're not forgotten in my heart. To the Binders for opening doors, sharing community, and providing resources so freely. To Debra Eckerling for inviting me into your community when I was brand new to Los Angeles. Thank you to Donna Talarico-Beerman for HippoCamp.

No writer can go without thanking the teachers who believed in her. To Ms. Nilsson, for letting me work on my first (very bad) memoir during freewriting in tenth grade; to Marcy Alancraig for all your "yeses" on the sides of my papers and for expanding my worldview; and to Professors Alma Alvarez, Craig Wright, and Kasey Mohammad for fostering my writing voice at SOU. Thank you to Jennifer Lauck for replying to my fan mail, long before my own journey, and for the opportunity to hone my voice in your class. To Carmiel Banasky for your words of wisdom in the LA Writers Group.

For the mixed-race friends who have become family: Kayla Briet and Debbie Ingram. Thank you to Mixed Remixed Festival founder Heidi Durrow and Topaz Club founder AF Bibbs for your life-changing spaces.

And to dear ones: Pamela Schwebach, Kelly Jones, Emily G., Krista Bannick, Jeanne Jones, John Riley, Gina Mendez, Holly, Niall, and so many others.

Lastly, to Dad and Grandma (and Great-Grandma) for instilling in me your love of writing. Though I don't believe in destiny, I was "destined" to become an author through being born of your genes.

And last but not least, thank you to those who supported me via GoFundMe as I finished writing:

Alice Anderson
Nabil Ayers
Krista Bannick
Shannon Berendes
Ingrid Boswell
Christina Cogswell
Dan Dawson

Santana Dempsey
Lauren DePino
Jacqueline Doyle
Anita Dugan
Susan Emmons
Colin Enriquez
Bess Fairfield

Karie Fugett

Lisa Gold

Kathleen Gorman

Jennifer Handy

Rebekah Henderson

Ariel Henley

Katie Ives

Jeanne Jones

Sonia Smith Kang

Erin Khar

Kim Ledgerwood

JoAnne Lehman

Ericka Lutz

Emily Maloney

Megan Margulies

Jamie Marich

Maria McVicker

Alyce Mitchell

Betsy Moore

Jennifer Morson

Miss D Mortimer

Svenya Nimmons

Jason Noriega

Lisa Rosenberg

Jordan Rosenfeld

Julia Schetky

Lisa Sheets

Michelle Hayden Smith

Francisco Sorto

Rebecca Spence

Leigh Stein

Kate Walker

Debbie Weingarten

Dennis Wilen

Emily Yellin

Michael Young